The 33rd

DREXEL UNIVERSITY
College of
Arts and Sciences

Editor-In-Chief	Scott Stein
Senior Editor	Kathleen Volk Miller
Layout Editor	William Rees
Graphic Design	Courtney Sabo
Editorial Co-ops	Brittany MacLean
	Melody Nielsen
Digital Design Co-op	Josh Weiss
Student Interns	Marquerita Algorri
	Maile Beal
	Rachel Croke
	Addison Davis
	Isabella Fidanza
	Hans Goerner
	Maggie Heath-Bourne
	Cassie Homer
	Jen Jolles
	Alexa Josaphouitch
	Sana Karim
	Maggie Leoffler
	Elizabeth Pollack
	Carl Roa
	Marie Ruisard
	Cayde Tanzil

Sponsors

Drexel University
The College of Arts and Sciences at Drexel University
The Department of English and Philosophy at Drexel University

Dr. Donna M. Murasko, Dean, College of Arts and Sciences,
Drexel University
Dr. Abioseh Michael Porter, Department Head, English and Philosophy,
Drexel University

The 33rd Volume 7
Drexel University
Department of English and Philosophy
3141 Chestnut Street
Philadelphia, PA 19104
www.drexelpublishing.org

Cover photo by Courtney Sabo

The 33rd is published once a year.

ISBN 978-1-58390-180-9

Thank you, thank you, thank you, and thank you to: Dr. Donna M. Murasko; Dr. Abioseh Michael
Porter; all the judges from the Drexel Publishing Group Essay Contest, the Week of Writing
Contest, and the First-Year Writing Contest (Pete Amato, Stacey Ake, Jan Armon, Ken Bingham,
Ron Bishop, Valerie Booth, Roman Colombo, Ingrid Daemmrich, Anne Erickson, Lisa Farley,
Leonard Finegold, Robert Gilmore, Susan Gurney, Charles Haub, Casey Hirsch, Katherine
Houseman, Monica Ilies, Rebecca Ingalls, Henry Israeli, Lynn Levin, Eva Litt, Deirdre McMahon,
Jonson Miller, Jill Moses, Karen Nulton, Anne-Marie Obajtek-Kirkwood, Emilie Passow, Margene
Petersen, Adam Rickert, Don Riggs, Gail Rosen, Sheila Sandapen, Fred Siegel, Jeanne Steuber,
Errol Sull, Monica Togna, Marshall Warfield, Scott Warnock); Department of English and
Philosophy, especially Mary Beth Beyer, Eileen Brennen, and Nicole Kline; contest participants;
Drexel Publishing Group staff.

The fonts used within this publication are Archer and Avenir

Credits:

Armon, Jan. "Toomey gave up too easily" was originally published in the opinion pages of *Main Line & Suburban Times*, 1 August 2013.

Cohen, Paula Marantz. "Glory at the Fountain of Coca Cola" was originally published in *The Smart Set* on December 9, 2013.

Daemmrich, Ingrid. "Humor as Celebrity-Maker: Recreating Lewis Carroll's Alice in Wonderland and Through the Looking-Glass in Multi-Media" was originally given as a talk at the 2013 International Society for Humor Studies Conference.

Davenport, Blythe. "The Lost Folktales of Laurel Hill" was first published in *Forgotten Philadelphia: Art and Writing Inspired by Philadelphia Heritage Sites* (PS Books, 2013).

Fitts, Tim. "Stripping Roses" was originally published in the Spring 2014 issue of *The Baltimore Review*.

Fox, Valerie. "Two Important Questions on Ant Individuality" was published in *Press 1* (2014). "Two Important Questions Concerning Seahorses" was published in *Apiary* (2013).

Israeli, Henry. "New Year in the Old Country" was originally published in *Pleiades* in 2014.

McVey, Donna. "Can mass shootings be prevented?" was originally published in *The Triangle* on January 18, 2013 (Volume 88, Issue 13).

Levin, Lynn. "Stay Lucky" was originally published in *Wild River Review*, April 2014.

Menon, Usha. "Hinduism, Happiness and Wellbeing: A Case Study of Adulthood in an Oriya Hindu temple town" was originally published in H. Selin and G. Davey (Eds.) (2012) *Happiness Across Cultures: Views of Happiness and Quality of Life in non-Western Cultures*. Dordrecht, the Netherlands: Springer.

Millan, Harriet Levin. "Yalla!" originally appeared in Volume 33, Number 1 (Winter 2011) of *The Kenyon Review*.

Miller, Kathleen Volk. A slightly different version of "Choosing Childfree" originally appeared in *Philadelphia Magazine*, 2013.

Obajtek-Kirkwood, Anne-Marie. "Banks and Capital: A New World Order" is an English version of a paper given in French at the 20th/21st Century French and Francophone Studies Colloquium Money/L'Argent in New York City, 6-8 March 2014.

Piety, M.G. "On Death and Dying" was originally published in the July 2013 Weekend Edition of *CounterPunch* under the alternate title "The Long Journey."

Sandapen, Sheila. "Rhetoric, Plato, The Fourth Doctor Who and How to Tell a Cracking Good Story" is adapted from a longer chapter, "The Doctor's Wondrous Wandering Dialectic Approach to the Universe," that appeared in *The Language of Doctor Who*. Eds. Jason Barr and Camille D. G. Mustachio. NY: Rowman & Littlefield, 2014.

Warfield, Marshall. "Motel Swimming Pool, Late Afternoon" was first published in the instructive anthology *Poems for the Writing: Prompts for Poets* in 2013.

Warnock, Scott. "Where do you keep your hoes?: Standardized tests are destroying education, part 4 (of 874)" was originally published in *When Falls the Coliseum*, 2013. <whenfallsthecoliseum.com>

Welcome

The 33rd anthology is a visible expression of the College of Arts and Sciences' commitment to interdisciplinary scholarship and writing excellence. Within its pages is an eclectic mix of short stories, essays, and scientific articles written by students and faculty from fields across the University. This volume demonstrates the incredible diversity of Drexel scholarship: we are one institution composed of diverse perspectives. These unique perspectives enhance our community and have the power to inspire others to pursue new insights and innovations, whether that's writing the next best-selling novel or discovering a new molecule. But powerful stories and miraculous discoveries are nothing without the skills of communication. These skills allow us to share our ideas, our research, our vision, with the world.

Whether you dream of being an author, an architect, or an environmental scientist, your training starts here, with the tools of communication.

Donna M. Murasko, Ph.D.
Dean
College of Arts and Sciences

Preface

As is often noted, the Department of English and Philosophy has established a well-deserved reputation not only as a place where instructors of all ranks are passionate about teaching and learning—derived from classroom and other such experiences—but also as the one locale at Drexel where excellent writing is seen as a daily, achievable goal. Because our ultimate objective is to make excellent writing a defining characteristic of a Drexel education, we will continue to help our students understand that a fine blend of traditional literary skills and modern thought and practice will help to make them excellent, even outstanding, writers. We, the faculty in our department, have therefore set as our primary goals the achievement of the highest academic standards, the creation of a congenial atmosphere for our students, and a dynamic teaching and scholarly environment.

It is thus with immense pleasure that we present the seventh volume of this yearly anthology. In *The 33rd* 2014, we aim to encourage our students to fuse insights derived from their varied experiences and knowledge to create a document that truly should impress readers because of the complex web of writing the authors present, even with an occasional undergraduate self-consciousness.

Using varying approaches that, even in these early stages, reveal the complexity, density of texture and meaning, and the richness of vision and artistry that often characterize good quality writing, the students—guided by their very able instructors—have carefully demonstrated in print some famous words of wisdom by Diane Stanley, author and illustrator: "Good writing is clear thinking." What I now hope the students, again with guidance from all of us, will continue to do from this point on is to apply the other half of Ms. Stanley's statement: "Reading is how you learn what good writing sounds like."

We are particularly heartened by the efforts reflected here because scarcely a false note is struck in this volume. The pieces in the anthology—though varied—continue to demonstrate the relevance and importance of high quality writing and good reading habits. Taken together, the contributions by both students and faculty reveal that literary and cultural exchanges between these two symbiotic groups continue to develop and improve. The pieces collectively address in a readable format and at the undergraduate level some of the aesthetics, concepts, theories, and debates that inform the various levels and perceptions of our contemporary culture (both highbrow and popular); they also attempt (successfully, I think) to analyze the role of writing in shaping culture, beliefs, identities, and social practices.

My personal congratulations—as well as those of the whole department—go to all who participated in this laudable and practically useful project. To those whose selections were published, I would like to conclude by offering some words by the writer Enrique Jardiel Poncela: "When something can be read without effort, great effort has gone into its writing." Bravo!

Abioseh Michael Porter, Ph.D.
Department Head
Department of English and Philosophy

Table of Contents

Faculty Writing
Introduction

First-Year
Writing

Introduction

The thousands of compositions written by students enrolled in the First-Year Writing Program at Drexel represent their extraordinary experiences and perspectives. Composed over weeks of reading, research, contemplation, rhetorical analysis, discussion, and revision, these compositions are a reflection of how students are learning to use writing as a tool for creative, complex inquiry, and are making their writing matter beyond the boundaries of the classroom: in the development of the self, in the crafting of proposals for change, in the building of ideas that lead to innovation.

The First-Year Writing category in this collection offers a showcase of some of the most excellent student work from this year. After a competitive multi-stage process of evaluating and narrowing down the submissions, the winners and honorable mentions are announced, and the awards are given at the English Awards Ceremony in the spring. I can say with confidence that these students, who hail from all corners of this institution, have made us proud not just as instructors and as a program, but also as a university that aims to create a culture of writing across the disciplines. We hope that these texts will serve as evidence to our writers and readers that—no matter what field you have decided to pursue—writing will be a critical tool for your exploration and success.

I want to thank the generosity of First-Year Writing faculty member Ingrid Daemmrich, sponsor of the First-Year Writing Contest, and the hardworking Drexel Publishing Group for bringing this book into being. I also want to extend my deepest gratitude to Department Head Dr. Abioseh Porter, Dean Donna Murasko, and Provost Mark Greenberg for their enduring support of writing pedagogy, innovation, and assessment. Finally, I want to especially thank our many beloved, wise faculty who continue to devote tireless inspired hours to make this program stronger each year.

Rebecca Ingalls, Ph.D.
Director of the First-Year Writing Program

Cindy Phan

For the Sake of Enjoyment

Personal Reflection...

For the sake of my research question (Why do I enjoy composing hundred-thousand-word-novels, but detest the thought of writing thousand-word academic essays?), I decided to blend the two into one. My project two composition provides an academic message as intended by the academic essay, however it is articulated in the form of a short story, a form of creative writing that also relates to novel writing.

Truthfully, planning didn't help my project as much as I'd hoped it would. Due to the nature of this project being exploratory, I couldn't clearly predict the end result even by planning. I didn't know my ending, and therefore had no control over its length. I wrote until I found an okay place to end. In a way, it doesn't ever have to end, because the exploratory process doesn't have to have an ending or a definite answer. But for the sake of this project, I stopped at the point when my fictional character could begin to take another step in her own exploration of writing, and I believe that is okay. Some stories don't have to end.

Story...

Some moments in life passed by too quickly, and some moments labored on too slowly. In the end, it all balanced out. But Dr. Roe's class was the one thing that threw my life off balance. Each second was an hour. Each minute felt like an eternity—sixty eternities until my freedom.

Dr. Roe had this book he loved to teach from—a collection of essays and academic journal excerpts from supposedly the best college writers in the nation. Every day it was the same meaningless praise for people I'd never met, whose writing I don't even enjoy.

"How do you infuse pathos into physics?" Dr. Roe once asked, regarding an article on fundamental physics that no one in the class understood.

"The exigence is very clear in this paragraph. Notice how the author drew upon his ethos as a fellow doctor to explain to his audience the difficulties of electromagnetism!"

Truthfully, it was lovely seeing a man express such passion. But after the first two days of class, I'd begun to zone out. Instead of paying attention to what Dr. Roe was saying at the front of the classroom, I'd allow my mind to wander. A natural inclination of my brain was to make up stories when I was bored. Really, there was nothing else to do in that class—nothing that wouldn't blatantly announce to the teacher that: "No, I am not listening to a word you're saying."

I'd look upon Roe's genuinely made totem pole in the back corner of the room and invent a story of him wearing something similar to Indiana Jones, engaged in some sort of ritual with aboriginals. The eagle, bear, and wolf heads on the pole were all twisted into snarls, and they were angled directly at me. It was hard not to look at them and invent a story to cure the boredom.

Twenty minutes through the class, I would have milked the totem pole for all of its potential stories, and moved onto the jade dragon statue sitting alone on Dr. Roe's barren bookshelf. As Dr. Roe preached on about some amazing essay regarding L. Frank Baum's *The Wonderful Wizard of Oz* as a political parable, I would imagine the dragon coming to life and burning down the entire school. Fire. We'd be engulfed in vermillion, and by God it would be a beautiful death.

"Emma," Dr. Roe croaked from the front of the classroom.

Panic struck. I could see myself, looking like a deer in front of headlights, staring back wide-eyed. "Yes?" I uttered.

Dr. Roe ran his hands through his hair—dark brown flecked with gray. He had to be no more than forty years old, but the pinstriped pants and the faded cardigan that hung off his body like he was a hat stand made him look a decade older.

"Emma," he sighed again, shaking his head and tidying up the papers scattered about the front desk. "Class is over."

"Oh." I glanced up at the clock. Nine-thirty, it read. "Sorry," I muttered, packing up the blank notebook and pencil I had back into my bag.

"Class ended ten minutes ago," my old teacher said as I began making my way through the labyrinth of desks to the door. "I would have informed you sooner, but frankly I'd forgotten you were here at all."

"Thank you," I replied, unable to hide a scowl from showing on my face.

"Wait a minute, please."

I stopped and turned around. "Yes, sir?" When he wasn't preaching about the brilliance of academic nobodies from places I'd never even heard of, Dr. Roe's voice was rather mellow and nice. It could lull a child to sleep.

He held up a set of papers, neatly stapled, black ink marked all over with red pen, a fat grade written and circled in the top corner. 90. Our assignment was to argue over which would be better for our district's education—school uniforms, or no school uniforms. I went with school uniforms just because everyone else chose no uniforms. For something so pointless, a 90 was good enough for me. "Your midterm, Emma."

"Thank you."

"I'd like to ask you something, if you don't mind."

I said, "I am actually late for my Creative Writing class."

He nodded, a small smile dancing upon his lips as if my tardiness had been by his design. "Yes, creative writing, that's what I wanted to talk to you about. Do you know why I gave you a 90 instead of a 100? I greatly enjoyed your essay—very persuasive!"

To amuse him, I flipped through the four double-spaced pages and concluded, "I'm guessing it's for grammatical errors?"

"No."

I stayed quiet, lips pursed, one eyebrow raised in expectance of an answer. "I'm sorry, sir. I don't understand," I said when he refused to relinquish one.

"No exigence," he answered at last.

Sadly, it took me a minute to recall what exigence meant.

"Why did you write this paper?" he asked. "What is your purpose?"

"Uh..."

"Because I assigned it to you, and you must do it for a grade, correct?"

I nodded. Internally, I cursed myself for being so stupid. I could have just lied and given him some satisfying answer. "Honestly," I confessed, "I don't really care about school uniforms."

"You'd rather argue for no uniforms?"

"No. I'd rather not argue at all. What is the point in making us write these essays? They're all the same anyway. There are two sides split among thirty kids. We all wound up repeating each other in different ways."

Dr. Roe tilted his head to the side, his gray eyes glazed over with a faraway look while he seemed to be studying me. "Every person has their way of writing, Emma. That unique style is even visible in academic writing, and what you wrote here is in fact considered academic." His voice grew louder when he noticed my accidental eye-roll. "I understand you enjoy writing contemporary fiction," he said. "Prof. Geralds told me so."

I nodded again. "I like novels," I answered.

"Why?"

The question shocked me. "They are stories, and stories are interesting."

"Why?" he asked again.

"Um, I like books...?"

He smiled, shook his head, and asked, "Tell me about books, Emma. Why do you like books so much?"

It was an awkward question to hear from an English teacher. I expected him to understand without the need for words, but I answered him regardless. "The voices of generations past," I began slowly, raw truth spilling from my lips, "of people who have already died and disappeared in their now invisible graves—we can still hear them, even talk to them in books. A million secret confessions, all recorded in between those pages. Books can be our friends. They can even show us the world. And the characters don't stay as fiction to us—not to me at least. They live in me, and others like me. They become people we remember—people who actually make us laugh, and cry, and scream because of how stupid they can be—"

Dr. Roe's face cracked into a wide, goofy grin. I stopped talking when I saw it, unhinged by the strange sight. In all the time I'd had him as a teacher, I'd never seen him smile that wide before. I guess he *did* understand.

"Why can't you display such exigence in your writing for class?" he asked me.

Feeling a little more comfortable now, I replied, "I don't care for the topics you give us."

"Is there a way that you can find a little exigence for my assignments?"

I frowned, trying to think of a polite way to say "no."

Dr. Roe clapped his hands together in realization. "Tell you what," he said, shuffling through papers in his backpack. "There is a contest coming up in which I will play a large part in judging. I'd like you to enter it. Find your exigence for academic papers."

"But Dr. Roe, I can't write academic—"

"It's a portfolio. It asks for more than academic writing," he said, handing me a bent packet.

I straightened the paper and placed it along with my midterm into my backpack, eager to get away from Dr. Roe before he strategized any more excuses for me to write pointless essays.

"Thank you," I told him, working up quite an honest and grateful smile before I fled from his classroom and my world moved in normal time again.

***

Prof. Geralds's Creative Writing class was located in a far off section of my high school, an added wing on the building's left side. The desks and chairs were brand new and the walls and windows were spotless. I stared at those white walls while writing. It was easier to see imaginary figures move upon them. It was easier to write and focus in that room than Dr. Roe's room where everywhere I turned, there was already a pre-established story.

Everyone was quiet. All twelve students of that class were busy typing up stories and poems. A few of us were writing by hand—the sound of pen scratching against paper a comfort to our ears, as were the clicking of the keyboard keys.

I'd halted progress on my novel to do research, scouring through Wikipedia pages for information about mythology behind the names of stars and constellations. Calypso. Atlas. Daphne. Cassandra. So many stars, so many stories.

But before long, I stopped reading about stars no matter how much I enjoyed it. I was seventeen—I couldn't explain everything about myself just yet.

Beneath the school laptop, I noticed part of my English midterm sticking out, as well as a corner of the packet Dr. Roe had given me. It was all because of curiosity that I actually started reading the bent packet, flipping through the rough pages, noticing a coffee stain from page four onward.

In the very back of the packet were the guidelines that I needed:

Morrison Debut Contest
Category: Writing Portfolio
      Required Pieces: Poem (No more than 50 lines)
                         Short Story (3,000 to 8,000 words)
                         Personal Essay/Memoir (500 to 3,000 words)
                         Academic Article (1,000 to 3,000 words)

Of the four, I had three of the categories ready to edit and turn in. My eyes narrowed upon the words, "Academic Article." It was an unwanted stain upon the paper, uglier than the light brown, broken circle coffee stain.

"You're planning on entering the Morrison Debut Contest?" Prof. Geralds asked.

I looked up, my eyes meeting the broad-shouldered man that towered in height over ninety percent of the population. "Yeah, Dr. Roe said I should enter."

Prof. Geralds nodded in agreement. "I brought the idea up to him. He didn't seem too keen on it at first, but we think with your writing abilities, you'd be able to get your name out there."

"Get my name out?"

"You want to write novels, don't you?"

I nodded many times. "Yes, get a book published."

"Literary agents will be more likely to notice you if they see your name attached to a writing award, especially one as prestigious as the Morrison. Have you heard of the Morrison Debut Award for novels?"

"Of course. Last year, *Where Things Come Back* by John Corey Whaley won."

"Think of how much help it would be to win this little writing contest here."

"But I can't write academically," I sighed, pointing to the ugly stain of letters at the very bottom of the last page. "I don't even know what can be considered an academic essay!"

He smiled apologetically. "Would you like me to give you a prompt?"

I shook my head. "No, because I may not understand it and then it'll lack exigence."

Prof. Geralds left me alone to write for the rest of class, but instead of writing, I kept staring at the white wall. I didn't know what to write about to pass as an "Academic Article."

When I wrote fiction, I could see the characters. I saw them rise up out of the page. They became real people to me, and they moved. Real people moved by themselves. I was not the puppet master pulling the strings, but simply a spectator who recorded everything. The characters enacted their own story, and it was fun watching them—it was like watching TV.

But academic articles were entirely different. There were no characters. No people, and they didn't move. In academic articles, there were only words— letters and spaces. I couldn't imagine them as easily.

***

By the time Creative Writing ended, I was hungry, frustrated, and ready to eat my feelings at lunch. But as I was heading to the cafeteria, I passed by Dr. Roe's empty classroom. The door was partway open, but the room was dark. From the corner of my eye as I passed slowly, I could see the milky glow of the computer screen in the back corner. Dr. Roe sat behind his desk, a halo of white light surrounding him as he studied his laptop screen.

On the spur of the moment, I entered the room. I knocked once on the door while standing at the threshold. The doctor looked up and beckoned me inside, neither smiling nor frowning.

"Questions?" he said calmly.

"Plenty," I nodded. "How do I write an academic article?"

It took a moment, but a smile flittered across his face at last. That one was of amusement. "So you're going to participate in the contest?"

"Yes, because Prof. Geralds said that it would help with my dream of getting published."

"That's exigence!"

"But not the exigence I need to write an academic article, especially one that will help me win the contest."

Dr. Roe sat back, crossing his legs and placing his hands on his knees. "So why do you dislike academic writing so much?"

I couldn't help rolling my eyes at how much he sounded like a therapist just then. "I don't get it."

"Why?"

"What I read is really pointless to me. No offense, since the class I have to read the most academic articles in is your class." Dr. Roe shook his head side to side, showing that he took no umbrage. "Yes, I like writing, but I don't care how sentences and paragraphs are formed," I said, addressing the endless essays he made us read on grammar. "And then those scientific ones—as kind and loving as Jane Goodall is, I don't care about her study of chimpanzees. I don't care about that physics paper you made us read last week. In fact, I don't even understand basic physics..."

"So your problem with academic writing may be the jargon," he said. "Oftentimes, authors of academic writing use in-group jargon in their writing. Their audience is often like-minded individuals or people from the same field of study as them. These people understand the jargon. For a general audience, you shouldn't use any in-group jargon" (Driscoll).

I shook my head. "No, no. It's not the jargon. These days, you can just look up those words on the Internet if you really try."

"So why don't you try? Reading and writing academically requires effort, Emma. You have to interact with it. In one article about reading rhetorically, Karen Rosenberg stated that, 'The final key to reading smarter, not harder is to make it social.' Making it social doesn't necessarily mean you go around with a bombastic attitude and talk empty words about it. Making it social means interacting with it—look up the words you don't know, write your own reaction if you will, or just grab a pen and underline the parts you like. Do you do that?"

"I do, actually. As lazy as I am, I actually do that. Otherwise, I would have never gotten through those quizzes you gave us."

Dr. Roe sat back, a soft laugh escaping his breath. He nodded, then said, "Right, decent scores on the weekly quizzes. So this is tough. Why do you enjoy novel writing, but detest academic writing? It's weird, right? You sit and churn out—how many—a *hundred* thousand words for novels? Yet it's so difficult to write just *one* thousand words for a little essay."

"I actually *like* novels. I can see it happening in my head. But I can't see the things written in the essays in my head. They're just abstract thoughts with no connections, nor relevance to me."

The distant gaze returned to his eyes, and we spent a long while in thoughtful silence.

My stomach was growling. I didn't know what time it was, but I didn't want to leave. I wanted to learn how to write an academic article, one that was good enough to stand a chance for a contest prize. I needed my name attached to that contest, because it seemed there was no easier route to getting a novel published than that. (And even so, it wasn't at all easy.)

After what felt like an eternity, Dr. Roe was the first to speak again. "I believe I've made a mistake assigning you such boring articles to read. Tell me, are there any books you don't like?"

I had to think about it for a moment. "I don't like romance much. You know, the ones you find in the back corner, guilty-pleasure sections of bookstores."

"So there are books you typically don't enjoy. Logically, there are also academic articles that you don't enjoy. I made a mistake assigning all the wrong genres to you."

"I seriously doubt that's the reason—"

"There are many genres to academic writing, did you know that? People can write academically about anything that interests them."

"They just have to put in sources and citations, right?"

"Well, not exactly. That's just so we give credit where credit is due" (Maddalena).

"So what is it then?"

"You just don't enjoy the things you've been asked to write academically about. If I asked you to create for me a novel about a whiny teenager with an irrational need to get a boyfriend, but not allow you to put any humor into it, would that be an enjoyable thing to write?"

"Not really...?" I thought of *Twilight*. I couldn't help it. Dr. Roe was describing *Twilight* by Stephenie Meyer, one of the few books I actually disliked.

"Exactly. It's the same logic as those who don't like to read. They just haven't found the right book. You haven't found the right article. That's why you don't like reading it, and in turn you are horrified of writing one.

"What you need is to read an academic article about something you actually like. And don't look at me like that." He smiled the moment I raised a skeptical eyebrow. "There has to be something that interests you. It's not impossible, you know. As a teenager, you're familiar with the young adult author, John Green, right?"

"I love his books," I nodded.

"Have you read *Looking for Alaska*?"

"Of course! It was his first, my first from him, and my favorite."

"If you recall, at the end of *Looking for Alaska*, our main character Pudge writes an essay for his history class about religion and the perspective on life and death. That essay, Emma, was Pudge's academic article. I told you, it could be about anything.

"John Green incorporated an academic piece of writing into a work of fiction. That is like working one of Stephen King's famous quotes backwards. The quote, 'Fiction is the truth inside the lie,' do you know it?"

"No," I said shyly. I never knew Dr. Roe memorized quotes. He was beginning to look more and more like a fellow book-lover, not a distant someone.

"Fiction is essentially a well-crafted lie, Emma. But facts gathered from academic sources help mold them into something that can be considered an askew reality. You do research for your novels, of course. You have to!"

"I do, actually."

"Those are sources—sources and citations."

For the first time, I liked listening to him talk. At last I could *understand* the passion he had. I knew he possessed passion before, but it was a stranger to me. This passion, however, this one I understood. I understood the love and admiration for books and stories. The love of fiction. I understood it well, and that was our even ground.

"I want you to enter this contest, because I'd like to see you publish a novel someday as well," Dr. Roe said. "You love books. I know that as a fact. I want you to write an academic article on books. The rest is up to you, and that's all the help I can give you." He paused and smiled again. "Well, I could help you a little more by reading your academic essay. I want sources and everything. Then I will give you feedback, and we'll work on from there."

I was a little apprehensive when I asked, "Do I have to write a whole essay in one night?"

"Of course not! Start small. Give me an introduction. I want to see exigence, and a good argument. Maybe an outline, a thesis statement, you know the drill."

I sighed. "Why are you helping me so much?"

Dr. Roe shrugged. "I am a teacher. It's my job." He bit his lip then added, "And because I'm bored. We need a new generation of writers. Why not help facilitate it?"

***

I spent that night scouring through Google page after Google page, searching for something academic about books that I could actually write about. Even after all the motivation and the long talk, academic writing was still an unfavorable thought.

It took hours typing in names of classics, hoping to find some interesting article that I could use as a source.

Fahrenheit 451 by Ray Bradbury.

The Great Gatsby by F. Scott Fitzgerald.

Wuthering Heights by Emily Bronte.

The Catcher in the Rye by J.D. Salinger.

After an hour went by, I typed in *The Wonderful Wizard of Oz* by L. Frank Baum. On the eighth link I clicked, my eyes finally lit up upon reading Henry M. Littlefield's article, "The Wizard of Oz: Parable on Populism."

There it was, an article about my favorite childhood story, relating it to something adults would actually care about! Dr. Roe mentioned it in class. It had to qualify as academic...

The rest of the night I spent reading over the twelve-page parable, and was pleasantly surprised at the level of understanding I had for everything Littlefield wrote about. The era of L. Frank Baum's lifespan was easily found after a Google search, and it was actually interesting to read about the author of, in my opinion, one of the greatest pieces of children's literature. All of Littlefield's references to the story were something I could actually interpret since I had the book lying on my bookshelf, and my mind could recall the story rather clearly. It was weird, reading the article, finding myself halfway agreeing with his argument. It was just weird overall, reading an academic piece of writing and actually understanding it.

It was the jargon, perhaps.

Or just the preference. I preferred this to some random article about physics with words I couldn't even pronounce.

***

I slept very little that night, because I spent it drafting an outline and starting on a rough introduction. Still, I didn't know how sources were supposed to look properly, but I supposed Dr. Roe could help me. He's actually helped me so much already...believe it or not. That boring old drone had passion and interest.

> *The Wonderful Wizard of Oz* by Lyman Frank Baum had been a beloved children's fairy tale since its creation—and no one really knew why. It could be the glorious childhood nostalgia it instilled as readers follow the odyssey of

Dorothy through the wonderful Land of Oz. Or it could have been the personal relation of the narrative to a different yet at the same time relatively similar life during one of America's most changing and active periods. Either way, Baum had successfully written a story that appealed to both children and adults alike. And in his creation, he'd created a world where all kinds of meanings and symbolism could be inferred—so fictitious that with the right wording, anything could be taken out of it. Henry M. Littlefield, for example, had pronounced the work of fiction as a parable on the political situation during Baum's era, which included works with the Populist Party, the free silver campaign, and the candidacy of William Jennings Bryan, as well as America's attitude towards the concerns and prosperity of western expansion. While many would stand to disagree with Littlefield's claim that Baum's fairy tale was a parable, it is inarguable that since the publication of Littlefield's article, "*The Wonderful Wizard of Oz* was no longer an innocent fairy tale (Parker, 1994)." David B. Parker argued that Baum was simply searching for meaning in what was a man's simple pursuit in crafting an entertaining children's tale. And as time wound on, the argument of whether *The Wonderful Wizard of Oz* was a parable or not remains. In response to the ever-existing question, Littlefield may have over-exaggerated the political relevance of this children's fairy tale, and Parker under-exaggerated. *The Wonderful Wizard* of Oz does possess political influences, but is not strictly a political story disguised as fiction—in fact it is simply a story written by a definite dreamer, with inspiration drawn from his existing reality, incorporating details that may be intentionally/unintentionally symbolic, with influences born from the Progressive Era, and carrying a self-prophetic air for the coming future.

It wasn't much, but it was a start.

I handed the introduction, crudely scrawled on three sheets of notebook paper, into Dr. Roe the next day. At the end of class, he returned the paper to me with no red markings, just a quick message scrawled in the back: *See me during free period; good start.*

Works Cited

Driscoll, Dana L. "Appropriate Language." *Purdue OWL: Using Appropriate Language.* N.p., n.d. Web. 15 Nov. 2013.

Green, John. *Looking for Alaska.* New York: Dutton Children's, 2005. Print.

Littlefield, Henry M. "The Wizard of Oz: Parable on Populism." *American Quarterly* 16 (1964): 47-58. Print.

Maddalena, Kate McKinney. "I need you to say 'I.'" *Writing Spaces* 1 (2010). Web.

Parker, David B. "Oz Populism Theory." Oz Populism Theory. N.p., n.d. Web. 26 Mar. 2013.

Rosenberg, Karen. "Reading Games: Strategies for Reading Scholarly Sources." *Writing Spaces* 2 (2011). Web.

Joe Wang

Alice in Normal-land

There is a wonderful quote which I will unabashedly borrow from the beloved essayist Phillip Lopate: "In the beginning, God created Fiction and Poetry, and saw that it was good; and then some whiners started demanding nonfiction courses" (Lopate). Of course, it's all delightfully facetious, but that spurious myth really does quite admirably encapsulate my philosophy on writing, at least as it stands at present. Of course, no one is debating the value and place of nonfiction—surely, journalism and data-backed analysis will always have its place in society—but fiction was my sanctuary. A mystical, secluded forest where adjectives and adverbs could prance about, free from the confining shackles of such arbitrators as "grammar" and "structure." Where writing was about *feeling*, not thinking, and one could ramble on for hours upon hours without having to sporadically stop to peruse copious volumes of studies and sources. Thus, without even realizing it, I had carefully constructed a barrier within myself, fashioning a clearly delineated world with the unicorns and angelic choirs of fiction on one side and the fire and brimstone of nonfiction on the other. And never the twain shall meet.

Creative writing became almost a second nature to me, and my immersion in its techniques and stylistic flairs gave me great confidence. However, with its more analytical counterpart, I felt like I was constantly floundering against the current, unpleasantly restricted by the rules, and my efforts turned out stodgy and awkward. However, in the deep recesses of my mind, that seldom-accessed part not permeated with whimsical fancies and fanciful whims, I had always wondered: how is it possible to be so enraptured by one genre of writing and yet be simultaneously so hapless at another? Certainly there must be some crossover, some aspect of fiction that may confer an advantage to nonfiction. And so, with trusty notebook and magnifying glass in hand, I bravely leapt into the rabbit hole.

Before embarking on the lengthy adventure to discern a correlation between fiction and nonfiction writing, I had to, quite obviously, learn what it was that distinguished the two. Now, the immediate easy answer is: well, nonfiction deals with true things, and fiction does not. Not quite, according to Marie-Laure Ryan; nonfictional works, such as biographies, "may be based on unfounded claims and controversial interpretations," just as novels may contain actual settings or events within its fictional narrative (Ryan 166).

Instead, she argues, we should examine each genre through the lens of validity and scope. Nonfiction cannot by itself establish a truth; it must be viewed within the context of other sources in the field: "To be accepted as true, the facts and interpretations of a biography must either harmonize with other versions regarded by the reader as reliable, or it must destroy the credibility of these versions" (Ryan 166). In contrast, fiction, quite paradoxically, can ensure its own truth. Since each work of fiction—barring series continuations or spinoffs—constructs its own world, it becomes the audience's sole point of reference for that world (Ryan 167).

Now, with the definitions relatively straightened out—I'll investigate some exceptions later on—what does this mean for my overarching analysis? Well, to begin with, one major difference between the two fields is that of language and style. Ryan mentions that "[t]he dissimilarity between fictional and nonfictional modes of narration is so much taken for granted that a reasonably close fictional imitation of a nonfictional genre strikes the reader as an ostentatious fabrication" (Ryan 169). That is, the difference in tone and diction is so ingrained, so natural to the reader, that he or she can immediately discern whether a piece is fiction or nonfiction from a few passages. However, that does not mean that there is absolutely no transference of expertise.

On one side, there is the advent of the so-called New Journalism, which utilizes nineteenth-century fiction techniques such as "the predominance of scene over summary, detailed record of dialogue, the depiction of everyday gestures, and variable focalization allowing direct access to the minds of characters" in an effort to personalize the topic and better immerse the reader (Ryan 171). On the other hand, there is the burgeoning realm of creative nonfiction, which strives to take historical events, such as the US Civil War, and imbue them with personalities and details not entirely grounded in fact; the major events, people, and locations may be factual, but it is sporadically sprinkled with fictional narratives, dialogues, and motivations. As such, perhaps it is not that there is an inherent crossover between fiction and nonfiction, but that the genres themselves are moving closer together, making certain skills more transferrable between the two.

For instance, the predominantly scientific and equation-riddled field of economics has recently experienced a shift in opinion as it relates to the importance of creative writing abilities. Though creative writing was rarely taught in traditional economics writing programs "because many professors believe that it cannot be applied within disciplines that lean towards mathematical modeling and theorizing," researcher Ophelia D. Goma believes that creative writing carries a value far beyond its purpose as a tool for communication (Goma 149). In fact, she argues, fiction writing has the ability to enhance mental faculties involved in the "construction and synthesis of knowledge" (Goma 149). Instead of being constantly hemmed in by the constraints of a formal writing style and structure, creative writing prepares students to think more actively and dynamically, better equipping them to tackle the unexpected and even outlandish economic problems they will encounter in the real world. Furthermore, one of the great strengths of fictional compositions is that they enable the author to truly discover his or her personal voice: "Through creative writing, students gain a voice [...] and their writing becomes more personal and insightful. They are no longer passive recipients of information but active disseminators" (Goma 150). From this study, it can be inferred that those with extensive creative writing experience tend to be more confident and expressive about their opinions in nonfiction writing as well—a clear advantage, if nothing else.

With the abundance of evidence espousing the burgeoning similarities between fiction and nonfiction writing, I wondered why more authors haven't elected to cross over and dabble in each category. Instead, there seem to be quite entrenched camps of "fiction authors" and "nonfiction authors"; what makes someone identify, as I do, as a fiction-focused writer as opposed to a nonfiction writer? The answer, as it seems to be with most controversial topics, comes down to perception. In an interview given at *The New Yorker* Festival in 2010, acclaimed authors Michael Chabon and Zadie Smith provided a glimpse into why one would feel a predilection towards one genre over the other. Chabon, a novelist and short fiction author, proclaimed that while some sort of fact or personal experience often trickles into his novels, he feels uncomfortable writing nonfiction as "the extent to which you do feel compelled to stick to the facts can be crippling" (Chabon). With fiction, "If I said there was a theater of war in Antarctica [during WWII], then there was, and I just needed to buttress all that so it sounded plausible" (Chabon). Smith, an essayist, disagrees, pointing out that she "[wants] to be right, and in fiction you can't be right"— interestingly subverting Ryan's earlier ideology on the truths of fiction—and referring to the facts as an "anchor" that helps keep her grounded and focused on the topic at hand (Chabon). This argument was all too familiar to me as it's one I've often contemplated as a writer; I was good at fiction because it gave me the freedom to express myself, whereas with nonfiction I was constantly hounded by the pressure to be accurate and adhere to the rules.

In order to truly determine the veracity of the above statement, I decided to conduct a minor experiment. I selected four pieces of writing from two authors, including myself, with each author providing one story and one analytical piece. Then, without revealing the details or origins of the papers, I asked one of my good friends, who is relatively familiar with my writing style, to comment upon the strengths and weaknesses of each composition, and try to determine their authors. Through this, I could figure out which aspects of my writing carried over the best between genres, and if an individual's writing style could be distinguished from both fiction and nonfiction exploits.

The results of the impromptu test were astonishing to me, as my friend was able to correctly identify which two pieces were written by me and which were written by the other author. He described both of my works as "vibrant," with "good storytelling ability," a "medium level of vocabulary," and "straightforward and simplistic yet with dark undertones" (Shanmugam). Conversely, for the other two submissions, which I commandeered from one of my other good friends, he categorized them as "conversational, with great emphasis on building believable character relationships," as well as possessing a "high level of vocabulary" (Shanmugam)—to be fair, she is a much better writer than I am! Though seemingly simple and innocuous at first glance, this study was able to clarify for me, on a personal level, which characteristics of my writing were most noticeably transferrable between fiction and nonfiction. For instance, my style of description and sense of humor seem to be good identifiers of my writing, while paragraph structure and diction can vary greatly depending on the purpose and audience of the piece in question. Similarly, my friend's tendency to write pieces focused on dialogue and establishing intimate character relationships can be easily discerned, regardless of the composition's content or purpose. Also of significance, when asked to disclose the genres of each piece, he mischaracterized one of the fictional short stories as a nonfiction personal anecdote, which again highlights the thin divide between fiction and nonfiction in many cases (Shanmugam).

Prior to this entire examination, I had a few notions as to how well certain aspects of writing translated between fiction and nonfiction. Obviously, fundamental mechanics such as breadth of vocabulary or a basic understanding of grammatical norms would remain constant across any form of written expression, while more malleable traits such as structure and process would vary widely. My investigation did little to dispel these preconceptions, but it did reveal some more nuanced and intriguing connections; for instance, fiction authors' flexibility and well-defined personal voice offer great value when it comes to developing innovative solutions in nonfiction scenarios. Even relatively minute touches like humor and dialogue idiosyncrasies may manage to seep through. Especially when it comes to my own personal writing, there were many more similarities between my fiction and my nonfiction than I had previously recognized; somewhat ironically, the largest gulf between the two might actually be my confidence.

Just as Alice was ultimately lifted from her reverie by a fluttering of falling leaves, so too must my journey through the intertwining kingdoms of fiction and nonfiction end. But, like many such journeys, the most fascinating element often lies not in the destination or conclusions drawn, but in the aftermath.

What happens to Alice when she is so rudely thrust back into the real world? Does she simply just fall back into her old routines and mundane reality, as if nothing had ever happened? I'd like to believe that, when she departed, Alice took a slice of Wonderland with her; though the post-Wonderland world is nearly identical to its pre-Wonderland counterpart, Alice as a person has been changed irrevocably for her escapades. And, taking a page out of the book of our titular heroine, I can borrow a sliver from my fictional sanctuary and take it with me as I trek into the unknown wilds of nonfiction. Perhaps—just perhaps—both realms will be better off for it in the end.

Works Cited

Chabon, Michael and Zadie Smith. *Writers on Writing: Fiction vs. Nonfiction.* Interview by ForaTV. The New Yorker Festival, 2010. Web. 5 November 2013.

Goma, Ophelia D. "Creative Writing in Economics." *College Teaching* 49.4 (2001): 149-152. Print.

Lopate, Phillip. "Curiouser and Curiouser: The Practice of Nonfiction Today." NonfictioNow Conference. 10 November 2005. Keynote Address.

Ryan, Marie-Laure. "Postmodernism and the Doctrine of Panfictionality." *Narrative* 5.2 (1997): 165-187. Print.

Shanmugam, Abi. Personal Interview. 15 November 2013.

Tirthak Saha

Humor—No Laughing Matter: An Exploration of the Merits of the Use of Humor in my Writing

It was a sunny summer's day six years back when I was still in high school. I remember how we had all been asked to hand in an essay on "my best qualities." I remember feeling supremely confident in my ability as a writer as my teacher skimmed through my essay with a smile on her lips as she read my playful writing interspersed with satire, wit, and humor. I also remember I got a C- on that paper.

This brings me to today, six years older, wiser, and with more facial hair (isn't that a sign of wisdom?). Today, as I look back on that fateful summer's eve, I can't help but wonder—was it my use of humor that sank that ship? I mean, I have always sprinkled my writing with a healthy dose of comedy because it felt so natural to me. I have always instinctively felt that humorous writing is easier to digest than the brand of serious and to-the-point writing that many prefer. Then again, what use is humor if it doesn't further the true purpose and topic of my writing? Should I have based my writing on the kind that I personally favor or should I have embraced the "dark side"? What kind of writing would actually have benefited me? This, finally and after a circuitous and tortuous route of introspection, brought me to the bedrock of the question that had been nagging me for six years—Was it a bad choice to have included humor in my writing?

This paper is written, primarily, for myself, as the question I have started with is very intimate to my writing experience. Thus, to start my investigation, I had to first define what I meant by humorous writing exactly. This turned out to be more of a roadblock than I could have imagined. I started out by collecting instances of my own writing where I had used different forms of humor and tried to recollect people's reactions to them. In the summer of 2006, I had received a copy of Edward Lear's *A Book of Nonsense* as a gift. Subsequently, my writing went through a limerick phase. I would churn out limericks by the dozen, some bad and some downright awful! But I recollected one such limerick that I had written:

We sent a man to the moon,

To humans it was a boon

Truly, a great feat it was,

Yet his wife said 'Alas!

Neil won't be home by noon!'

I fully expected this limerick to crash and burn and yet, when I presented this to my parents, it was met with much laughter and appreciation. As I started recollecting all the other times my use of humor in my writing had produced a desirable result, I realized the first problem. People laugh at such different and unexpected types of humor that it is near impossible, as a writer, to say for sure "this is going to click with my audience!"

Laughter and humor, unlike other human behavior, has evaded an all-inclusive theory to date. According to eminent humor theorist John Morreal, "The major difficulty here is that we laugh in such diverse situations that it seems difficult, if not impossible, to come up with a single formula that will cover all cases of laughter" (1). As such, it became difficult for me, as a writer, to depend on a particular type of humor in my writing in order to appeal to my audience.

Thus, I changed my direction of thought to a different aspect. I realized that regardless of the type of humor used, my writing experiences show that people did react to humorous writing favorably! All I had to do now was field-test writing of mine that was serious, factual, and basically precluded the use of humor and see if it fared better than my writing in which I had used humor.

To test my premise, I wrote two versions of an essay titled 'India—The Colonial Puppet' and e-mailed them to a group of 10 people. The first version was a factual outline of the topic filled with serious introspection and factual evidence for my beliefs on the subject. The second one included humorous anecdotes, satirical views of the British government's apathy and cruelty towards their subjects, and a smattering of puns. These instances of humor were interwoven with serious philosophy and hard facts about the independence movement. After a week, I asked my test group to give their feedback on which essay they preferred and how much of it they remembered. Surprisingly, six people out of the 10 had not bothered to read the serious version in its entirety. On the other hand, nine of them could remember almost the whole of the humorous version word for word (one person was too slothful to read either version).

Although the test had shown conclusively that my test group had reacted favorably to my use of humor in writing, the question that remained to be investigated was 'Why?' In response to this, I revisited the following points, which I had distilled from my research on the nature of humor.

Humor results from a psychological shift from the expected to the unexpected.

Therefore humor disarms the audience of any preconceived notions and judgments, even if momentarily.

Humor leads to the negation of tension. As Morreal again suggests, "... laughter is seen as the venting of nervous energy" (20).

These points led to the realization that humor increases the effectiveness of communication. "There can be no doubt that humor has social value and practical usefulness beyond measure. Most observers would agree that humor has an immense impact in erasing social conflicts, relieving tensions and fostering interpersonal rapport" (Chapman and Foot 248). This clearly shows that the major advantage of humor is its communicative power in social contexts. This, ultimately, brought me to the power of humor in, specifically, my own written communication or writing. I realized that use of humor in the second version of my essay received a favorable response because the addition of humor to a message enhances its persuasiveness. The humor makes the source of the message (the writer, or in this case, me) be perceived more favorably by the readers (my test group), leading to enhanced credibility of the message being delivered (my thoughts on India's Independence struggle). The humor draws the wavering attention of the reader to itself and, by continuation, to the message. This was proved by the fact that most people read the humorous version in its entirety and didn't bother to finish my factual, descriptive version. In addition, humor, by nature, suddenly disarms the reader and throws him off balance. This sudden shift has the effect of distracting the readers from their objections to the message. "It has been hypothesized that humor in a persuasive message might distract audience members so that their counter argumentation would be precluded..." (Sternthal and Craig 14). This probably was the reason why not a single test subject objected to any of my views outlined in the essay.

These realizations conclusively answered my initial question—"Was it a bad choice to have included humor in my writing?" and this time the answer was clear—a big resounding no! My initial instinct as a young writer, that the use of humor in my writing increases it efficacy, was vindicated. I also realized that one must be careful of being too liberal with its use lest the writing be perceived as frivolous; which is probably what went wrong with my essay all those years ago. However, there remains no doubt in my mind now that humor is a great rhetorical tool and I was justified in using it in the formative years of my writing experience. Having said that, I must also mention that while we may yet be far from a comprehensive understanding of humor in written communication as a theory, perhaps the best way to appreciate its power and beauty is how I perceived it in my childhood—instinctively.

As the great essayist E.B.White put it, "Humor can be dissected, as a frog can, but the thing dies in the process and the innards are discouraging to any but the pure scientific mind" (White 1).

Works Cited

Chapman, Antony J. and Hugh C. Foot. *Humor and Laughter: Theory, Research and Applications.* New York: Wiley and Sons, 1976. Print.

Morreal, John. *Taking Laughter Seriously.* Albany: State University of New York Press, 1983. Print.

Sternthal, Brian, & Craig, C. Samuel. "Humor in advertising", *Journal of Marketing,* 37.4 (1973): 12-18. Print.

White, E.B. Preface. *A Subtreasury of American Humor.* New York: Coward McCann, 1941. 1-13. Print.

Avital Breverman

Writing for a Score

I used to have a recurring nightmare in which students in my high school walked around with their SAT scores floating above their heads, like players in a videogame. I did not refer to my friends by their respective names, but by their scores. I sat down in math class next to "2250" and "2080." I had lunch with "1900," "2160," and "2210." Any time that "2400" passed by, everyone else parted to let her through.

That was junior year: the year that I gave up my sanity for a bunch of numbers and scores. Two years later, I still reflect on my less-than-fond memories of junior year. I have to admit that I scored well on the SAT, and that my highest score was in the newest section, the writing section. As I began my first quarter at Drexel, just two months ago, I wondered whether my strong SAT score had any implication on how I would fare as a college student. When presented with an assignment to write about writing, I decided to explore the following questions: "What effect did the SAT writing section have on my writing?" and "What do my SAT writing scores indicate about my success in college (if anything)?"

First, I decided to research the conception of the SAT writing section. The SAT writing section was implemented in March of 2005. It was developed to emphasize "the importance of writing skills for future success in college and beyond" to high schools and to their students (Norris, et al. 6). The SAT writing section includes a 25-minute timed essay and 49 multiple choice questions.

The differences between college writing and the SAT essay are numerous and openly acknowledged by College Board officials. Some of these differences were pointed out to me by Dr. Karen Nulton, who worked as a Senior Assessment Specialist for the ETS, specializing in the writing and reading sections of the SAT. Dr. Nulton is now a professor at Drexel University.

College writing assignments ask students to write with a purpose and address an appropriate audience while considering their own voices. As Dr. Nulton pointed out, the SAT essay, on the other hand, dictates the purpose and the audience for the assignment. According to Professor Nulton, the predetermined audience (the graders) "keeps students from really exploring a topic since they are trying to please an audience so thoroughly." The SAT does not abide by the "do not write to please the grader" maxim, an unfortunate result of its standardized nature and the large quantity of exams that must be assigned a score quickly. The SAT essay is administered under a time limit. College writing is rarely, if ever, assigned a time limit. Most adults have not written a timed essay since high school.

Since the essay is limited in time and students are not given the prompt ahead of time, graders allow students to make up facts and supporting details. College writing, on the other hand, encourages students to base their arguments and reasoning on facts and to use and cite outside sources. Obviously, it would be difficult to require SAT takers to pump out five paragraphs and three MLA citations in 25 minutes. Therefore, the SAT essay is a quick-and-dirty exam response that does not resemble college writing. However, as Professor Nulton says, "at least now the SAT encourages writing" in some form. A formulaic five-paragraph essay is "better than no writing and no essay" (Nulton).

Although the SAT essay is vastly different from college writing, SAT officials found that the inclusion of the writing section catalyzed schools to change their curriculums to include more writing. The addition of the SAT writing section sent a message to high school administrations and English departments that writing is essential for success in college and beyond. My high school was among the schools that integrated more timed writings and multiple choice practices into all levels of eleventh grade English, in order to prepare students for the SAT writing section. The addition of SAT practice in my junior year English curriculum helped prepare me for the SAT writing section; however, the time spent on SAT preparation detracted from the amount of time spent preparing for the AP English exam and on the class curriculum.

If there are so many differences between the SAT essay and college writing, what is the purpose of the SAT? I am sure that readers have already heard many different answers to this jaded question. The SAT was originally designed to test for scholastic aptitude (what is that, anyway?). SAT scores are used as a prediction of a student's success in the first year of college. SAT scores, however, have no predictive validity for a student's overall college GPA or of success after college (Nulton). Now equipped with an understanding of the SAT's purpose, I sought out data and sources that confirmed that there is indeed a correlation between test scores and first-year college GPA.

A 2006 College Board study, entitled "The College Board SAT Writing Validation Study: An Assessment of Predictive and Incremental Validity," involved the administration of a prototype version of the SAT writing section to 1,572 students during their summer freshman orientation or during their first semester at college. The results were used to assess the predictive validity of the SAT writing section for the students' first year GPAs and writing GPAs. The study uses various models (orders for taking the various SAT sections and high school GPA into account) for determining the incremental validity for predicting first-year college GPA. The corrected and adjusted values from Tables 13 and 15 (found on pages 10 and 12, respectively) were used in this analysis.

In Table 13, a student's high school GPA (HSGPA) was the first factor used to predict freshman GPA, producing a validity, or correlation, of 0.40 units. By adding the student's SAT verbal and math scores, the validity was increased to a stronger correlation of 0.59 units. The addition of the student's writing score added a mere 0.01 units to the validity. In Table 15 (which represents a different model), the addition of the SAT writing to the other two sections of the SAT adds 0.01 units to the SAT's ability to predict first-year college GPA. Considered holistically, a student's HSGPA and SAT score has 0.60 units of validity for predicting first-year college GPA.

Admittedly, this study was conducted using a prototype of the writing section, which closely resembled but was shorter than the true writing section. Also, the population that participated in the study could have been larger to ensure more accurate results.

While interviewing Dr. Nulton, she pointed out that SAT scores are "being asked to make predictions that they are not intended to measure." In another study, discussed in "SATs for Writing Placement: A Critique and Counterproposal," by Emily Isaacs and Sean A. Molloy, the SAT writing scores of incoming freshmen to Georgia State University (GSU) were used to place the students into one of two English courses, College Writing (the more advanced course) or Introduction to Writing, for their first semester. Previously, GSU used an "in-house writing assessment" but discontinued it because of the cost (Isaacs and Molloy). GSU found that when it used an arbitrary SAT writing cutoff score of 410, it placed 9.5% of incoming freshmen into Intro to Writing, a drop of one-third from previous years. Did each successive incoming class contain more capable writers or is using SAT writing scores a more lenient method of placing freshmen into college writing courses? The study found that there was a "misplaced cohort" that was placed, unprepared, into College Writing as a result of the arbitrary cutoff score (Isaacs and Molloy). Therefore, SAT scores, particularly writing scores, have *some* predictive validity, but this predictive validity is not enough to serve as the only factor used to place freshmen in college writing classes (especially when an arbitrary cutoff score is used).

It is important to remember that students take the SAT at 8 AM on Saturday mornings. The essay is the first section that they must get through while they are still probably half asleep. It may be unreasonable to expect these scores to consistently and accurately reflect students' true writing capabilities given the known sleeping habits of high school students.

After reading this paper, I hope that I have provided enough information for readers to make the following conclusion: poor SAT scores do not signify an unsuccessful life nor do strong SAT scores guarantee a 4.0 throughout college and a seven-figure income. There is some correlation between SAT scores and first-year college GPA (although the addition of the SAT writing score to the pre-existing SAT adds little to the test's ability to predict first-year college GPA), but the relationship is not a causation.

Too often we confuse SAT scores with intelligence and success. We are not defined by SAT scores, nor should we allow ourselves to define others by their scores. If, in my sleep, I have a dream about high school, it will be a dream filled with fond memories, not a nightmarish SAT déjà vu. I will sit next to and joke with Julie and Matt, not "2250" and "2080," in math class. I will eat lunch with Ruth, Sarah, and Neil (real friends, not bodies with floating numbers). Most importantly, when I see a certain girl passing me in the hallway, I will smile and wave to Jasmine, not to "2400."

Works Cited

Dwayne Norris, Scott Oppler, Daniel Kuang, Rachel Day, and Kimberly Adams, "The College Board SAT Writing Validation Study: An Assessment of Predictive and Incremental Validity," College Board, New York, NY, Rep. 2006-2, 2006.

Isaacs, Emily and Molloy, Sean A. "Texts of our Institutional Lives: SATs for Writing Placement: A Critique and Counterproposal." *College English*, 72. 5 (2010): 518-538. *ProQuest*. Web. 2 Nov 2013.

Nulton, Karen. Video Interview. 15 November 2013.

Nidhi George

No Time to be Breathless

"Nid, it's happening again."

They say that life isn't measured by the breaths we take, but the moments that take our breath away. For the number of times I've heard that cliché one would think I'd know who the omniscient *they* is, or that I would be able to attest to the aphorism's validity. But I can't. I don't know if my life's true worth is the sum of the times I've found myself gasping for air. All I know was that in that moment, as I lay on my bed with the phone pressed up against my face, I was completely breathless.

My friend Veronica has suffered from depression for her entire teenage life. Her insecurities have catalyzed a constant paranoia and an eating disorder. And while these struggles are significant parts of her identity, they were not part of the girl I met my freshman year of high school. The Veronica I passed notes to in chemistry was vivacious. She had a laugh that could make Mondays enjoyable. Ronnie was the definition of *people pleaser*; she'd constantly ask about my day while never complaining about her own. Because of her secrecy, I didn't find out about her struggles for months. Eventually, a few friends and I learned to pick up on unspoken cues to gauge her mental state. We'd notice the days she looked particularly tired despite the extra concealer on her face, and the lunch periods when she'd only eat carrot sticks, claiming to have eaten more substantial food during class. These were signals of her regression and we'd collectively force her to talk to us about the problem. Being my clueless 16-year-old self, I often handled the situation rashly. I did the only thing I knew to; I lectured her. I would constantly remind her of the minimum calories she should be consuming a day, chastise her for being irrational, and threaten to tell her parents. The pleas didn't work. She would appease me, telling me what I wanted to hear and then pretend like everything was okay. Veronica knew that this was how I coped. She elected to regard my lectures as acts of love, and never called me out for not really knowing what I was talking about. In the end it was the presence of her friends, and not what we said, that helped her deal with her issues. She, like so many of us, derived the greatest comfort from the simple act of being cared for.

Senior year rolled around and Veronica was as healthy as she had ever been. She had been eating regularly for months and had only the occasional spout of depression. We spent the few weeks before Veronica went to Vassar talking about the pros and cons of our looming higher education. On the one hand we'd have freedom, interesting classes, and parties, but on the terrifying other, we'd have to part with the safety net that is our group of friends. The night before she left I told her the only thing I could, "I love you, and I'll always be here for you, Ronnie."

It was about a week and a half later that I got the call.

"Nid, it's happening again."

At that moment I was breathless not because I knew that she was feeling down—to be honest, I had foreseen an initial period of loneliness—I was breathless because I knew that for her to be reaching out to me, something had to be very wrong. The instant I found the ability to speak, I made up for lost time by firing a barrage of questions.

"How are you? Have you made friends? You're not spending all day in your room, right?"

Silence. All I could hear was the sound of her breathing.

"Ronnie, talk to me"

"I haven't been eating."

My heart dropped to my stomach.

"How long has it been?"

"Two days."

The gravity of the situation hit me and I knew that for her sake I couldn't become overly emotional. The reality was that if I didn't manage to get through to her during this phone call, she would descend into a downward spiral without anyone around to pull her out. It was then that I resolved to convince her to go to therapy—a challenge that would require the use of every rhetorical strategy I knew. The first of which would be pathos.

"Ron. You know I love you, right?" I asked.

"I know," she whispered.

"I love you so much, and I see in you a person who is capable of such great things. A person who I know will change the lives of many, and I know this because you've changed mine. Remember this and hear me out."

She sniffled, "I love you too, and I will."

By starting the conversation in such a manner, I appealed to her emotions. The establishment of love above all else was what I thought would make her receptive to my following argument. Next, I had to address something that I struggled with during high school, establishing credibility. But I had learned from my mistakes, and I knew that this time my goal shouldn't be to try to build up myself but to vouch for the credibility of someone more qualified than I.

"Ron. You need to see somebody. I know that when you tried therapy freshman year you felt worse, but that's only because you didn't find the right therapist. But just because it didn't help the first time, doesn't mean it won't now. I understand that it's scary for you to open up, but I promise whoever you talk to will know the right things to tell you. They'll understand where you're coming from more than me."

By saying that I wasn't qualified, I showed honesty. She was more inclined to believe what I said about therapy because it was clear my prerogative was not selfish. I also managed to foster credibility in therapists by emphasizing their training with the issues that Veronica was battling. Finally, I attempted to employ the all-important logos.

"Most importantly, Ron, things are different now. I'm not around to make sure you're doing okay, and neither are our friends or your parents. Nobody is there to make sure you're healthy all the time. I know after a while you'll make close friends, but till that happens, you're going to *need* somebody to be there for you."

She sighed, "You're right."

This final component of my rhetoric was what I believed made the most difference. My use of logic gave Veronica no choice but to face the situation she was in. She knew her darkest times took place when she felt isolated.

"Please think about it, Ron, okay?" I begged.

"I will, I promise," she replied.

Two days later she called me back and told me she had signed up to meet with her university's counselor. This call, much like the first, filled me with emotion, but this time it was a wave of relief. None of this would have been possible without the proper use of rhetorical devices that presented my request in an appealing manner.

Allison Law

The "New Art" of Letter Writing

According to Maslow's Hierarchy of Needs, communication and the need to fit in have long been an integral part of human lives, psychologically needed for fulfillment. However, communication comes in many forms. Whereas handwritten letters convey a sense of emotion and sentiment, technology brings an entirely new dimension, offering a wide variety of speedy communication, specifically e-mail, which has commonly been used to convey brief and factual messages. With the incorporation of technology into everyday lives, it is easy to be sucked into an Internet world. Consequently, many have coined the term "the lost art of letter writing." Because means of communication create a virtual sense of oneself, the students of today must distinguish the usefulness and purpose of each form. After the implementation of technology, letter writing should now serve a different purpose: for emotional connection and deeper reflection.

Handwritten letters have been present for hundreds of years, giving historians primary sources, which act as a window into the minds of great figures. Household names such as Einstein, Beethoven, and Churchill each wrote letters to loved ones and colleagues, revealing the inner thoughts of these great figures in our society. These letters uncover emotions, desires, and creative processes, contributing to our knowledge of these people, outside their accomplishments. Valentinuzzi complains that with the implementation of technology, specifically e-mail, it will be difficult for historians of the future to reconstruct "facts, discover secret romances, find undercover political deals, war or revolution plannings, learn about inceptions of scientific discoveries, and developments and evolution of ideas and concepts!" (1). He speaks of the importance of letter writing and is afraid that "this beautiful, ancient, and traditional custom has been essentially extinguished" (Valentinuzzi 1).

Many critics like him agree that e-mail has had negative influences on letter writing. The postal service undoubtedly lost income due to the Internet, when e-mail took over as the main vehicle of communication. Our society has been shaped to take the most convenient route, sending a quick e-mail, rather than opting to sit down to write a letter. The U.S. Postal Service "lost $8.5 billion in 2010 and has cut nearly 200,000 workers in the past decade," largely due to the shift in communication modes ("Commentary: Technology Threatens U.S. Postal Service." 2). As the article exaggeratingly describes, "technology has been the demise of the postal system" ("Commentary: Technology Threatens U.S. Postal Service." 2).

Truth be told, e-mail and handwritten letters are extremely different. While handwritten letters are more personal, old-fashioned, and allow for deeper communication, e-mails are more generic, modern, and are best for functional communication. Handwritten letters are tangible and can be kept. They have sentimental value and display an array of handwriting, which is much more distinctive than a typed font. Although letters may slow us down, they allow for deeper thought and a more reflective piece of work. The letter-writing process requires a well-thought-out plan, rather than a spontaneous impulse to send e-mail. Therefore, this drawn-out process is considered an act of thoughtfulness, especially in our society, where other forms of communication are so much more convenient.

Although e-mails and handwritten letters present very different forms of communication, their underlying similarities are undeniable. Both are a reliable source of communication, and are readily available to the public at a minute cost, if anything at all. They are both, after all, forms of communication through the written word, electronically or with a pen and paper. Most importantly, both e-mails and letters strengthen our relationships, giving us the opportunity to connect with others without being with them in person.

As Callisen explains, we are able to create a sense of the human mind through words. Using language, one can articulate himself without being interrupted by others. Callison deems this false presence through words a "telepresence," "an imagined body, and a spiritual, almost telepathic sense of [an]other's presence" through their correspondence (1). Our telepresences generally resemble our actual personalities and can be manipulated to create relationships with others. Our presence through words, when read by another, can be extremely persuasive, since "presence as integrally related to the phenomena of disembodiment and intimacy" (Callisen 2). And, it is often found that these "constructions of presence are concerned with a sense of shared experience, or involve conversations around topics of common interest," therefore further strengthening relationships (Callisen 2). Neither letters nor e-mails can be "matched by the flesh and blood of the physical self," but there is still "persistence, despite changes in technology, of certain ideologies and desires" (Callisen 2-3). E-mails and handwritten letters therefore allow for a kind of connection that is a lot more similar than we initially perceive.

Spoken or written, communication is not uniform; it has many functions. Intimate conversations often take place in a quiet, secluded setting, while casual conversations take place in the public, workplace, or school. Conversations can be meant for sharing personal thoughts, desires, and experiences with loved ones, or they can be used for setting up meeting dates, and passing information. They can be intimate, casual, or formal. Like setting and topic, mode of conversation should embody the kinds of conversation that exists. There should be an appropriate correlation between mode of communication and its purpose.

In a study done on young adults and the effect of technology on language use in their formal writing, researchers found that the use of "textisms," informal abbreviations and slang, in formal writing was quite low, "varying most strongly among those without a college education" ("The Relationship between "Textisms" and Formal and Informal Writing among Young Adults." 1). The study "reflected negative associations between reported textism use in daily communications and formal writing and positive associations between textism use and informal writing" (Ibid 1).This illustrates the human ability to separate form from function, where different situations call for different language. If this is true, young people should be able to also distinguish between appropriate times for e-mail and handwritten letters.

As many have noticed, e-mail quickly has taken a huge role in professional communication. It is functional, quick, and formal. A standard format can even be applied to an e-mail to create authenticity for an organization or business. Because e-mail and technology are inevitably an integral part of our society, in order to stay up to date, a firm grasp on the technological world is critical. A firm line, however, must be drawn between what kind of technological connections can be made professionally and socially.

In November 2011, the Illinois School Board District took the initiative to safely incorporate technology in its school system. The school recognized that teachers must embrace this new technology without being careless, since it also has many potential negative effects. It acknowledged that "these forms of communication are dynamic, mobile, and quickly reach their audience through technologies that have become an integral part of our online lives" (Todoric 2). However, it has also established definite technological rules for teachers in their classrooms. It asked teachers to "choose words that are courteous, conscientious, and generally businesslike in manner" (Todoric 2). Most importantly, it said that a "wall between the role of a public educator and personal friendships with students should always be visible and strongly communicated" (Todoric 3). These successful guidelines for technological communication set the standard for many like-schools to follow. Obviously, e-mail has proven to be a very effective mode of professional and functional communication.

So, while e-mail is ideal for clear, informative communication, it greatly lacks the individualism that comes entwined with handwritten letters. Letters are more meaningful to both the sender and receiver because they are more time-costly and thoughtful, where the sender must make a trip to a post office to send it. Because e-mail lacks individualism and intimacy, the telepresence of the writer is slightly lost. Additionally, Isaacs emphasizes that we should all "nurture and treasure our handwriting" (2). "Handwriting incorporates something of our personality and perhaps something of our humanity" and is "unique, as distinctive as a fingerprint" (Isaacs 1). Handwritten letters allow the reader and writer to connect and learn more about each other through this unique form of communication, recognizing handwriting as an important identity of a person. He also explains that although "the content and meaning of what we write is the most critical thing," "we lose something deeply personal and meaningful if we stop writing by hand" (Isaacs 1).

The impact and significance of handwritten letters can be seen in their role in our American soldiers' lives too. They "still retain immense importance in America for an audience that can sometimes only receive snail mail" ("Writing Letters and Sending Packages to Soldiers Helps Boost Their Morale" 1). The article explains how simply receiving letters from loved ones is something memorable; "it's always easy to Skype or e-mail, but letters are special; they can be read over and over again" (Ibid 3). Even from strangers, letters "make a difference and a large impact on the morale of the protectors of the country" (Ibid 1). A nurse who was on duty during the war described how "the change in soldiers when they received mail is reason enough to write to them," and how "handwritten letters have a particular power to make an emotional impact on soldiers' lives" (Ibid 2). For soldiers, a handwritten letter "shows that you go the extra distance" and that fellow citizens from home are thinking of them (Ibid 2). It lets soldiers know that they are not forgotten and that we are appreciative of their service.

Letter writing should, in no way, be a "lost form of art." Although e-mail has created an alternative, much more convenient vehicle of communication, it should not, in any way, be handwritten letters' demise. Historically, letters have been used as a means of deep communication. The differences between e-mails and letters are obvious: e-mails are formal, quick, and convenient, while handwritten letters are personal, slow, and allow for intimate communication. However, the two have many similarities as well; both are ways to create a telepresence and convey messages through the written language.

Neither mode should be used exclusively. Instead, letter writing should now serve a different purpose than it had in the past: for emotional connection and deep reflection. E-mail, on the other hand, should be used for informative and professional conversations. This should ultimately lead users to quickly distinguish between the writing and typing for different functional purposes. Our future generations need to embrace technology as it continues to make our lives more convenient and faster-paced. However, they should never neglect the significance of a good handwritten letter, as demonstrated to us by generations past.

Works Cited

Callisen, Christian Thorsten. *Letters, Postcards, Email: Technologies of Presence.* 62 Vol. Oxford, UK: Blackwell Publishers Ltd, 2012. Print.

"Commentary: Technology Threatens U.S. Postal Service." Wisconsin Law Journal, 2011. Print.

Isaacs, David. "Handwriting." *Journal of Paediatrics and Child Health* 49.8 (2013): 609-10. Print.

"The Relationship between "Textisms" and Formal and Informal Writing among Young Adults." *Communication Research* 37.3 (2010): 420-40. Print.

Todoric, Mary E. "Guidelines for Acceptable Electronic Communication with Students." *Education Digest: Essential Readings Condensed for Quick Review* 77.3 (2011): 47-9. Print.

Valentinuzzi, Max E. "Manuscript Letters... are they Forever Past? [Retrospectroscope]." *IEEE Pulse* 4.3 (2013): 48-51. Print.

"Writing Letters and Sending Packages to Soldiers Helps Boost Their Morale." *The Collegian.* N.p., 12 June 2012. Web. 22 Nov. 2013.

Gregory Przybylski

To My Dearest

While not a common office supply for college students, my stamps and my envelopes were two of the most important things I packed when preparing for my fall term. Since classes have begun my girlfriend, Linda, and I have been in a long-distance relationship. While texts, phone calls, and Skype are all great ways of keeping in touch with someone, I have found letters to be romantic. In an age when almost no one sends letters, finding one in your mailbox is a big surprise and a big deal. That is why I wrote with anticipation of hearing her opinions and thoughts about my letters. However, I am new to writing about my emotions. I have been used to writing formal essays so I felt inexperienced about my letter writing. Going over these thoughts in my head, I decided I wanted to share them with Linda in my next letter. I got out my writing pad and pen. As my hand painted words of love across the page, I wondered how I could improve my love letters.

I dropped my pen and decided to do some research before writing my next draft. I first looked online and read any love poem and letter I could find. In my research, I found many famous people have used the mail to keep in touch with those they love. I found the introduction to Beethoven's first love letter to his Immortal Beloved. "My angel, my everything, my very self. – only a few words today, and in pencil (with yours)..." (Beethoven). The power in that opening line began my inspiration. I wanted to be able to write like the great composer himself.

To write like him I decided to find out why people write love letters. In doing some more research, I found that in eras with less communication, correspondence through the mail was the only way people could talk over long distances. "At their core, letters were men's attempts to sustain their emotional relationships with family and friends" (Hunter 339). In reading Hunter's article about an army officer and his lover from World War I, I realized how much I shared his plight. Due to circumstances outside of his control, the army officer was separated from the person he loved. He and his lover wished to remain together during and after their physical separation, just like Linda and I. Hunter writes, "Denied the opportunities for physical intimacy, their letters had to replace walking home in the dark after a dance and other moments of unobserved togetherness" (351). Letters allowed for communication to still occur as a form of physical interaction. The first time I visited Linda, I saw my letters taped up above her desk. For her, my letters were a physical reminder of me, and she kept every one of them so that she could read my handwriting and my words. Hancock further describes, "Passion has its physical manifestations, then, but it also prompts us into conscious activity; as we can see, the writing of poems is such an activity" (208). I now understood that while we spoke on the phone and Skype, the physical trait was a benefit of letters. While intriguing to me, I wanted to search further to figure out what to include in my next letter.

I looked for more letters online. Continuing to read, I realized some were passionate and full of loving words and thoughts, and some focused on simply what was happening around them in their daily life. Others looked to popular culture and historical culture in their letters. "Lovers declare their love, not only in the statement 'I love you' but in quoting (or sometimes disputing) popular songs, poets, preachers, writers or 'experts'" (Teo 344). Like me, these writers probably consumed a bit of their time reading other sources and immersing themselves in the love-writing process. By exposing themselves to more and more literature, they had found something that matched exactly how they felt about their recipient. Similarly, Linda and I share love songs and music videos with each other. In this distance apart, the both of us along with many others wanted to keep our love continuing.

These writers, just like me, needed these letters to continue their loving relationship. As Cancian writes, "Separation between individuals who were intensely involved in a relationship required them to mediate their intimacy" (759). Love letters were a way of keeping in touch and staying together. All of these writers were in love, yet were separated by distance. I then stumbled upon something rather peculiar. Many of these couples felt they became closer to each other during their separation. Cancian analyzes the migrant letters between two lovers separated by their occupations in Montreal, Canada and Venice, Italy. She writes:

> "Separation and idealisation were often integral to letter writing. In the letters of Antonietta, idealisation of her beloved Loris, and an enhanced feeling of their mutual love are frequently underscored. For instance, in the first weeks following their initial separation in 1946, Antonietta wrote: Tonight I think of you, you whom I cannot see. I reread your letter from Venice, an affectionate letter as usual, I can honestly say, like you, that the distance does not make us forget our love and affection. Instead, love grows (as you say) through distance. Yes, I feel that I love you more" (758).

How could this separation improve a relationship? Distance causes couples to lose a lot of intimacy they had experienced earlier in their relationships. Without dates, dinners, and activities, relationships became focused on communication.

If a relationship boils down to communication, I wondered what kinds of things people talked about. In my letters, I have written about romantic events I've witnessed during the week. I have written about my excitement for our next visit together and what we planned to do. In doing further research, I found that there is a trend in what writers include in their letters.

"Lovers often inhabited several timeframes in their letters: the actual moment of writing, the anticipation of the reading, reminiscences of previous encounters—which served to reaffirm the bonds of love—and then a projection of love into the future. Through this imaginary movement of love to and from the past, present and future, the experience of love at the moment of writing was thickened" (Teo 346).

Overall, Teo made a lot of sense to me. Writing about all moments of the relationship incites the imagination. The sheer concentration of love in a little letter is so dense that writing and receiving it warms the heart. As I finished reading this article I jotted some more notes down in the margins of my notebook. Teo also analyzes the purpose of a love letter. He writes, "Thus one of the main purposes of the love letter is to produce and maintain love: to provoke desire in periods of separation" (348). This was my epiphany. My letters were a way for me to continue expressing my love while we were apart.

I felt that my next letter would certainly surprise Linda. As I skimmed over my research, I became truly inspired. Now I knew why people wrote letters, what I could include in my letters, and why they brought us closer together. My new knowledge would help me write to my inspiration. I got out another sheet of paper and began:

To My Dearest,

Works Cited

Beethoven, Ludwig. "Letter One." Letter to Immortal Beloved. 6 July 1812. *Ludwig Van Beethoven - Letters to the Immortal Beloved*. N.p., Apr. 1998. Web. 11 Nov. 2013.

Cancian, Sonia. "The Language of Gender in Lovers' Correspondence, 1946–1949." *Gender and History* 24.3 (2012): 755-65. *Wiley Online Library*. Blackwell Publishing Ltd, 24 Oct. 2012. Web. 4 Nov. 2013.

Hancock, T. "The Chemistry of Love Poetry." *The Cambridge Quarterly* 36.3 (2007): 197-228. JSTOR. Web. 31 Oct. 2013.

Hunter, Kate. "More than an Archive of War: Intimacy and Manliness in the Letters of a Great War Soldier to the Woman He Loved, 1915–1919." *Gender and History* 25.2 (2013): 339-54. *Wiley Online Library*. John Wiley and Sons Ltd, 23 July 2013. Web. 31 Oct. 2013.

Sun, Linda. *Love Letters*. 2013. Photograph.

Teo, Hsu-Ming. "Love Writes: Gender and Romantic Love in Australian Love Letters, 1860–1960." *Australian Feminist Studies* 20.48 (2005): 343-61. EBSCO Host. Web.

Maria Raggousis

Performing Music and a Student's Personal Identity

As I sat in the Wenger Posture Chair below me and leaned on a Manhasset music stand in front of me with the letters BHS poorly spray-painted on it, I looked around my high school band room and saw intelligent, self-sufficient, and friendly peers. As soon as I would walk out of that room I encountered rowdiness and immaturity. Did all of the people in my high school who I could easily tolerate just happen to be involved in the instrumental music program? I could see a relationship between music and these slightly more intelligent peers of mine but I did not know if this was caused by learning music at a young age, was developed over time, or just happened randomly. It is not the first time I have thought about this correlation throughout my musical career and it certainly will not be the last. In the future perhaps my own child may have the choice between playing and not playing an instrument and that moment can potentially define a child's demeanor in the end. What I really have always wondered is if it is true that performing instrumental music changes the outcome of a child's academic achievement and personal identity. If music is in fact a factor for academic success, then I would consider myself a child with this outcome; however, before I can label myself as such I would like to inquire further to see if it is proven adequately.

From a general musician's standpoint, most would be biased to think that musicians were in fact superior and that musically inclined children would develop life skills more thoroughly. I visited a local Bucks County area high school and spoke with their music program instructors to gain some insight on their opinions on this matter; their answers surprised me to some extent, but after giving them some thought I agreed with what they had to say. All three of the teachers unanimously said that they believed music programs help kids do better in school. One question in particular that was asked was if the child's developmental success was formed because of the music or because it was an involvement in a group, and, could sports accomplish the same thing. We all concluded that the GPAs of students involved in instrumental music were higher than those of the general student body, but they did not share my initial point of view that it was the music specifically that made children 'smarter.'

Ms. Susan Hinson, with a Bachelor of Music in Music Education from the College of New Jersey and a Master of Arts in Music and Music Education from the Teachers College, Columbia University in the City of New York, thought that "although music and sports accomplish the same thing, sports have to try harder; with music it just happens naturally." What I took from that statement in combination with a recollection of my soccer involvement and my music involvement was that although things like teamwork, confidence, and communication skills were developed in both cases, a sport must verbally teach and enforce those standards; music on the other hand, accomplishes those tasks in the subconscious. By playing music, students become the ensemble; there is no way for a band to play music without becoming a team, without communicating, without having confidence in themselves, their ability, and each other. It is holistic experience. In a sport, I realized, all the students are not forced to behave in that mature manner and can in fact succeed at the sport without gaining these skills.

The jeopardy as I see it now, having been influenced by the research of Lois Hetland and Ellen Winner, in claiming that instrumental music can improve academic achievement, is that "the arts will quickly lose their position if academic improvement does not result, or if the arts are shown to be less effective than [promised]" (3). The teachers I interviewed would have agreed with Hetland and Winner in that "arts educators should never allow the arts to be justified wholly or even primarily in terms of what the arts can do for mathematics or reading. The arts must be justified in terms of what the arts can teach that no other subject can teach" (3).

We cannot assume that because the arts achieve group ethics in their student body, that they are the sole cause of academic flourishing. One factor may simply be that music attracts students who are more capable of higher level thinking skills, skills such as analyzing, evaluating, and creating. Music combines these things in applicable ways: improvisation, hand-eye coordination, spatial reasoning. Similarly, music can also be related to learning a new language (Hallam 1). It cannot be understood by anyone at random and uses similar functions in the brain as linguistics and logical-mathematical areas (Colwell and Davidson 57). Society can then argue that the number of languages one person can speak fluently makes them more intelligent in the long run. Music educators across the country are fighting the wrong battle if they believe telling the administrations that music helps academics will push the arts into the forefront.

Statistically, there are multiple studies done with various age groups and demographics that show the effect of music education on academics. Kate Fitzpatrick, of Northwestern University, used the Ohio Proficiency Test on fourth, sixth, and ninth grade students of varying social classes to study the effect of instrumental music participation on the score (73). Fitzpatrick accumulated data and it shows that upper class students involved in instrumental music outperformed the other students in every grade level and in every subject. In many cases, the lower class musicians scored just as well if not more than the upper class non-musicians. The students who scored the lowest consistently were the lower class non-music students (Fitzpatrick 81). That music has helped the Ohio children tested exceed their peers by such a large margin does not surprise me. My question is why these results cannot be supported by scientific proof of brain stimulation or something quantitative instead of qualitative. Donald A. Hodges and Debra S. O'Connell from the University of North Carolina at Greensboro collected the results of many different studies of how academics were affected by music. They begin by generalizing, "students who participate in music education frequently do better than their peers on many measures of academic achievement such as grade-point averages and standardized tests like the SAT or ACT" (2.1). That is a statement that most people can agree on, but why this is the case is what has been debated by professionals and amateurs alike.

Is this correlation between academic successes related to a child's self-awareness, confidence, and social development? What about their personal identity? Does music change the students in an irreversible way in their development? I would imagine that it does, for everything has a factor upon someone's personal development. Susan Hallam, from the University of London, explores different areas of a child, from intellectual and social development to the effects on their physical health and all the numeracy and literacy skills in between. She explains some of the relationships between music and a child's development:

> Participating in musical groups promotes friendships
> with like-minded people; self-confidence; social skills;
> social networking; a sense of belonging; team work;
> self-discipline; a sense of accomplishment; co-operation;
> responsibility; commitment; mutual support; bonding to
> meet group goals; increased concentration and ... makes
> a major contribution to the development of self-identity
> and is seen as a source of support when young people are
> feeling troubled or lonely (2).

Hallam realizes that music has these benefits to a child's social development, thus making them better at academics because they have become better people. A question raised here is if it is the fact that it is music that is making these positive effects or the fact that it is a group activity. Hodges and O'Connell also touch on this and the effect of these developmental qualities, where "musicians (band or choir), athletes, or non-participants...were statistically equivalent in fifth and sixth grade," but, "[in] seventh, eighth, and ninth grades the musicians achieved significantly higher academic achievement scores than the athletes" (2.4), which goes back and enforces what Susan Hinson had commented on about music achieving the stated developmental processes more naturally than sports, and in the long run more effectively and permanently.

A prime example of instrumental music's effect on the whole child is through el Sistema, which originated in Venezuela, where it "now teaches music to more than 500,000 of Venezuela's most vulnerable children, demonstrating the power of ensemble music to dramatically change the life trajectory of...a nation's youth" (el Sistema). Even if there is no proof that playing music can increase a student's academic achievement and demeanor, there is no denying the fact that music is a gateway to teaching underprivileged children how to interact in a self-fulfilling way. It gives them an opportunity to "'[overcome] material poverty. From the minute a child's taught how to play an instrument, he's no longer poor. He becomes a child in progress... who'll later become a citizen' –Maestro Jose Antonia Abreu" (el Sistema). These children will become citizens of the world and have values instilled in them that would not have been there before. Music has given these children a hope and a will to become more educated than they ever thought they could be. We can see the same results happening with Fitzpatrick's study in Ohio, where the lower class musicians met and exceeded their upper class peers who were not musicians. These effects on underprivileged children can be described as the arts "used as entry points into academic subjects" and maybe "certain students—those lacking academic interests or strengths in specific subjects—benefit" (Hetland and Winner 6). This line of thinking is more widely accepted and supported because of the immediate results that come from it: having nothing to having some kind of improvement is still an improvement. If we can say nothing else, at least we can say that music has a positive influence upon those who are less fortunate and that music can both lift their spirits and open opportunities for success that were not available before.

Although children are noticeably different when playing music, will their personalities be changed in a positive way that will then in turn *allow* them to be more successful academically? Is it all chance that the studies of music students in half the cases report higher test scores and in the other half there is no difference? We may never know the answers to these questions, but I think the biggest thing to take away from all of this is that music has an effect on the body, mentally, physically, and spiritually. Even if we cannot measure by how much and by what means, humans react to music, whether it changes their career path, influences their personality, or allows them to be well-rounded; every choice we make changes the way that a person makes their way through the world, and as a child, choosing to play an instrument is in fact an instrumental moment in their life.

Works Cited

Colwel, Richard, and Lyle Davidson. "Musical Intelligence and the Benefits of MusicEducation." *National Association of Secondary School Principals*. NASSP Bulletin, (Nov 1996): 55-64.

Fitzpatrick, Kate R. "The Effect of Instrumental Music Participation and Socioeconomic Statuson Ohio Fourth-, Sixth-, and Ninth-Grade Proficiency Test Performance." *Journal of Research in Music Education* 54.1 (2006): 73-84.

Hallam, Susan. "The Power of Music: Its Impact on the Intellectual, Social and Personal Development of Children and Young People." *Institute of Education, University of London* (2010): 1-32.

Hetland, Lois, and Ellen Winner. "The Arts and Academic Achievement: What the Evidence Shows." Arts Education Policy Review (2001): 1-6.

Hinson, Susan, Keith Wilson, and Philip Kaufman. Personal interview. 2 November 2013.

Hodges, Donald A., and Debra S. O'Connell. "The Impact of Music Education on Academic Achievement." *The University of North Carolina at Greensboro*, (2004): 2.1-2.33

"el Sistema USA." National Alliance of El Sistema Inspired Programs Home Comments, 2010. Web. 24 Nov. 2013.

Shorner-Johnson, Kevin. "Building Evidence for Music Education Advocacy." *Music Educators Journal*,(2013): 51-55.

Publishing Group
Essays

Introduction

Researching, thinking, and writing are at the core of the College of Arts and Sciences. No matter what field they're in, students must be able to research, to find and evaluate the best evidence and information on a topic. They must be able to think, to formulate original ideas and take a fresh approach to a problem or question. And, of course, they must be able to write—excellent research and thought must be communicated to others to have value. After all of their reading and thinking about the work of others, students must make their own contributions to the field by writing.

The constant exposure to accomplished works published in their field of study can intimidate students when they sit down to write. Or inspire them. It may do both as students strive to explain complexity. Fortunately, this striving often yields remarkable writing. The following works, selected from student submissions to the seventh-annual Drexel Publishing Group writing contest, exemplify a firm grasp of subject matter and a facility with language.

The essays in this section of *The 33rd* cover a host of subjects from a range of disciplines in the arts and sciences. The topics are as diverse as the students who wrote about them, but the essays all demonstrate originality and boldness as well as great skill in researching, thinking, and writing.

Sarah Adigba

Change

Lagos was hot, but that was hardly new. Lagos was always hot, always bustling, always moving. That seemed to be an intricate character of she, of Lagos.

The airport stunk: not just of the toilets that always carried too much, tottering and overflowing, but of sweat, from the men and women who had just escaped the hot sun. The stink was deeper than that though. It didn't just feel like a stink, it felt like a darkness, like an abscess, like something was missing, but you didn't quite know what.

This airport was always under construction: even the elevator hadn't been fixed in more than three years. But again, this was nothing new. This was Murtala Mohammed Airport; along with the dirt roads and roadside debris, you could expect some sections of it to always be "under construction." *Under construction* meant that it would never be fixed, and the money allocated for the fixing was probably in one big man's pocket, being used for a private jet.

Things had changed, though, I tell you. The *polity continued to be heated up* while I was away, and politicians and their apparatchiks continued to throw low blows, but with perhaps more spite. When I had left, there had been talks of a new political super group called APC, a conglomeration of much smaller, much less influential political groups called the CPC, ACN and the ANPP. They were going after the main prize, seizing power from the PDP (People's Democratic Party, the leading political party since 1999). Now, this group had solidified and had begun to give the PDP a run for its money. I found it funny: old men, men who could father my father, slinging thinly veiled insults on the pages of newspapers, all while a part of the country burned, and had been burning since the insurgency in 2010.

Some roads were definitely better than I left them, and finally traffic lights had been installed in busier areas. But Lagos was still the same. With the same slap-me-I-slap-you attitude, the attitude that the Spartans must have had, but of course to a much lesser degree. Other drivers still hurled insults at you if they felt you had *chanced* them, taken their turn. In fact, many street fights between car drivers started like that. One driver, frustrated after a long day of work, drove around like a bomb looking for an ignition. Another driver, just as frustrated, or maybe even more so, would of course overtake him, because that was just how everybody drove in Lagos. That would be the ignition, and boom, the fight. Then a free-for-all. If the fight attracted enough people, the *agberos* (street boys) would use the opportunity to steal from the cars of the spectators.

Lagos was and is still very colorful, nobody cannot deny that.

Lekki, a part of Lagos that is just beside the Atlantic Ocean, still got drenched with gray water, sometimes so high that your lower body could be covered. The little boys, street urchins, who would later grow up to be the *agberos*, still continued to beg to wash your mirror with dirty soap water for 100-200 *naira* (around one dollar). And the music, music I so disliked, was still brash, hard, unyielding.

The music, electronic, computer-generated, trite. The new Nigerian musicians were all liars. Stylistically, they claimed to have been influenced by Fela Anikulapo-Kuti, but they were at best bastard descendants. Politically, there were even further apart. (I feel like I could write an entire paper on how popular Nigerian music is just danceable nonsense, but that doesn't mean I won't dance to it. I guess they have won, in a way.) The artistes (if they can be called this) routinely stole one another's catchphrases, used each other's beats, dressed similarly, and the most infuriating of all, carried their pre-recorded CDs when called to perform and just lip-synced along.

Perhaps the greatest changes lay at home, things that somehow managed to not get mentioned in the long, weekly phone and Skype convos I had with my mother, and how there was a new maid—and judging by the looks of her, she wouldn't last. The new maid was too grasping, had eyes that shone just a little too bright at the sight of material things. My mother would tire of her after a while and she would join the list of maids who hadn't survived at the Adigba home. There wasn't an actual list. My mother was actually very patient with the help, and much more kind than some "madams" were to their help. Our next-door neighbor was so brutal to her help that they usually left after a month or two. Some after a week. The woman was pure evil, with her shaved head and eyes that seemed to see all your sins from all past lives to this one. She beat her help for the smallest of things, and heavy beatings they were. Being so close, we could hear everything and we routinely intervened. It was during those times that I wished you could call the police for things like that—I mean, you could, but she would just wriggle out unharmed because she was rich.

The arrangements worked like this: a woman, like my mother, needing someone to take care of the house and her children when she worked, would arrange for a young person from a relative or friend. That young person would come and work a year or two, and my mum would then proceed to train her however she wanted, or she could earn a salary if he or she so wished. Each arrangement was different, though, although my mum usually offered to provide all the basics, pay salary, and still provide education.

You could say that a huge percentage of the help in Lagos were teenagers and tweens, most younger than I. However, my mum always employed girls older than 20. Another house down the street from mine had this little boy who didn't look much older than nine, who would walk at least five kilometers every day running errands for the wrinkled, old woman that lived there.

Other things had changed, too. My dad had remodeled the house, as he was so fond of doing, and my room was now bright pink at the request of my sister. My sister had taken my bamboo frame handbag and had begun to use it as hers, leaving biro marks in the bag's lining. The stairs felt different, so low, so smooth. The marble flooring seemed unnecessary now; my legs were so accustomed to walking on wood, although with room slippers.

Once I stepped off that Virgin Atlantic flight from Newark to Lagos, I became Nigerian again. No, not simply Nigerian; it is never that simple with Nigeria. In Nigeria, I am Idoma, my father's tribe. And if I want to be more correct, Igala also. My mother's tribe. Whenever two Nigerians meet, home or abroad, after general introductions, the first question is, What is your tribe? That is your identity in Nigeria and among Nigerians, your *raison d'être*.

However, in America, I am now black or sometimes, African. Two terms I am not sure I am comfortable with. The African because it allows people here to ask me about Rwanda, a place I know just as much about as any American and besides, Rwanda isn't in my part of Africa: I am West African. Also, Africa is a very complex place. Prior to colonization, Africa contained about 10,000 tribes and kingdoms, many of which still exist today in the 53 nations. I cannot speak for all 10,000; I can only talk for the about twenty tribes I am familiar with inside my own country (Nigeria has about 350).

Neither am I comfortable with the term "black," because I think it is too wide a term to define all peoples of Sub-Saharan heritage. There are several differences between the Africans and the African-Americans, whom I consider the true "blacks." For one, they are American. We are not. I feel that the 300 years of slavery and oppression that African-Americans went through here divide us even more. This is not to say that Africa has not had its fair share of problems; in fact, I think I was alive when Nigeria had its last dictator, Abacha (who many said died under exotic prostitutes from India). And several other African nations still continue to suffer under tyranny and civil wars. But, that is still different, in my opinion, from slavery. And after slavery, living as second-class citizens for another 100 years. The issues that mostly concern the Africans "fresh off the boat" (I hate this term so much because we didn't come on boats, but on planes — *planes.*) is simply succeeding and getting the most out of the education. African-Americans, though, seem more concerned about race, and with due cause.

In America, I simply want to be Nigerian. For now, my only identifier remains my accent (which, by the way, may act as a barrier for me; I've noticed that some people may treat you like you are stupid if you speak English in a different accent, even if it is just as good as theirs). And maybe not simply Nigerian, but maybe a privileged Nigerian, living and schooling in the US, expanding her mind, and constantly thinking of home. Yes, that's it.

Alissa Falcone

Suicide by Way of Conrad

When Joseph Conrad was 18 years old, he deliberately attempted to take his life after losing a large sum of money through illegal smuggling and gambling. Rather than shooting himself in the head, Conrad shot himself in the chest and planned it just before he knew someone would visit him. The self-wounding, as described by C.B. Cox, professor of English literature and the director of the Poetry Centre at the University of Manchester, "represents a cry for help." Stranded in France with no money, Conrad must have run out of options—until he created an entirely new one by shooting himself in the chest. Conrad's uncle, Thaddeus Bobrowski, heard the "cry for help" and rushed to Marseilles to pay off his nephew's debts and get his affairs in order (Cox). With a loved one dedicated to fixing his life, Conrad recovered and went on to have a successful career as a sailor and a writer, but his suicide attempt deeply impacted the rest of his life. According to Paul Wake, a Conrad scholar and senior lecturer of English at Manchester Metropolitan University, "It is only necessary to recall how often suicide crops up in his work to realize how profoundly he must have been affected" (Wake 96). Conrad eventually created several suicidal characters that, despite differing means or motivation, committed suicide in a desperate effort to preserve their individual agency.

Some Conradian characters chose death rather than face a forthcoming punishment for the murder they committed. Both the method of suicide and the final resting location were deliberately chosen by Kayerts in "An Outpost of Progress" when he hanged himself from the cross marking the grave of the man he killed. He was obviously affected and traumatized by Carlier's death before the Director came, as evidenced by how Conrad describes Kayerts as being "deadly sick" as soon as he sees Carlier's "pair of turned-up feet" on the ground ("An Outpost of Progress"). While still wracked with guilt after shooting Carlier in an argument, Kayerts committed suicide only after "hearing the return of the Managing Director's steamship" (Kestner 101). The Director's arrival announces a staunchly European man with civilized ideals, and the Director might not excuse Kayerts like Makola. Kayerts killed himself in the short amount of time it would have taken him to greet the Director— which was much, much shorter than the amount of time that Carlier had been dead. Guilt may have played a part in the suicide, but the Director, the physical embodiment of both the societal values and punishment for going against those values, triggers the suicide. Kayerts would rather kill himself than be imprisoned or killed by the authorities, which would have happened if the Director reported the crime.

The fear of receiving a death sentence also proves too much for Winnie Verloc, who drowned herself after stabbing her husband in *The Secret Agent*. Her first reaction after the murder is to open the bedroom window "with the intention of screaming Murder! Help! or of throwing herself out. For she did not exactly know what use to make of her freedom" (*The Secret Agent* 165). Winnie later considers another type of suicide when she fully absorbs that she could hang in the gallows and "She could not stand *That*. The thought of it even was not bearable. She could not stand thinking of it. Therefore Mrs. Verloc formed the resolution to go at once and throw herself into the river off one of the bridges" (*The Secret Agent* 174). Ultimately, she does commit suicide after "the lecherous Ossipon," who is aware of her suicidal thoughts, "deceives Mrs. Verloc in her hour of need, takes her money, and abandons her to self-destruction" (Sullivan 127). She later commits suicide by jumping off a cross-Channel boat in an "act of madness or despair" (*The Secret Agent* 197). Completely abandoned, Winnie finally acts upon her previous suicidal thoughts after too much time alone without money, options, or anything besides her fractured, terrified thoughts of the gallows. Though her death ultimately appears in the papers, she would rather it be for suicide than a public hanging.

The threat of the gallows also looms for the Professor in *The Secret Agent*, but it's not as near as it was for Winnie or Kayerts. The Professor is willing to kill himself to avoid any punishment from the police, but he would only do so if provoked by someone else. Armed with a powerful homemade bomb that could be detonated on his person in 20 seconds, he "is always moments away from a violently destructive suicide" (Wake 81). The reason behind his odd lifestyle choice is that "the possibility of his suicide acts as a constant deterrent to the authorities that would otherwise have him arrested," and his taking control of the situation means that "his potential death becomes a mechanism through which he orders his life" (Wake 81). Like Winnie Verloc and Kayerts, the Professor prefers suicide to a death controlled by the authorities. The difference is that the Professor is always prepared to make this decision and always has been, even though he's had more time to consider suicide and has never needed to use it as a method of escape. When the Professor states, "I depend on death, which knows no restraint and cannot be attacked" (*The Secret Agent* 21), he reveals that he does not believe in a death forced by the police, who could arrest him and take him to the gallows. By the end of the novel, the Professor doesn't end up killing himself, but suicide is such a significant part of his life and defined personality that he merits inclusion with other Conradian characters that have also considered suicide.

For all of the power that the authorities and their prosecution hold over some characters like the Professor, it plays very little part in the deaths of other Conrad characters. In those instances, the person's own self-identity and personal standards are the deciding factors to end someone's life. This crisis of confidence happens to Captain Brierly, a young, successful and respected judge who served on Jim's trial and, as Conrad describes, "jumped overboard at sea barely a week after the end of the inquiry [...] as though on that exact spot in the midst of waters he had suddenly perceived the gates of the other world flung open wide for his reception" (*Lord Jim* 41). As a consequence of the trial, Jim ends up receiving the most negative attention focused on him, but Brierly is the one who kills himself. Brierly's exact motivation is unknown, but Marlow's inclusion of a previous discussion with the Captain suggests that he finds it important that the Captain referenced his ego and confidence. Brierly was discussing Jim when he said, "Such an affair destroys one's confidence. A man may go pretty near through his whole sea-life without any call to show a stiff upper lip. But when the call comes..." (Nook file 49). But Marlow's description of Brierly's unfinished thought suggests that Brierly dreamed up something so horrifying he didn't want to articulate it, least of all to an obsessively nosy man like Marlow. Ultimately, Brierly realizes that he has more in common with Jim, the cowardly deserter, than he would like to admit. He's terrified to think that one day he might commit a mistake as disastrously impactful as Jim's *Patna* jump, which is why "Brierly commits suicide by drowning himself at sea when he finds his own honour" (Wake 81). His dignity and moral code, rather than the looming threat of criminal prosecution, spur him to take his own life instead of accepting a life with his new realization. He doesn't want to be a Jim-like Brierly, but he doesn't know how to be any other Brierly. His inability to escape his personal entrapment makes him just one of the many Conradian characters "to choose suicide deliberately and consciously as a proper response to the meaninglessness of their lives" (Cox).

The titular character of *Lord Jim* caused Brierly's death, but not in a literal sense. In an interesting turn of events, the same could be said of Jim as well. Jim's lofty personal values and sense of self also contribute to his death, which is a suicide like Brierley's even though Jim does not actually take his own life. Jim's "suicide" occurs when he deliberately faces Doramin, a man whose son was a casualty of Jim's actions, even though Jim knows that the furiously grieving father would kill him. Before facing the man, Jim even acknowledges the deliberateness and possible consequence of his action when someone cries, "'He [Jim] hath taken it upon his own head'" and he replies, "'Yes. Upon my head'" (*Lord Jim* 278). Of course, Doramin shoots Jim in the chest, and Jim lets it happen after his realization that he is no longer accepted in the last place left that could accept him. Even though he does not shoot himself, Jim is also implicated in his death because he was a voluntary martyr to his romantic and ideal notions of honor. He felt that he did not deserve to live after failing to live up to the identity and salvation he had found in the obscurity of Patusan (Cox). The cowardice he displayed at past life-or-death moments of his life, most significantly his abandonment of the *Patna*, factored into his decision to die at the hands of another instead of shooting himself. Jim's death is marked by his two most definable characteristics as a coward and romantic, so of course he couldn't kill himself, but felt no qualms about letting someone else do the killing. Jim's motives and methods of suicide require some unpacking to fully understand. On paper, his death would not have been ruled a suicide. The actual cause of death was that someone shot him in the chest, but the hidden cause of the suicide was that Jim couldn't live after failing so many times. This crucial information is gleaned after his history and personal information are revealed throughout the course of *Lord Jim*, and the proximity allows for a sense of his character to emerge from the writing.

Conrad did not always take so much care to show the exact reasons for a suicide that his character commits. In fact, the mysterious suicide of a Swede in *Heart of Darkness*, as well as a possibly impending suicide of another misplaced Swede in Africa, is purposefully left unexplained and unknown. Marlow learns about the suicide from the Swedish captain of a sea-going steamer who saw the other Swede's body, and the secondhand narrative does little to answer the question of why the Swede killed himself. The captain tells Marlow that the man "hanged himself on the road," and his simple, detached take on the suicide continues when he answers Marlow's question of why the suicide happens. As Marlow describes, "He kept on looking out watchfully" before replying, 'Who knows? The sun too much for him, or the country perhaps'" (Nook file 15). The Swede, who had suspiciously brought up the suicide only after Marlow said he expected to see him soon, was not able to know what caused the suicide, but his guesses—that the unfamiliar sun and country became overbearing—reveal that he can relate a little too much to his dead compatriot. He suggests that the inability to cope with being thousands of miles in a foreign climate in a foreign country could have contributed to at least one Swedish suicide, and possibly his own future one. Marlow doesn't recognize the connection, and his failure to follow up with the Swede leaves that captain's state of mind, as well as any hope of a future, in a very ambiguous position. The Swedes' personal crises, both recognized and unnoticed, drive them to think about suicide as a result of their reaction to a whole new world and their inability to want to survive in it.

Most of the suicides in Conrad's *Heart of Darkness*, *The Secret Agent*, *Lord Jim* and "An Outpost of Progress" are reactionary. Each death is committed after some sort of crisis, as well as various direct and indirect causes. Internalized factors, like an identity crisis or a perceived weakness of character, are prevalent in some of the suicides committed by people who hung themselves or purposefully drowned. External factors such as avoiding punishment for a crime or murder are also prevalent across several of Conrad's works. The similarities show that the people's personal ideals and values, whether failing to be a good person or wanting to avoid a harsh punishment, will usually contribute to their suicides. This is as true for the Conradian characters as it was for Conrad's own suicide attempt. Having internalized his depression and fears caused by the impending trouble with the law until the resulting suicide attempt, Conrad had more than enough experience to relate to the stimuli he created for his characters. The difference is that Conrad proved both stronger and weaker than the characters he would go on to create.

Works Cited

Conrad, Joseph. "An Outpost of Progress." *Tales of Unrest. Project Gutenberg.* Web. 6 Mar. 2014.

Conrad, Joseph, Robert Kimbrough, and Paul B. Armstrong. *Heart of Darkness.* New York: W.W. Norton, 2006.

Conrad, Joseph. *The Secret Agent.* New York: Modern Library, 1998. Nook.

Cox, C.B. *Joseph Conrad and the Question of Suicide.* Rep. The University of Manchester. Web. 6 Mar. 2014.

Kestner, Joseph A. *Masculinities in British Adventure Fiction, 1880-1915.* Farnham, England: Ashgate, 2010. Print.

Sullivan, Walter. "Irony and Disorder: The Secret Agent." *The Sewanee Review* 81.1 (1973): JSTOR. Web. 7 Mar. 2014.

Wake, Paul. *Conrad's Marlow: Narrative and Death in 'Youth', Heart of Darkness, Lord Jim and Chance.* Manchester: Manchester UP, 2007. Ebrary. 2007. Web. 6 Mar. 2014.

Hajer Karoui

My Beautiful Sin, My Grapes of Wrath

"How are you even comparing yourself, a girl, to me when I was teenage *boy*?" –Dad

That was probably the quote of the day. It was one of these typical and unexceptional days of mine, standing here in my room, baptized in my thoughts gazing at the shut roller blind of my window. My very black sugar-free coffee was burning hot. I was sipping it, slowly, drowning my mouth at every gulp with every bitter atom of this liquid, in a wavy movement. Not that I have no taste in food; I am gourmand indeed, so I accompanied my beverage with small portions of Oreo, black ones. Well, it is filled with a thin layer of pure white milk, but I could only see the black side of the biscuit. It was on the night of August 31st of this year when the argument happened; and let me be precise, "argument" as it is in our culture as "a strong disagreement (...) with rash words and harsh feelings."

It was all about me having a Facebook profile picture my father did not like, then with me going to cultural events in summer but coming home around 10 PM, then with me having a boyfriend. As simple as these facts may sound, the case was not that simple, according to my parents. I bit on my biscuit, and drank coffee afterwards; I bit, then I drank, and drank more. Every time, at the end of the process, I rolled my tongue through my jaws and my teeth, up and down, constantly trying to extract the sweet particles of my mouth, keeping the sour taste of the coffee invading my orifice for several seconds, minutes, until it vanished. And I replicated it with no respite...I heard my father talking to my mom after I came back home: "Who is this guy? How can you be okay with your daughter going with him in the car?"

Shortly after, I was summoned to this family meeting. My father had these concerned looks towards me, and asked me loads of questions, useless questions. At some point I thought I was a 15-year-old teenager, because I was actually treated like one. "Who is he? Does it sound or look so ordinary to you to go into his car in everybody's eyes? If he wants anything from you he should come and *propose*." No, he didn't say that softly in a father-daughter friendly way. Also note that I was 19 at the time. He said it with a firm tone. I didn't expect it at all from my dad because we were close; he trusted me, I never failed him, and already knew a little about my boyfriend. He would tease me once in a while about it. However, he made a scene, claiming and insisting that I was not the person he thought I was.

He was "shocked" when he found out that we, teenagers, are actually pretty intimate with each other, friends, boys and girls. We are close, we take pictures together, we hug, and we have fun. I was told it was a sin to even hug a boy, supporting that with the prophet's saying, "To thrust any of you in the head with an iron needle is better than touching a woman who is not permissible for them." "Did you know that?" he asked. "Have you got the slightest idea about what you are doing? I am extremely disappointed in you, Hajer. I thought your religion was the landmark in your life. If I knew this about you I wouldn't have let you go to the States by yourself. What else do you do, you 'modern teenagers,' besides hugging each other and taking pictures? You are not allowed to see this boy anymore, because apparently you failed to remember that in our religion you are not allowed to have any kind of close relationship with a male unless there is something official. Most of all, do not compare yourself to me because you are a girl and I was a teenage boy. You are supposed to stay inconspicuous. I cannot understand what happened to you, Hajer."

That was the situation. It was literally keeping me awake late at night from time to time. What did I do wrong? What went wrong? My dad knows me very well, so I couldn't let him be mistaken or let a misunderstanding ruin our relationship. Though I knew it wouldn't be a piece of cake, I tried to convince him that he needed to help me with my transition to adulthood. Most importantly, I needed him to accept me like an adult and treat me like one. As it was discernible in his words, my father is a very committed person, in a religious way. He wasn't like that a few years ago, so when he embraced religion, he was "slightly" driven by it. He looked at things from a certain angle that is, from my point of view, not the right one to look from since we are now in the 21st century and most of all because he has six daughters. He has six girls but he didn't seem to consider that when trying to approach us, my sisters and me. He looked at religion as if it was a lifestyle that a person shows in every single aspect of our daily and modern life. I don't think he ever thought of the fact that it is more of a personal matter that should probably not interfere in some things. However for him, no exceptions are to be made. I also feel like he makes it sound as if it [religion] was mostly about fear, more than passion and willingness. What kind of person would enjoy telling their daughter, "To thrust any of you in the head with an iron needle is better than touching a woman who is not permissible for them"? The strange paradoxical thing about my father is that he is more of a person to use logic when he talks, but his religious affiliation always influences his opinion and way of thinking and made him a bit narrow-minded. Also unfortunately, he is not the kind of person who is usually willing to listen to others' explanations, because that's how it works with him: he sees the facts, judges and has a conversation with the subject to get justifications. However, that conversation will actually make it worse. The purpose of it is to prove you are wrong, and that he is not happy with you, period.

My ethos played a big role in my process of convincing him that I *am still* the girl he always knew, the one who never lied to her parents or did something behind their back. If I didn't do that in the rebellious teenage years like all my peers, why on earth would I do that now, when I am 19 and will be leaving my parents' home to another continent? However, this paranoia he had at that time is in some way understandable. My elder sister has been the rebel ever since she was 14 and that created a lot of problems at home. He had always been happy with me because I was this shy, hard-working, and religious girl who is neither interested in fun or parties, nor in boys. So I pretty much spared him the trouble of dealing with another "riot" at home. I told him that this is my first-time boyfriend, and I did it after having given the matter serious thought, reminding him that I've always shown responsibility in everything I undertook so far; thus, I gained his trust.

In my use of logos, on the one hand I told him that he knew about that guy already months ago; he met him, they talked, and he knew he was not just a friend. So there was no point in making a scene. He actually knows his family, which is a very known and noble one in my city. I made it clear that the picture he saw and did not like was one among many pictures my friends and I took at the end of our senior year. He sees those shots, described as "lacking ethics and being the embodiment of sin itself," he says, as a very serious matter, even though they go unnoticed in our everyday lives. I asked him to try to remember when he was my age and try to feel how it was, but then he pointed out that I shouldn't compare myself to him because I am a girl. He's made it clear that his mind was still set to the old image religion or conservative cultures had given about life hundreds of years ago. Some things are not feasible anymore; life has changed and societies are not as conservative as they used to be. Values are for sure still highly considered, but maybe not to be taken from a religious angle.

I avoided using pathos because my father was not much of an emotional person. I certainly wouldn't have been able to tell him that I love this person I am with, and that it was completely natural for someone at my age to start thinking about their love life. Trying to get to him emotionally would've been completely useless.

With my father having had a past in politics and a big interest and involvement at the present time, the kairos was not really on my side because of the deep political divide in Tunisia for two years between the Secularists and the Islamists. Everyone wants to set up their own ideas claiming that there's no room for senseless statements, as they refer to people who didn't have the same opinion as them. So everyone was pulling from their side and each of them was heading more towards the abyss of extremism. My dad was very affected by this, because he hated to see his homeland in this sad situation, but he was also in the middle of all of it. He was nervous all the time, in grief, and every tiny little thing that went against religion irritated him.

If there was anything I would change today it would be...absolutely nothing. I was honest with my parents; I never lied about where I was or who I was with. I strongly believe that honesty is the pillar of keeping a good relationship with anyone. If I am going to change my attitude towards them, it will eventually endanger my credibility. Unfortunately, I couldn't convince my father that at this age having a boyfriend is not something he should worry about because I am not 15 anymore. He raised me with great values and it is high time he saw the fruit of his labor. I am sure I am becoming more mature through time and experiences, so he should have definitely been more understanding and closer to me as his daughter. He could've tried to know more about this person I am with in a friendly way, maybe meet him one day. He could've advised me and listened to me just like he used to do 15 years ago, when I was telling him about the monsters under my bed...He listened.

References

Steinbeck, John. *The Grapes of Wrath*. Los Gatos, CA: The Viking Press, 1938. Print.

Clark, Carol Lea. *Praxis*. 2nd ed. custom. Southlake, TX: Fountainhead Press, 2012. Print.

"To thrust any of you in the head with an iron needle is better than touching a woman who is not permissible for them." From Maakal Ben Yasar. Reported by Al-Bayhaqi. Translated from Arabic by Hajer Karoui.

Brittany MacLean

Assigning Identity: A Critique of Testimony as Memorial Practice

Of all the things that human beings seek to claim ownership of, there is something incredibly intimate and personal about our memories. We view memory as an individual process, to which no one else is privy, and if they are, we tell ourselves that they still do not truly own it. The role that memory plays in our individual lives and in our position in society is partly dependent on the way in which the process of remembering is enacted. These practices of memorialization are entwined into our very understanding of the past, but also of our present. In this essay, I will first discuss memorial practices in a broad sense, offering my interpretation of their purpose. I aim to show the inability of the participator to divorce the memorial practice from how he or she constructs a present identity. I will then examine a particular memorial practice, the act of giving testimony, and use the specific example of testimony given after the violence of apartheid in South Africa. Lastly, I will seek to problematize testimony as a memorial practice because, although effective, it is dependent on the unreliability of memory and, by its very nature, politicizes the identities of individuals as a result.

Remembering a person or event, a tragedy or triumph manifests itself in many ways. It partly depends on who is doing the remembering, whether it is an individual, group, or society. However, the way the memory is expressed is equally as important. In the introduction to his book *The Texture of Memory: Holocaust Memorials and Meaning*, James Young writes, "The shape of memory cannot be divorced from the actions taken in its behalf" (15). The way or practice of remembering is inseparable from the form the memory takes. Remembering could be enacted through a visit to a gravesite, a funeral procession, a poem written in the privacy of one's own home, an oral tradition passed down, or a museum erected by a government. These are all valid forms of memorial practices, for they are acts whose purpose is to give the past a place in the present. Generalizations cannot be made that group every memorial practice together, because their functions are dependent on the people perpetuating and taking part in the practice. Maybe for a widow visiting her husband's grave, that memorial practice is meant to elicit memories and show his continual role in her life. School children who visit the Vietnam War Memorial may have no personal connection with the tragic events of the war, however they are still valid participators in the memorial practice by learning and paying respect. Whatever the case though, as Young writes, the form of memorialization shapes the very memory itself.

This is to say that the sole function of a memorial practice is not simply to remember an event, because for many who participate in memorial practices there are no direct memories connected with the practice. A memorial practice brings the past into a present context of understanding by revisiting that which is being memorialized and reconstituting it based on present circumstances and attitudes. Said understanding may be individual, group, or societal, but whatever the case, the work of the memorial practice is inseparable from the present. In that same Introduction, Young explains this connection between past and present when he writes, "... the memorial activity by which minds reflecting on the past inevitably precipitate in the present historical moment" (15). The memorial practice is not only a reflection on the past, but a contemplation of what is being memorialized in the context of the present. An individual's participation in a memorial practice, therefore, not only causes them to think about the past, it also shapes the present he or she is living in. This contextualized present is not only an understanding of the memorialized event, but of the individual as well. The way a person sees him or herself in the present is fundamental to how that person constructs his or her identity, particularly in the context of society as a whole.

In her book *Country of My Skull: Guilt, Sorrow, and the Limits of Forgiveness in the New South Africa*, Antije Krog explores a crucial notion in her reporting of the Truth and Reconciliation Commission in post-apartheid South Africa. In quoting another scholar she writes, "Identity is memory" (32). The individual's present, and therefore identity in the context of various groups and in society as a whole, is shaped by the memorial practice. In this way, the practice constitutes a fundamental understanding of identity. The implications for the synonymic relationship between memory and identity become more consequential to varying degrees in the enactment of all memorial practices, but are certain. Young writes, "...understanding of events depends on memory's construction, and that there are worldly consequences in the kinds of historical understanding generated by monuments" (15). Young specifically cites a type of memorializing structure, monuments, however his conclusion is applicable to any type of memorial practice. Memorializing has very tangible consequences. I would argue this is in part due to the unbreakable connection between memory and identity.

One memorial practice for which the connection between memory and identity is irrefutable is that of giving testimony. First, it must be said that testimony is in fact a memorial practice as I have defined it. Like other memorial practices, it brings the past forward as a context for understanding the present, and shapes individual and group identities. The issue with testimony is that, like the construction of a public memorial, testimony is highly politicized. By its very nature, testimony is formal and civic, understood primarily in the context of judiciary processes. As a result, the identities shaped are not only based on the testimony given, but on the decisions rendered by a governmental body. While testimony does lend a space for the individual to share firsthand memories, it is intrinsically placed in a political context.

There is perhaps not a better example of testimony as a memorial practice than that of the Truth and Reconciliation Commission in South Africa. Formed by the new South African government after the abolition of apartheid, the Commission functioned to redress the violence committed from the mid to late 20th century as a result of the institutionalized segregation based on race. It did this in three separate committees: The Human Rights Violations Committee, The Reparation and Rehabilitation Committee, and The Amnesty Committee. Instead of being a prosecutorial body, the TRC was tasked with recording victims' and perpetrators' stories in order to determine if compensation or amnesty should be granted. In explaining the process of constructing the Commission, Krog quotes Minister of Justice Dullah Omar as saying, "'...there was a strong feeling that some mechanism must be found to deal with all violations in a way which would open up the truth for public scrutiny. But to humanize our society we had to put across the idea of moral responsibility—that is why I suggested a combination of the amnesty process with the process of victims' stories'" (8-9). In this way, the truth was viewed as a healing mechanism, one that would set South Africa on the right path to a more peaceful future.

The TRC's purpose was to expose the truth of apartheid and thus prevent violence in the future. The difference between the testimony given in South Africa from other testimony given after a massacre or genocide was the aspect of reconciliation, characteristic of the South African effort. The array of committees and functions of the Commission meant that many different rulings could be made about an individual. The testimony that was given by individuals and the decisions rendered by the branches of the TRC were instrumental in constructing an identity for the individual. A person could be a victim, perpetrator, forgiven, or condemned, all based on memory. What happened in the TRC not only determined what an individual was in the past, but also branded them with a label in the present.

Testimony by its very nature is based on individual memory. Young writes, "Memory is never shaped in a vacuum; the motives of memory are never pure" (2). This, as well as its civic nature, makes it easy to problematize as a memorial practice. The shape that memory takes has an important impact on both the individual and collective memory. This warrants concerns about testimony as a shaper of present contexts. For one, memory is fickle, and in the case of testimony it is often unclear when a witness is forgetting on purpose or from trauma. Krog encountered this in the testimony given at the TRC: "Several perpetrators claim not to remember certain things and the committee obviously is not sure whether people are genuinely traumatized or whether they are deliberately hiding information and so do not fulfill the amnesty requirement of full disclosure" (98). This issue is raised in the TRC as to whether perpetrators are failing to disclose information because they are being untruthful or because they truly do not remember. Though it is difficult to call the perpetrators true victims, a psychologist testifies at the TRC as to the different types of memory loss, which could explain perpetrators' testimony. Krog also writes, "The truth is validated by the majority, they say. Or you bring your own version of the truth to the merciless arena of the past—only in this way does the past become thinkable, the world become habitable" (112).

There is a tendency to beautify memories, or remember in a way that favors the speaker. However, this is not always a conscious effort. In this way it is problematic that the decisions made and identities assigned by the TRC are based on memory, which must often be sifted through to find the truth. For the truth is inseparable from identity, as Krog writes: "Is truth that closely related to identity? It must be. What you believe to be true depends on who you believe yourself to be" (125). In the case of testimony, the truth is not only shaped by identity, but also, conversely, identity is shaped by truth as well.

Secondly, the very nature of testimony politically charges memory, and thus identity becomes so too. This is especially true in the context of a committee like the TRC, where memory forms testimony, which in turn shapes judicial decisions. The practice of testifying indeed serves its function as a memorial practice of causing the past to be understood in a present context. The decisions made based on testimony are the foundations for ascribing a label to participators. Especially in a country like South Africa, where the violence of apartheid was predicated on the ruling group assigning value to racial identity, newly politicized identities are problematic. It is problematic when the government fetishizes memory, makes it into something that people want to claim ownership of. With testimony, the political context means that it is in a sense the government claiming ownership. By taking claim of the reconciliation process, they are in a way claiming ownership of the memories and the subsequent process of assigning labels to individuals. With amnesty and reconciliation, labels are inevitably placed on individuals based on the decisions of the TRC. These labels can then spread from individuals to groups, not only in the context of the past, but of the present as well.

Testimony in front of the TRC was no doubt effective, but there is an inevitable conflict that arises from the fickleness of memory and the labels assigned to individuals as its result. Just as the discrimination and segregation of apartheid were viewed as natural, so is the process of reconciliation. In reality, the goals of the TRC are rendered unnatural by the very nature of apartheid. While reconciliation may be viewed as key for the future of the country, its institutionalization should in no way be viewed as natural.

Memorializing a trauma like apartheid through testimony forever shapes how the individual views their very identity as a product of the event. Sometimes, identities may be adopted based on false, incomplete, or misinformed memories. While there is no denying the need to let victims be heard, apartheid quickly becomes about what individuals did to each other. Identity is then ascribed, and it becomes about what one group did to another. However, it never truly becomes about what environment fostered the violence. Through testimony, victims can rightly received justice and perpetrators can rightly be punished, but it is unclear whether the causal societal values will truly be prevented from resurfacing. While it is safe to assume that apartheid itself will never return, the TRC is evidence that the institutionalization of assigning identity will continue in various forms.

Any memorial practice is a paradoxical act. In constitutes looking back at the past and forward to the future at the same time. While chronologically it is sound to argue that the past must be examined in order to shape the future, it is simultaneously the vision of the present and future that lends the context for interpreting what the past holds. Hopefully through truth, we can understand the past, present, and future in the purest terms.

Works Cited

Krog, Antije. *Country of My Skull: Guilt, Sorrow, and the Limits of Forgiveness in the New South Africa*. Broadway Paperbacks, 2000. PDF.

Young, James Edward. *The Texture of Memory: Holocaust Memorials and Meaning*. New Haven: Yale University Press, 1994. PDF.

Alina Toporas

Multilingualism as a Survival Toolkit in the 21st Century and How America is Sabotaging Itself

"Language is the blood of the soul into which thoughts run and out of which they grow." —Oliver Wendell Holmes

I will begin by kindly asking the reader to imagine the following scenario. You are walking down the street when you hear an individual yelling frantically: *Cuidado!* You don't pay attention. Then he agitatedly continues: *Prends garde! Attento! Остерегаться!* You just think the person is having a stroke, so you would rather call an ambulance than anything else. Ten minutes later, you are the one in an ambulance with a million-dollar impending hospital bill due to an unfortunate collision with a "brakeless" and "no-honk" vehicle. To the skeptics, this seems like an unlikely scenario. Karma cannot hate someone that much. Even if it does happen, it is by no means your fault that you are now in a much poorer health condition and without your million dollars. Alternative explanations could include faulty car infrastructure or "wrong place at the wrong time"...

The truth of the matter is that you were blind...hopelessly and irrevocably blind, handicapped by the placement of a *language barrier*.

Language Acquisition in History

In early history, ancient philosophers believed that the acquisition of a foreign language is an actual subset of the acquisition of knowledge, in general. They put a great deal of emphasis on the methods through which one can be trained in the study of a foreign language. From Plato, who believed that foreign language abilities are innate, to Hobbes and Locke, who looked at this capability through the lenses of a sensorial practice, every important philosophical figure seemed to have an opinion on the best approaches towards foreign language learning (Palmer). The Classical Method, associated with the learning of Latin and Greek, used to focus extensively on syntactical and grammatical structures, along with translation of literary texts and memorization of vocabulary. The only reason for learning these two languages was to create an "illusion of erudition" and not to actually use it in oral communication (Thanasoulas). Contrastingly, Charles Berlitz introduced the Direct Method, which put a spotlight on oral interaction, very little translation and limited use of grammatical guidelines (Thanasoulas). But why the fuss over language in the first place? What does *language* really mean?

Different schools of linguistic theory have distinctive understandings of language. On the one hand, there is the structuralist definition proposed by Ferdinand de Saussure. This approach looks at language as a formal symbolic system in which grammar has a leading role (Saussure). On the other hand, a more primordial approach is to focus on language as an organ, instinct or mental faculty that permits people to engage in linguistic behavior. This view is attributed to Descartes and Kant who, much like Plato, look at language as mainly an innate process (Hauser & Fitch 2003). The one particular definition that we are primarily interested in for the purpose of this essay is language as a means of communication. It views language as an enabling factor in cooperation and chiefly focuses on the cognitive skills amassed with every new language acquisition, those precise cognitive proficiencies that are less and less used by Americans (Pinker 2007).

Return to Sign Language?

America's foreign language deficit is paradoxically both an increasingly worrisome and equally neglected problem. According to Forbes Magazine, only 18% of American citizens speak a foreign language (Skorton & Artschuler 2012). That would not seem like such a small number when taking into consideration the large population in the U.S. However, when comparing it with the European Union, this 18% is by no means a match for Europe's 53%. I have experienced this firsthand as an exchange student in Philadelphia. For instance, in my Spanish class, five out of eight students are European. Moreover, the professor is also European. This is rather peculiar considering that Spanish is not one of the most widespread languages in Europe, but in the U.S. it most definitely is. Still, besides the official Spanish language instruction signs seen at the airport, people do not seem to want to engage with the study of Spanish on an individual level.

Nevertheless, multilingualism is needed for immediate practical purposes, such as mere communication. There are some idealists in the world that are still impatiently waiting for a universal language to be determined. To those, I regrettably say that Esperanto, with its political nonpartisanship, is unlikely to gain any ground. The same applies to English, the latest *lingua franca*. The problem lies in the fact that languages continuously modify their structure and phonetics. Since people from manifold linguistic groups are using English in a multilingual environment, our beloved *lingua franca* becomes cemented in a simplified form (Rajadurai 2007). That can only lead to multiple oral variations, which can give birth to numerous types of English (Trudgill 2004). Variety is usually a positive thing, but since communication is at the center of human interaction, having such diversity in dialects only leads to the English language inevitably dying out. This can already be seen in the United Kingdom where people from South West England have difficulty understanding those from the Highlands and Islands region. Remember, we are talking about mere communication skills that are gradually "vanishing in the haze," as the famous Beatles band accurately puts it in the lyrics of their *Help!* song.

Living in Fear

So far, I have demonstrated why, in the very near future, we will no longer be able to understand one another. What else will we not be capable of doing? One answer to this question revolves around our inability to have any sort of perception of what world understanding is supposed to mean and, thus, endangering ourselves. As stated by Vivian Cook, a professor of Applied Linguistics at Newcastle University, "A person who speaks multiple languages has a stereoscopic vision of the world from two or more perspectives, enabling them to be more flexible in their thinking" (Cook). Consequently, having more than one worldview allows people to understand different outlooks, see their own native culture through multiple lenses (as both insiders and outsiders) and be able to employ critical thinking, contrast skills and comparison dexterities in relation to other cultures and civilizations. This focus on global understanding has at its core the idea of stepping inside the minds of people from different cultures by being conscious of their national and cultural context. Once this first step is achieved, it becomes a lot easier to create bridges of trust and acceptance. Under the name of multilingualism, many aspects of international relations can be facilitated, such as international trade and all types of economic partnerships that, in the long run, promote peace in a world where pacifism equals individual security.

The reality is that America is in desperate need of a reform that would make its inhabitants more "geoliterate." According to former President George W. Bush, being multilingual is not just about education, it is also about economic security, public diplomacy and, most importantly, national security. The American linguistic isolationism hurts its own creators, especially since new axes of economic growth are constantly emerging and the relative power of the United States is declining. What the former President observed is that devoting a small fraction of your time to the acquisition of someone else's language makes you appear less ignorant and more willing to discover somebody's heritage and culture (Kolb). These are the messages that need to be sent by Americans in a progressively interconnected world if we want to avoid a second World Trade Center catastrophe.

In what other ways are American monolinguals exposing themselves to national security hazards? One possible answer would be by not being able to participate in the process of gathering intelligence. During the past decades, the U.S. has focused on the acquisition of intelligence through means that were more technical. After 9/11, however, the lack of personnel that could translate messages collected through intelligence was severely felt. Thus, expertise in terms of multilingualism became overwhelmingly requested, but not many people could state that they had it. Hence, it is clear to see how shortages in polyglots undermine national security and, implicitly, individual security.

What else can disrupt peace and affect security? Discriminatory practices are seen as the "big, bad wolf" in this case. Being a polyglot and understanding other people's cultures makes others automatically assume that one is less likely to nurture feelings related to racism, xenophobia or intolerance, in general. Individuals that speak at least one other language besides their own are more disposed to "possess a second soul," as Charlemagne, the king of the Franks, gracefully put it. Personally, I have experienced being "bullied" in college by the monolinguals, simply because they could not understand my culture and all the habits that come with being an Eastern European orthodox. I would have never asked them to have a "second soul." What they needed to understand is what Fernando Fellini understood a long time ago, that "a different language is a different vision of life" (Reehan).

Presidents and secretaries of state around the world that are working to ensure our security understand very well the need for the recognition of the multiple "visions of life." They are required to master multilingualism in order to communicate in a clearer and more open fashion. For instance, the ability of former President John F. Kennedy to speak German and deliver the "I am a Berliner" ("Ich Bin Ein Berliner") speech allowed him to create a stronger bond between West Germany and the U.S. Even though he unintentionally introduced himself as a jelly doughnut, he was able to make the Germans understand that America recognizes the predicament that they had found themselves in as a divided nation. That obviously benefited Germany, but ensured America's security as well.

Multilingualism undoubtedly helps communicating to large masses. However, it also facilitates the process of business dealings and negotiations. It assists world leaders in the delivering of their messages in a clear and accurate manner. The sensitive situation developing in Iran, in which negotiators have to deal with the prospect of nuclear weapons, is an illustrative case in point. There, deterrence is of maximum priority. Consequently, the perfect grasp of a common language is of utmost importance in delivering overt messages and drafting unambiguous resolution points. Therefore, according to Henry Boye, the simple recognition of the fact that in negotiations "the most important trip you may take is meeting people half way" can sometimes prevent the planet from being blown up into little atomic pieces.

Not Just a Job, but a Career

Multilingualism does not unfold only on an individual level. Certain international organizations such as United Nations Educational, Scientific and Cultural Organization (UNESCO) or the World Health Organization (WHO) are becoming increasingly aware of the fact that they need to make access to health and cultural information more proportional. In a report released by the Secretariat of the World Health Organization in April 2007, it was revealed that "a multilingual WHO is better equipped to communicate health messages, to produce and disseminate health information and to generate, share and use knowledge about health in an equitable manner. It is also better placed to meet today's major public health challenge: strengthening health systems in order to provide essential health care for all" (WHO 2007). In their extensive goals, these international organizations need highly trained multilinguals, something that most Americans cannot identify themselves as. Isn't it a shame that a potential career in such a prestigious institution is simply off-limits to the average American even though he or she might have the knowledge, but not the linguistic skills?

Isn't it also a pity that Americans do not seem to want to take advantage of the incredibly diverse multilingual pool of cultures coexisting in the same geographic space? People of different cultures are most certainly taking advantage of this fact. They are using their multilingual abilities and, inherently, boosting their brainpower (Hitti). Studies have shown that multilinguals have denser gray matter within the brain and that their brains are generally bigger. Growth in areas of the cerebral cortex and the hippocampus determine their ability to further learn new things with ease. This essentially relates to all areas in which personal development is possible, but, most specifically, in the career field where opportunities are becoming more and more available. That is to say, one good thing leads to another. Contrastingly, for monolingual Americans, this process is seen in terms of a downward spiral. Lack of mastery of a second language leads to less brainpower, fewer career prospects and, ultimately, to the "dumbness" of America.

It is an overstated fact that the 21st century is not particularly known for an easy path to a career. The fact that the society is highly mobile does not make it any easier for Americans to have careers or even obtain jobs. The vanishing of territoriality assumes that people are no longer bounded by geographical constraints. As the famous philosopher, Emil Cioran, stated, "One does not inhabit a country; one inhabits a language." Thus, it is safe to say that non-Americans inhabit multiple countries and languages. In cyberspace, both native and non-native speakers are interacting with one another. Identities represented by nationality, geography, or history are simply inconsequential and that facilitates the mutual development of foreign language use by creating universal opportunities. In that sense, the Internet represents a blessing for non-Americans and a curse for Americans. That is, the citizens of the Land of the Free have reached such a level of self-inflicting sabotage that, in this case, the very development of technology is not seen in positive terms.

Can We Make it Through the 21st Century?

By the looks of it, if Americans continue to refuse the benefits and essential survival toolkits that come with the acquisition of a foreign language, English itself will become a burden. Expressing oneself in their mother tongue will increase in difficulty due to loss of awareness of grammatical structures, conjugation of verbs, and sentence design. The decrease in the quality of writing and conversation will finally lead us to agree with Wolfang von Goethe's statement that "those who know nothing of foreign languages, know nothing of their own."

As proved, multilingualism is gaining more and more opportunities to create momentum for intercultural interactions. Thus, it is essential to acquire as many languages as possible to create cultural openness and appreciation but, most importantly, to *survive*. We should all live by philosopher Ludwig Wittgenstein's mantra, in which he states that "the limits of my language are the limits of my world."

Works Cited

Cook, V. (2011), "Requirements for a multilingual model of language production." Retrieved from http://homepage.ntlworld.com/vivian.c/Writings/Papers/RequirementsForMultilingualModel.htm

Palmer, K. (2009). "Understanding Human Language: An In-Depth Exploration of the Human Facility for Language." *StudentPulse.com*. Retrieved from http://www.studentpulse.com/articles/82/2/understanding-human-language-an-in-depth-exploration-of-the-human-facility-for-language

Hauser, M.D., Fitch, W.D. (2003). *Language Evolution: The States of the Art*. M.H. Christiansen, S. Kirby (Eds). New York: Oxford University Press.

Hitti, M. (2004). "Being Bilingual Boots Brain Power." *WebMD Health News*. Retrieved from http://www.webmd.com/parenting/news/20041013/being-bilingual-boosts-brain-power

Pinker, S. (2007). *The Language Instinct: How the Mind Creates Language*, New York: Harper Perennial.

Kolb, C. (2012). "Foreign Tongues." *Huffington Post*. Retrieved from http://www.huffingtonpost.com/charles-kolb/foreign-tongues_b_1506451.html

Rajadurai, J. (2007), "Intelligibility Studies: a Consideration of Empirical and Ideological Issues." *World Englishes*. Retrieved from http://onlinelibrary.wiley.com/doi/10.1111/j.1467-971X.2007.00490.x/full

Reehan, S. (2014). "Difficulties of Vocabulary Learning and the Use of Songs to Promote Vocabulary Learning Part 3." Retrieved from http://shurooqreehan.blogspot.com/2014/03/difficulties-of-vocabulary-learning-and_18.html

Saussure, F. (1998). *Course in General Linguistics (Open Court Classics)*. C. Bally, A. Sechehaye, A. Riedlinger (Eds.). Chicago, Illinois: Open Court.

Skorton, D., Altschuler, G. (2012). "America's Foreign Language Deficit." *Forbes Magazine*. Retrieved from http://www.forbes.com/sites/collegeprose/2012/08/27/americas-foreign-language-deficit/

Thanassoulas, D. (2002). "History of English Language Teaching." *English Club*. Retrieved from http://www.englishclub.com/tefl-articles/history-english-language-teaching.htm

Trudgill, P. (2004). *New-dialect Formation: the Inevitability of Colonial Englishes*. Oxford,UK: Oxford University Press.

World Health Organization, *Multilingualism: plan of action*. Retrieved from http://apps.who.int/gb/ebwha/pdf_files/EB121/B121_6-en.pdf?ua=1

Bhavya Sharma

The Curious Case of Arab Spring

Lately, much has been in the news about the revolutionary protests and uprisings that have taken the Arab world by storm. The series of protests, known popularly as the Arab Spring, began in Tunisia and Egypt and spread to other nations such as Libya, Yemen, Bahrain, and Syria. The Arab Spring began in response to the citizens' growing dissatisfaction with their governments and the heightened sense of autocracy in these countries. Consequently, the "major slogan of the demonstrators in the Arab world has been 'the people want to bring down the regime'" (Abulof).

While from a distance, it appears that these protests have been consistent and successful, resulting in a favorable outcome, that is, a democratic regime replacing a former dictatorship, a closer observation would reveal that that is, in fact, not the case. The Arab Spring protests have differed in their outcomes across nations. A major division can specifically be observed between the Muslim Arab and non-Arab worlds. In countries such as Libya and Egypt, the rulers were overthrown after massive protests by the masses. However, in the Arab nations like Saudi Arabia and Oman, there were only mild protests that were subdued by the government by making minor concessions. Why has an outcome this varied occurred across these two worlds? While there are many complex aspects related to the problem, three particular ones have been massively researched by scholars. These three aspects are: a. religion, b. income of a country, and c. presence of a natural resource. Scholars have tried to analyze if these factors have a relation with the absence of democracy in the Arab world, and if revolutions in the future would result in a more liberal regime.

1. Religion

It is often believed that the presence or absence of democracy and religion are correlated. According to some scholars, some faiths such as Islam and Catholicism are incompatible with democracy. This theory has been applied to explain why the Arab Spring protests were not as successful in more conservative countries like Saudi Arabia. In the non-Arab Muslim world, the traditional bans on freedom of speech and prevalence of censorship are not as prominent, which allowed the masses to take to social networking websites as a way to propagate the revolution. Thus, while countries like Tunisia and Egypt saw a burgeoning "twitter revolution," the more conservative Arab world did not witness any such outcomes. It is important to note that many political analysts correlate the words "conservative" with "religious" (DeLong-Bass). However, critics of this theory have pointed out that many Islamic countries have had democratic regimes in the past and sustained them.

In their book called *The Principles of Comparative Politics*, Golder and Golder point out that seemingly conservative religions such as Islam preach many democratic principles such as consultation and decision-making. Thus, the degree of religious conservatism has nothing to do with the magnitude of outcome of the Arab Spring protests. Dr. DeLong-Bass, in her speech at Georgetown University, also pointed out that the ongoing Arab Spring protests are a sign of the masses' desire for a democratic regime. She pointed out that the success of the Arab Spring protests in some countries is not coincidental, and that their failure in other countries is not an expected outcome. Thus, just because countries like Saudi Arabia and Oman are more religiously conservative does not imply that they have no prospect of becoming a democracy. Her claims are supported by many other scholars such as Sprusansky, who mentioned that many times, Westerners tend to "disrespect values [of people in the Middle Eastern societies]" by assuming that they do not want the Arab Spring protests to yield a successful outcome. Thus, religion and the presence of democracy have no direct correlation, which subsequently implies that failure in regime change in the Arab world is not due to religious conservatism present in the society.

2. Income

Proponents of the Modernization Theory believe that the wealthier a country, the better the chances of it emerging as and sustaining a democratic regime. To test this theory, Stepan and Robertson applied quantitative and qualitative findings by categorizing Muslim countries into primarily two categories: Arab and non-Arab. The countries were then placed under categories separating them on the basis of their income levels, identifying them as either being "electoral overachievers or underachievers" (33). The term "overachievers" refers to countries that, despite having a low GDP ($1,500-$3,500) and contradicting the modernization theory, are democracies. The term "underachievers" refers to countries that, despite having high levels of income (more than $5,500), continue to be autocracies (although, according to the Modernization Theory, they are expected to be democracies). The empirical evidence showed that countries in the non-Arab Muslim world were electoral overachievers. Albania, Niger, Nigeria, Bangladesh, etc. are democracies despite having low-level GDPs. This, when applied to the Arab Spring protests, also shows that African countries of Egypt, Libya, and Tunisia are capable of becoming electoral overachievers. But more interesting were the findings through these quantitative analyses of the Arab Muslim world. Not a single Arab nation was an electoral overachiever. What was more surprising was that almost all the nations fell under the "electoral underachievers" category, i.e. despite having high-income levels and a GDP of over $5,500, these countries still happened to be autocracies.

When applied to Arab Spring, these studies reveal that the ongoing Arab Spring protests disprove the Modernization Theory. Low-income countries like Libya and Egypt have managed to overthrow their regimes, while high-income countries like Saudi Arabia and Oman have continued to be autocratic and only provided a few concessions to their citizens. Thus, the level of income has little to do with the emergence of democracy and has more to do with its survival. But the specific question that researchers wanted to address was why countries like Saudi Arabia, despite having high GDPs, did not become democracies even after the emergence of Arab Spring protests in these nations. As observed, income is obviously not relevant to the question. This brings one to analyze the final aspect that differentiates the non-Arab world from the Arab world.

3. Presence of a Natural Resource:

Scholars have attempted to examine whether the presence of natural resources is inversely proportional to the chances of the country being a democracy. One of the main countries that has been researched is Saudi Arabia. Saudi Arabia is the "world's second largest [oil producer]" and the oil industry comprises about 45% of Saudi Arabia's GDP (Wynbrandt 296). This makes Saudi Arabia a rentier state. By definition, a rentier state "derives all or a substantial portion of its revenue from the rent of indigenous natural resources to external clients" (Golder and Golder 197). Countries rich in natural resources face what is commonly known as the "resource curse" or "rentier effect," which suggests that "resource-rich countries use low-tax rates and patronage to relieve pressures for greater accountability" (Ross 327).

To understand this paradox, an EVL (Exit, Voice and Loyalty) game tree is used. An EVL game plan is studied which suggests that groups or organizations can respond to a change in three ways: 1. By exiting (withdrawing their investment), 2. By showing loyalty and adapting to the change, or 3. By voicing their opinion for a change in their favor. To understand how oil hinders democracy, it is essential to know the difference between fixed and liquid assets. "Fixed assets cannot easily be converted into cash, while liquid assets, such as cash, bank deposits and the like, can easily be converted into other assets" (Golder and Golder 196). If, hypothetically, the government imposes a law that is viewed by the citizens as unfavorable, the citizens can respond in three ways, to which the government will then respond.

The game becomes interesting when the citizens do not have the option to disinvest and exit the economy, i.e., they have fixed assets. Countries such as Saudi Arabia have people who are dependent upon the oil industry (a fixed asset) and cannot exit the economy if the government imposes a law that is unfavorable to them. The citizens cannot voice their opinions either. This can be explained by the "Repression Effect" of oil-rich economies. Countries that are not rich in natural resources depend upon their citizens to invest in the economy and utilize taxes to help the country flourish economically. But resource-rich countries have a steady source of income due to oil production and thus, they do not depend upon their citizens for investment. This makes the ruler(s) oppressive. They no longer require the citizens to remain loyal to them.

In another case scenario, by extracting substantial revenue from oil production, "[the rulers] are likely to tax their populations less heavily or not at all, and the public in return will be less likely to demand accountability from—and representativeness from—their government" (Ross 332). The government is also able to utilize its internal security mechanisms in its favor by oppressing the citizens. Thus, the citizens are unable to voice their opinions, thereby leaving them with the only choice, i.e., to remain loyal to the rulers. This has been noted during the Arab Spring uprisings.

In countries such as Libya and Egypt, the rulers, though oppressive, did not have the power to use oppressive forces on the citizens. The masses were then able to overthrow the regime. But countries like Saudi Arabia unleashed a reign of terror on their citizens by making swift arrests of people involved in these uprisings. According to Toby Jones, "[the regime's] power and willingness to pursue a counterrevolutionary agenda [was] on full display" during these protests. Another look at the EVL game will reveal that the government, like the citizens, can respond to protests in three ways, 1. By entirely rejecting the demands for freedom by its citizens, 2. By accepting these demands and changing the regime, or 3. By providing some concessions to avoid accepting the demands entirely and to pacify the citizens. The last option is what countries like Saudi Arabia and Oman chose when their citizens demanded a regime change. This way, the rulers did not have to switch from an autocracy to a democracy and at the same time, they were able to pacify citizens to some extent.

Scholars and political scientists have come to the conclusion that the presence of natural resources hinders democracy due to the aforementioned reasons. However, critics of this theory point to the fact that there is not enough empirical evidence to support this, as many other Muslim non-Arab nations are autocracies as well. A majority of scholars still believe that oil-rich countries sustain dictatorial regimes by repression and that a resource curse surrounds these nations.

In conclusion, the different outcomes of the Arab Spring protests have been the subject of discussion of many researchers who have tried to analyze the scenario to explain this variation. Currently, the only theory that explains failure of the revolutions in the Arab Muslim world is the "rentier effect" or "resource curse" theory. This theory has been accepted widely and has met little or no criticism. Scholars such as Dale Sprusansky believe that the real problem does not lie with what regime type the country is, but by how the West (in particular, America) views these countries. "[These] stereotypes could be misleading and harmful because the U.S. tends to view the Kingdom through [its] own values and fails to understand Saudi culture and society" (Sprusansky 57).

The ultimate question is whether the citizens of countries like Saudi Arabia and Oman in fact desire a regime change. These questions cannot be answered due to the lack of transparency in the Arab world. Thus, the prospect of democracy in the Arab world is hard to predict with no statistical evidence to support the view. But the hope for democracy in these countries is not altogether absent, as scholars like Dr. DeLong-Bass point out that "Saudi Arabia has the second largest Facebook usership in the Middle East (2.9 million users) and YouTube has emerged as a means of forcing accountability and fighting corruption" (Sprusansky 58). Arab Spring has resulted in not just changing the political atmosphere of the countries it has spread to, but it has empowered the people in these resilient states to stand for what they believe is right and what they deserve as denizens of a nation. A time will soon come when the people would not just want to, but will change the regime of their country and replace the age-old oppressive dictatorships and monarchies with the freedom that is the essence of modern democracy.

Works Cited

Abulof, Uriel. "What Is the Arab Third Estate?" *The Huffington Post*. TheHuffingtonPost.com, 10 Mar. 2011. Web. 09 Mar. 2014. <http://www.huffingtonpost.com/uriel-abulof/what-is-the-arab-third-es_b_832628.html>.

Briefing: *"Saudi Arabia and the Gulf: Looking for the Arab Spring"* Perf. Dr. Natana DeLong-Bas. 2012. Video. ACMCU, 21 Mar. 2012. Web. 20 Feb. 2014. <http://vimeo.com/41035909>.

Golder, Matt, and Sona N. Golder. "The Economic Determinants of Democracy and Dictatorship." *Principles of Comparative Politics*. By Williams R. Clark. 2nd ed. California: Sage, 2013. 171-209. Print.

Jones, Toby C. "Saudi Arabia Versus the Arab Spring." *ABI/Inform Complete.*
McClatchy – Tribune Information Services, 4 July 2013. Web. 20 Feb. 2014.

Ross, Michael L. "Does Oil Hinder Democracy?" *World Politics* 53.03 (2001): 325-61. Print.

Sprusansky, Dale. "Saudi Arabia and the Arab uprising." *Washington Report on Middle
East Affairs* June-July 2012: 57+. Academic OneFile. Web. 20 Feb. 2014.

Stepan, Alfred C., and Graeme B. Robertson. "An "Arab" More Than a "Muslim"
Democracy Gap." *Journal of Democracy* 14 (2003): 30-44. Print.

Wynbrandt, James. *A Brief History of Saudi Arabia.* New York: Facts On File, 2004. Print.

Edward Seamans

Ada

"Forget this world and all its troubles and if possible, its multitudinous Charlatans—everything in short but the Enchantress of Numbers." —Charles Babbage to Ada Lovelace[1]

To get an idea of the sense of discovery inherent in the mind of our subject, imagine, in 1828, a short carriage ride southeast out of Canterbury, England. The carriage would bring you to a rolling and palatial noble estate called Bifrons.[2] Had you taken this journey at that time, you might have seen a young girl of thirteen years dashing across the sprawling lawns, flapping huge and elaborate wings strapped to her arms, arching and leaping into the wind with the hope of taking to the sky.[3] And if you were fortunate enough to distract her long enough for a conversation, she might tell you that her name was Augusta Byron of Lovelace (but that you could call her Ada).

If she were tired enough from all of that wing-flapping, the conversation might continue for a bit, and she might tell you about her father, the celebrated poet Lord Byron. She might also confide that she had no memory of ever meeting him, since he had left England when she was just a baby. Ada might then sadly reveal how, four years before in 1824, her father died in Greece on Easter Sunday campaigning against the Turkish.[4]

After catching her breath, she might have turned into the wind to stretch out her wings once more. "I'm busy," she might say. "I'm writing a book called Flyology."[5]

***

In late 1834, Lady Augusta "Ada" Byron of Lovelace attended a dinner party hosted by noted astronomer and mathematician Mary Somerville. Among the guests was Charles Babbage, an accomplished mathematician and engineer who held the Lucasian Chair of Mathematics at Cambridge University.[6] As 19-year-old Ada listened in rapt fascination, Babbage imparted to Somerville an idea he had for a new and wonderful invention.[7]

Babbage spoke of his visits to the burgeoning textile mills springing up all around London and of the new forms of manufacturing machinery he saw in them. In particular, Babbage mused about a particularly novel machine that was becoming commonplace in the textile industry: the Jaquard loom. He explained how this loom was capable of swiftly and automatically weaving very complex patterns from raw fabric using instructions encoded on rigid cards punched with holes and how the arrangement of these holes could be made to produce any desired design. Babbage speculated on the possibility of a new device similar to the Jacquard loom in that it could also be controlled by instructions on punched cards and would also be powered by steam. But rather than assembling designs in fabric like the loom, this "Analytical Engine" would instead be able to execute complex mathematical operations in a specified sequence, speedily and without error.[8]

Though Mary Somerville warned Babbage that people might not be ready for such radical innovation,[9] young Ada's imagination soared as she listened. Maybe she remembered her girlhood dream of building a flying machine, and how that dream was cut short by the illness that forced her to hang up her wings in favor of crutches for a time.[10] Childhood dreams may have been forced aside by the realities of life, but her genius for brilliant, inspired, and fearless inquiry never abandoned her. She had become a grown woman comprehensively schooled by some of the finest minds in mathematics. One of her tutors,[11] the renowned mathematician Augustus De Morgan, noted in a letter to Ada's mother that her daughter had the necessary mathematical skills to become "an original mathematical investigator, perhaps of first-rate eminence."[12] Upon hearing Babbage's idea, Ada somehow knew that she was witness to something very special. In fact, this "Analytical Engine" would turn out to be the precursor of the modern general-purpose computer.[13]

From that day forward, Ada was fascinated by the concept of the Analytical Engine. She corresponded often with Babbage[14] as he gave lectures at technical centers of learning across Europe trying to raise funds for the construction of the Analytical Engine. During one of these trips, Babbage travelled to Turin, Italy in 1840 where a young engineer named Luigi Menabrea took notes on some of his lectures. Soon afterward in 1842, Menabrea published an article in the journal *Bibliothèque Universelle de Genève*, titled "Notions sur la machine analytique (Sketch of the Analytical Engine)." The article quickly reached England. Seeking to further interest in the idea of his machine at home, Babbage realized at once that he needed someone to translate the article from Menabrea's French.[15]

Babbage did not have to search very far; by this time Ada was fully versed in the theory of the Analytical Engine and she also happened to be fluent in French. Babbage asked her to translate the document into English, and over the winter of 1842-43 she labored over the task, correcting many errors made by the original author. Upon seeing the finished product, Babbage was so impressed with the depth of her understanding that he suggested she add notes to the completed project to develop her own ideas and insights on the Analytical Engine.

The resulting "Notes by the Translator" (hereafter referred to as the "Notes") were published in London along with the translated version of Menabrea's article in 1843. The Notes turned out to be three times the length of Menabrea's original article, and the quality of Ada's work along with the nature of her insights are today considered far more relevant than the article they accompanied.[16]

***

Through her "Notes," Ada prophesized many more varied and versatile uses for the Analytical Engine than the straight-forward number-crunching envisioned by Babbage. For example, she foresaw the potential of computerized music: "Supposing, for instance, that the fundamental relations of pitched sounds in the science of harmony and of musical composition were susceptible of such expression and adaptations, the engine might compose elaborate and scientific pieces of music of any degree of complexity or extent."[17]

In "Notes," Ada also appears to be the first to imagine that a machine such as the Analytical Engine might be able to manipulate symbols of language, a notion of course taken for granted today: "Many persons who are not conversant...imagine that the *nature of its processes* must...be *arithmetical and numerical*...This is an error. The engine can arrange and combine its numerical quantities exactly as if they were letters or any other general symbols."[18] (All italics in Ada Lovelace's quotes are retained from sources and appear to express her own emphasis. Italics are retained in this way for the remainder of this essay.)

Ada's most important contribution, however, was most certainly buried in Note G of "Notes." After warning us that "[t]he Analytical Engine has no pretensions whatever to originate anything. It can do whatever we *know how to order it* to perform,"[19] Ada proceeded to lay out a mathematical problem that today is familiar to many in the field of computer science: the calculation of the Bernoulli numbers.

The mathematics for calculating the Bernoulli numbers are beyond the scope of this essay, but suffice it to say that they represent an infinite series of specific numbers. The values in this series can be algorithmically calculated, but is a computationally intensive task and becomes more so as successive values of the series are generated. After describing the problem of deriving the "numbers of Bernoulli" in an earlier portion of her "Notes," in section G she lays out a specific algorithm intended to be used with the Analytical Engine to compute those numbers. Publishing this in 1843 made her *the first to publish a computer program*. Considering the impact that computers have had on the way we live, in terms of significance to the human race Ada's contribution is of the highest order, comparable even to the invention of the wheel or the taming of fire.

Sadly, the Analytical Engine was never built, as Babbage's fiscal problems persisted for the remainder of his life. However, Babbage and Lovelace kept copious records (most of which survive) and mainstream engineers today believe that Babbage's designs of the Analytical Engine provided a workable organization of a complete machine.[20] That being said, Ada often corrected Babbage's mistakes (which he himself acknowledged) on subsequent algorithms,[21] so it seems reasonable to surmise that if his machine had ever been realized, Ada's original algorithm would have been able to run on it.

Ada had several bouts of serious sickness during her life, but it was uterine cancer (in combination with the bloodletting that was the fashionable treatment of the time) that would finally get the better of her. On November 27, 1852, Ada succumbed, fighting to the last, in the neighborhood of Great Cumberland House, Westminster, England, just two weeks before her 37th birthday.[22] She had asked to be buried next to her father, Lord Byron,[23] whose face she could not possibly have remembered.

When Byron had been buried in the family tomb at Nottingham, England, his body had travelled in a hearse "drawn by six black horses." Twenty-seven years later, his daughter Ada was taken to meet him aboard a train operated by the Midland Railway.[24]

***

In a journal entry dated 29 October, 1851, a little more than a year before her death and almost certainly after she had contracted the disease that would kill her, Ada wrote in her diary: "If I *could* ever help to give the *despots a shove*, I should certainly feel that I *had not lived in* vain."

On December 10, 1980, the United States Department of Defense released a computer programming language intended to standardize systems across the U.S. Military. The language was named Ada, and the manual was designated MIL-STD-1815 in honor of the year of Ada Lovelace's birth.[25]

Endnotes

1. History-computer.com, <http://www.history-computer.com/ModernComputer/thinkers/Ada.html>.

2. Benjamin Woolley, *The Bride of Science*, (London: McGraw Hill, 1999), p. 111.

3. Ibid., p. 112.

4. Ibid., p. 93.

5. Betty Alexandra Toole, "Ada Byron, Lady Lovelace, an Analyst and Metaphysician," *IEEE Annals of the History of Computing*, Vol. 18, No. 3, (1996): p. 5. Print.

6. "Charles Babbage," Wikipedia.org, <http://en.wikipedia.org/wiki/Charles_Babbage>.

7. Ibid 5., p. 6.

8. History-computer.com, <http://www.history-computer.com/Babbage/AnalyticalEngine.html>.

9. Ibid 5., p. 6.

10. Ibid 2., p. 115.

11. John Fuegi & Jo Francis, "Lovelace and Babbage and the Creation of the 1843 'Notes'", *IEEE Annals of the History of Computing*, October-December (2003): p. 17. Print.

12. Ibid 5., p. 7.

13. Ibid 10., p. 1.

14. Ibid., p. 17.

15. Ibid 11., p. 18.

16. Ibid 11., p. 18-19.

17. Augusta "Ada" Lovelace, "Notes by the Translator on the Sketch of the Analytical Engine Invented by Charles Babbage," *Scientific Memoirs* 3:666-731 (1843): Note A.

18. Ibid., Note E.

19. Ibid., Note G.

20. Allan G. Bromley, "Charles Babbage's Analytical Engine, 1838," *IEEE Annals of the History of Computing*, Vol. 4, No. 3, (1982): p. 1. Print.

21. Ibid 5., p. 8.

22. Ibid 2., p. 372.

23. Doris Langley Moore, *Countess of Lovelace*, (New York: Harper and Row, 1977), p. 325

24. Ibid 2., p, 372.

25. "Ada Lovelace," Wikipedia.org, <http://en.wikipedia.org/wiki/Ada_lovelace>.

Taylor Bush

Anamnesis: An Exploration of Memory

I just had it in my hands. My special memory. A glowing conch shell with barnacle-licked ridges, and emanating from within—the call of the ocean. But it was wet and I was careless and it slipped right through my fingertips. Now the tide's coming in. Will my memory be swept out to sea or stay lodged in the sands of my memory bank?

The concept of memory is far from a simple mechanism. It's mystical, even magical. There are countless diagrams, charts, data, and paradigms that try to paint a picture of memory. But unlike, say, phylogenetic nomenclature (which you need a diagram just to pronounce), it is next to impossible to attain a proper schema that encompasses all principles, elements, and facets of memory. And as anyone with a memory can tell you—which is everyone on the planet—memory can never be properly articulated.

But a small shaft of light *can* be shed upon its mechanics.

Beginning with semantics, memory is best defined as "the mental capacity or faculty of retaining and reviving facts, events and impressions" (Oxford English Dictionary). The Atkinson-Schiffrin 3-Stage Model is the most common and accepted diagram concerning memory processing used within the scientific and academic community. It begins with an external event being transmitted into sensory memory. Let's use, for an example, walking into my mother's kitchen and discovering a pleasant balmy aroma hitting my nostrils. Nutmeg. Or pumpkin pie. The fragrance will be processed instantaneously from my sensory memory to my short-term memory, where it will hover for three to 15 seconds. Then it is encoded into the long-term memory where it waits to be recalled again. The act of retrieval occurs when I think back to that kitchen and connect the smell to the given circumstances. A substantial amount of time may pass and I may be unable to retrieve the smell from my long-term memory. Obviously, this means the detail has been forgotten.

The Atkinson-Schiffrin Model has its limitations. Some information skips the first two stages and enters long-term memory automatically. Also, the model is fairly simple and fails to encompass the fact that humans tend to select sensory details that are important to them or catch their attention—like my mom's home-cooked pumpkin pie—more so than all sensory information that we encounter. But just as emotions such as love and lust are too abstract to be classified into mere words, it would be impossible to pigeonhole memory into a tangible classification.

Sensory memory, short-term memory, and long-term memory are essentially the "storage bins" of memory. How I retrieve, sort, store, and consolidate the items from said bins are a whole different matter entirely.

There are essentially two types of long-term memory, each with different ways of retrieving from the bin. Procedural memory, or implicit memory, is primarily concerned with *recognition* and inherent recollection. This encompasses motor skills, learned information, muscle memory, et cetera.

Then there is declarative memory, or explicit memory, which refers to facts and information that can be consciously *recalled*. It is subdivided into episodic memory—which is information from autobiographical events— and semantic memory—which concerns facts and concepts independent of personal experience.

Say I take a romantic getaway with a loved one up to a cozy cabin. I put a log on the fire, pop on some Marvin Gaye, bust out the *pinot noir*, smoke some Cubans from the private humidor, and make sweet, sweet love with my bonnie lass on the bearskin rug. These events or "episodes" are classified as episodic memory. The loveliness of the evening, including intangible emotions such as excitement and tranquility, comprise your autobiographical sketch. Obviously there are discrepancies when it comes to this form of memory due to its subjective nature, but the annals of one's memory are the fulcrum of one's sense of self, providing the proper tools necessary to navigate your life.

Semantic memory, on the other hand, concerns mostly objective material, with little disagreement concerning its importance or definition. The rules of cricket. The capital of Yugoslavia. The sound the letter "Y" makes. Most of these are indisputable facts that do not contain the same autobiographical significance as episodic memory.

There is overlap with both of these types of explicit memory, yet episodic and semantic memory both possess distinct qualities. When one thinks of those special individuals on *60 Minutes* who claim to have "perfect memory," usually it is in only one of these specific areas. While a person with perfect recall can remember what they ate twenty years ago, they may be completely unable to memorize basic functions for a Calculus test. By the same coin, a savant might be able to be a genius when it comes to arbitrary information, but they may be incapable of retrieving the details of a personal encounter they had just a few days ago.

The various models, categories, steps, divisions, and sub-divisions can make the science of memory appear rather confusing. And as stated above, the classifications don't even come close to touching the true nature of memory, mainly because it is a subjective entity changed and challenged with each respective context and personal circumstance. And when you add in varying scientific viewpoints and opinions, memory can certainly become quite the tangled web. My bet is that, because of the way memory becomes embedded in us or not, you will remember the sensory details I've fashioned here more readily than the scientific material. Can't recall the nomenclature I mentioned in paragraph 2 of part C (don't look back and check!)? That's because you didn't attach emotional significance to what I was saying. Things that are funny or poignant tend to "stick" in your memory. Conversely, things that are mundane and boring mostly tend to pass through your memory's grip. A boyfriend's kiss. The intimation of summer in a May breeze. That feeling of flying when everything in the world is going your way. Those are the instances that really hit the memory dartboard.

As far as memory reinforcement is concerned, some techniques are frequently employed to strengthen memory: exercise, pneumonic devices (such as acronyms or music), playing games that challenge one's mind, and regular sleep habits. Some foods that provide anamnestic aid are cantaloupe, blueberries, salmon, eggs, red wine, green tea, soy foods, and anything that came from a tree. And think in words rather than images. Words are easier to recreate than a mood or impression.

Rehearsing, or the constant retrieval of information from long-term memory, can also help to prevent forgetting. Forgetting is generally caused when there is a blip in the encoding or retrieving process. Thus, the more you rehearse—the more you retrieve and encode—the easier it is to remember a memory.

And the easier it is to prevent your shell from slipping through your fingers.

James Warren

Ghosts Out of Time

Human beings are obsessed with extinction. There is something about the idea of a species having vanished forever from the Earth that makes it iconic, something that both fascinates and terrifies people. Extinction is even more final than death, obliterating whole species, but like death, extinction is inevitable: it is the ultimate fate of every species that has ever existed or will ever exist. It seems that it is this fascination that has led some particularly sensationalist scientists to seek to clone certain extinct animals back into existence. With some exceptions, the animals that are most frequently targeted by this goal are those thought of as most iconic: Wooly Mammoths, *Smilodons*, and Passenger Pigeons often topping the list. Often they are not species whose extinction human beings played any role in, and even less frequently is there any viable plan for reintegrating these species into ecosystems once they have become "de-extinct." Not only would this be an impractical use of funds that could be much better spent on conserving extant species, it would be incredibly unethical, as it would likely result in only a few isolated individuals of each species, with no hope of propagating their race or reintroducing them to the wild.

With the famous cloning of Dolly the sheep, the first mammal to be successfully grown to adulthood from cloned cells, a new era was ushered in. No longer was there a question of whether or not it was possible for large animals to be cloned. Cloning techniques were then and still are now in need of improvement—Dolly herself died quite young—but it became inevitable that more cloning would take place, and on an ever larger scale. Indeed, since Dolly, numerous other clones have been produced—from animals such as pigs, cows, and deer—and within five years, the first endangered species was successfully cloned, a European Mouflon (Trivedi 2001). This was seen as a triumph for species conservation; no longer were conservationists limited to working with existing populations; they could buffer them with human-made clones if need be. This was a particularly important step along the way, as it was the first time that a clone was produced using a surrogate mother of a different species, something that would be necessary if trying to produce clones of an entirely extinct species (Trivedi 2001). This seemed to open limitless possibilities, starting with bolstering existing populations of endangered species by expanding their gene pool, and ultimately leading to the idea that it might be possible to resurrect species that were already extinct.

The idea of cloning extinct species was first introduced to the public before even Dolly became a reality—with Michael Crichton's *Jurassic Park*, where a theme park full of dinosaurs goes disastrously (and some would say predictably) awry. Somewhat strangely, and certainly not in accordance with the message Crichton intended, the message that many people got out of this book and film was that it would be thrilling if extinct animals came back to life. This began a fascination by the public with cloning particularly iconic species, which, at the time, was a dream quite far away from being able to be realized. However, public fascination with the idea did not die down over the years, and it became increasingly evident that, when the technology became available, someone was likely to try to turn that dream into a reality—not with dinosaurs (it has long since been agreed upon that dinosaur DNA is far too old for cloning), but with other long-extinct animals.

The animal that is always favored to get the "Jurassic Park" treatment above all others is the Wooly Mammoth, with popular news sites always magnifying any buzz around the possibility of a cloning attempt (Cotroneo 2014). It's not surprising, really—the mammoth is a well-known behemoth from another era, and it bears the most similarity to the dinosaurs that came roaring onto the silver screen decades ago: huge, loud, and something that we have no real experience with whatsoever. The possibility of cloning mammoths raises two critical questions, however, which, in the excitement of potentially raising a giant, hairy ghost from its peaceful grave, many people have overlooked: why should we? And, perhaps even more importantly: would it be ethical for the mammoths? Any population of mammoths cloned into existence would be an anomaly; there is no real hope of repopulating the wild with them—their habitat largely disappeared millennia ago, and what little of it they would find today is shrinking with shifting climates. With this in mind, the mammoths would be condemned to a life behind bars, never able to have a natural population, and with no intent by scientists of that ever changing. If we were to subject living animals to such a fate, there would need to be a very good reason for it, and curiosity value certainly would not cut it.

This quandary becomes even more disturbing when one considers the possibility recently brought up by some geneticists: that of cloning a Neanderthal. Neanderthals, one of human beings' most recent cousins, likely possessed intelligence on par with that of our own; so this would mean bringing an intelligent hominid into existence with no relatives and no companions, into a world where he or she would almost certainly be ostracized for their entire life (Hughes 2014). This would be the height of irresponsible, unethical science, and would be tantamount to human experimentation. Nothing that could be gained by studying a living Neanderthal would be worth the lifelong psychological torture that this individual would be forced to endure.

There exists another sort of resurrection proponent entirely: those who claim to be interested in it for the sake of conservation. Such people are usually more interested in cloning species that human beings have directly driven extinct. In particular, Passenger Pigeons have received a great deal of attention of late, as a group known as Revive & Restore has begun a project intending to clone the pigeons back into existence (Rich 2014). This is hardly the first time scientists have dreamed of resurrecting a recently extinct species: there is perennial talk of reviving the Thylacine, an extinct carnivorous marsupial, and a project aimed at cloning the extinct Pyrenean Ibex actually succeeded in creating a short-lived infant. Such projects present two ethical conundrums. The first is that, as is the case with Passenger Pigeons, it is wildly impractical to expect that it will be possible to integrate a population of the animals back into the wild; Passenger Pigeons survived in flocks of billions, moving from chestnut forest to chestnut forest, a habitat that is all but gone now, thanks to the ever-ravaging chestnut blight. The niche they occupied has all but vanished from the earth, and even if it had not, it is simply not practical to attempt to clone a billion Passenger Pigeons back into existence. This leaves the pigeon project in the same ethical quandary that faces those seeking to clone mammoths: the birds would likely live their lives in captivity, with no real hope of ever living natural lives with members of their own species.

The second ethical problem is one of funding: those who are seeking to clone animals driven extinct by human beings require millions of dollars to do their research, before ever even obtaining viable offspring. In doing so, they are passing over thousands of other, still extant species that that funding could just as easily be helping. In the case of the Thylacine, the Ibex, and a recently extinct species of frog from Australia that is the subject of a similar project, it is not too difficult to imagine a recovery plan, once a sufficient number of each species has been cloned. However, this would involve spending millions of dollars for each individual species. To put this in perspective, each individual endangered Whooping Crane is estimated to represent a funding cost of greater than $100,000, and these are birds that are born naturally, not cloned, so there would be a huge initial cost to get each individual of an extinct species into existence, only to spend even more money to keep them alive and integrate them into the wild (Haywood 2012). As much as it makes all conservationists go starry-eyed to imagine Thylacines prowling through the Australian brush after a century of absence, the fact that so much money would be lost to other conservation causes for the sake of that one species makes it an unconscionably wasteful pursuit.

As fascinating as the subject of cloning species back into existence is, there is no way in which it can be ethically justified. In many instances, such animals would be freaks out of their own time, doomed to a lonely existence in a cage. In those few instances where species could be successfully reintroduced to the wild, and form viable populations, it would likely doom dozens of other species to the axe in favor of that one species. It would be a set of scales wildly out of balance, with one species on the left and whole ecosystems on the right, thrown away because the funding that could have saved them went instead into trying to misguidedly fix mistakes we made in the past. For our sake, and the sake of the species we still have left, I hope we can instead learn from those mistakes in the future.

Works Cited

Cotroneo, Christian. "Wooly Mammoth Clone is Now Possible, Say Scientists." *The Huffington Post*. 14 Mar. 2014. Web. 20 May 2014.

Haywood, Joe. "Indiana DNR News Release." *Whooping Crane Eastern Partnership*. 16 May 2012. Web. 20 May 2014.

Hughes, Virginia. "Return of the Neanderthals." *National Geographic*. National Geographic Society, 06 Mar. 2013. Web. 21 May 2014.

Rich, Nathaniel. "The Mammoth Cometh." *The New York Times*. The New York Times, 01 Mar. 2014. Web. 20 May 2014.

Trivedi, Bijal P. "Scientists Clone First Endangered Species: A Wild Sheep." *National Geographic*. National Geographic Society, 29 Oct. 2001. Web. 21 May 2014.

Week of
Writing

Introduction

Drexel University's eighth annual Week of Writing (WoW) was held in May of 2014. WoW is a weeklong celebration of writing sponsored by the Department of English and Philosophy and the College of Arts and Sciences. Each year, in conjunction with the Week of Writing, the Drexel Publishing Group runs the WoW Writing Contest, and faculty judges determine the best fiction, poetry, and creative nonfiction submitted by Drexel students.

Creative writing is among the most challenging fields. Even experienced authors who have been writing for years often struggle to find just the right word. As author Gene Fowler famously said, "Writing is easy. All you do is stare at a blank sheet of paper until drops of blood form on your forehead." The writers whose work appears in this section have stared at that blank sheet of paper, or that computer screen. Whether or not blood formed on their foreheads, they have struggled for the right words to touch their readers and bring their vision to life.

Joseph Esposito

Beyond the Panes

The tilt wand pivots 360 degrees,
hunching the flimsy vertical slats,
to complete the nightly ritual.

Every remaining inch of incandescent street light
empties
into a King's throne of fabrics.
To my liking,
Even an eyelash could no longer slip into appearance.

On the floor below,
red curtains called.
My mother searches for the pillow's warmest surface,
One eye open,
For the return of his familiar blue-collar uniform.

She lays toward a window that
barely kisses the trim,
the entrance of gaseous fumes would
defeat the past,
and a fresh primer aroma would
accept the future.

But his presence hung on door hooks,
like a robe that never saw the morning.
Little did he know
Her eyes were the hooks,
and mine
stayed buried in the sheets.

Taylor Bush

Fat

One day I'm going to be fat.

One day I'm going to be fat and you're going to be nothing. Just a skinny sliver, like you've always been. I once thought you were powerful, but you never were. I just made you powerful by believing in you. Now you'll be looking up at me and I'm going to be so god damn big you won't even be able to see my face.

And I'm going to make you pay, pay so much that Rich Uncle Pennybags will be crying over your overdraft fee. I'm going to step on every barb you ever threw at me and I won't even feel it. For the first time in your life, you'll know what it's like to feel small.

One day you won't even be able to walk down the street without seeing my ugly mug everywhere you look. I'll be ubiquitous. My name, my voice, my soul, every part of me will be fat. I'll be in the papers. I'll be on blimps. That nagging sensation, that prickling on the back of your neck, that's me and it's never going away ever again...so get used to it.

You made me feel so small. But that won't matter once I'm big. Big, big, big, so fucking big that Paul Bunyan and Jack's beanstalk will invite me to their pissing contests. You'll bow down and kiss my size 100 bunions. So don't shit yourself when you see me in the Guinness Book of World Records.

I'll be the obesest motherfucker in the whole universe. Alice's mushroom is going to make me extra-solar, baby. I'll scratch my back with stars and floss my teeth with the Milky Way. One day man-boobs, muffin tops and bubble butts are going to rule the world.

I'll be fatty-fat-fat-fat, high glucose levels, osteoarthritis, W.H.O.'s most wanted, Mr. Sedentary, a bowling ball of sweaty cellulite, Godzilla's worst nightmare, too big for my britches, bursting at the seams, earthquakes under my feet, saggy nipples and belches, I'll be the most obscene, I won't move my knees, I won't see my junk, and my BMI infinity will be soaring. Oh, you may not miss me now, but you're going to miss me when I'm fat. And even if you beg for me to come back down to Earth, I'll be too big to ever go back to the way it was.

Once upon a time we were something else. We went out to eat and danced to rock-n-roll. You fed me pies and slim jims and words that cracked my teeth like rock candy. I wanted to have your world. I tried to turn your liquid fantasy into my solid reality. But I'm not sure there was ever anything but artifice on your menu.

I wish I had never gotten a taste of you.

Because you didn't want me when I was anorexic. You didn't want me when I made touching my tonsils with a toothbrush a nightly ritual. You didn't want me when the L-B's on the scale were only in double digits. You didn't want me when you could see my bones. I know I vomited all over everything we had, and even the Asian dry cleaners couldn't scrub out the mess I made, and I know the stain will always be there, but I am sorry.

You didn't even give me a shot at forgiveness. Didn't you see how much pain I was in? Every swallow hurt, and every swallow still hurts...

But, fuck it, I'll push through it now and head into triple digits, quadruple digits, quintuple digits, and way, way beyond. Soon no scale will ever be able to contain my ever-expanding mass.

Because happiness is my secret weight pill. I'm going to turn my happiness into a buffet and I'm going to eat and eat and eat until my belt buckle snaps.

You won't even recognize me; I'll be all over magazines and on TV screens. Oh, and lunchboxes too! The fattie, the hero, the very best.

I'll be at some fancy-pantzy award show making a nice long speech at a big shining podium, decked in my three-piece wool blend suit with the lapelled waistcoat and flapped pockets, accentuated with a polyester bowtie, all from Casual Male XL. And you'll sit in the crowd and realize that could've been you up there, the greatest acknowledgement in my speech. And after the show you'll come up to me and I'll be holding Krug champagne and you'll try to give me a handshake and offer to take me out for a drink. But I'll refuse, because I'll have places to go, people to see and things to eat. I won't even shake your hand.

So you'll go home and nurse your regret with some cheap horse-piss beer. Because you'll *know* that we could've both been fat, if you had just given me a second chance. I wanted you to be up in the clouds with me. I wanted you to be at the other head of my banquet feast. I wanted you to be all the digits on my scale. But now I see that I can do it all without you. I no longer need your words or your dreams.

I'm telling you—one day my heart will be stronger than my vendetta. And I'm going to be everywhere.

Steven Goff

Dear Diana (a poem for Diana by Augustus Saint-Gaudens)

Dear Diana,

I have seen you in constant conversation
with the ghost of Alexander Calder.
You are naked and he is blushing
lively red plumes;
thrashing out from the ethereal Philadelphia air.

I have seen randy bullies on the Parkway
willing to pay their last eight dollars to see you.
With questions cocked like arrows;
atop countless balls,
eternal ether,
endless plumage.

"I have come all this way. What are your aims?
Is that your natural color?" They will ask these questions.
Diana, you are not ready for them.
These are not the Grecian planes
(though the columns may have had you
fooled). This is no Pantheon.
Your stairs are no Olympus

Listen Diana I have stripped naked.
I have checked all of my clothes,
my arrows, my ball, my lively red plumes,
into the coat check.
Here is my tag.
They are there waiting for you should you need them.

Jen Jolles

Cuyahoga

I remember that summer in thunderstorms. I remember the big, gray, barreling clouds that seemed to come out of nowhere. That's how it goes with summer storms in Washington D.C. They begin with languid, determined winds that eventually give way to bone-rattling thunder. I remember that summer in soaked through t-shirts clinging to cold skin. Pulled over on the side of the highway, I would sit warmed by the comfort of my Toyota as enormous pellets struck the exterior of my car. I would watch intently as the wind would whip around traffic patterns. Like a gentle massive hand, just barely nudging the bigger cars around one another in a spectacular display of vehicular Tetris.

I spent most of that summer in a tent. Every few weekends I'd pick up and relocate west across my home state. From the Shenandoah Mountains down to northern Virginia and back up to western Maryland, I lived out of the trunk of my car and wherever I could start a fire. Experiencing a thunderstorm in a tent solidified my belief in a greater power. As the violent wind hissed through the zipper seals that insulated me from the outside world, I could feel the hand of God shaking the flimsy fiberglass infrastructure. My sunset-orange tent would tremble violently in harmony with loose, low-hanging branches. I lived like a nervous stutterer, forever terrified by the prospect of utterance.

I remember that summer in left turns and missed exits. The First Julia and I visited three of my favorite campsites that summer. Of course, these places only became my favorites after we broke up. I have revisited them all many times. I have revisited them with other women, with more profound loves. But I still remember them all bathed in the torrential downpours of that summer.

It was July and we hated each other. It was the summer she was breaking up with me. It took her almost the whole summer, but we both knew it was over. She slept with a mutual friend at the end of August—placing the proverbial final nail in a shoddily constructed coffin. I would sprawl out along the queen-sized air mattress in the tent, big red headphones over my ears. She would curl her body away from mine, poring over a book written in a language I couldn't speak and didn't understand.

Le Petit Prince was the chosen work for this particular weekend. When she tossed it into the front seat of my car as we packed up to leave, I picked up the tattered copy. As I fingered the splintering spine, I said, like a Philistine, "*lee pet it prince?*" The First Julia was a fluent French speaker. I can recall in painstaking detail how she would draw out the long a's and catch the "eu" sounds just perfectly in the back of her throat. "*Lep tee prawnce,*" she noted, pointedly. When she would whisper "*je t'aime*" into my hair before I fell asleep, I never once doubted her honesty.

That summer was different though. I only ever remember falling asleep to music. R.E.M has this song called "Cuyahoga." It has been covered a multiplicity of times by numerous bands since it was first released. But my favorite cover of all is the one rendered by The Decemberists. I listened to it on repeat for the first half of that summer, falling asleep to it many nights as sheets of rain inundated our nylon fortress.

I became enamored with the subject matter. Cuyahoga: the river, the falls, the county, and the city in Ohio. It all became so ceaselessly interesting. From the clumsy bass line that pervades the opening measures of the song, to the hauntingly poetic lyrics, I could only imagine how intriguing the eponymous place must be.

The First Julia was the first girl I thought I truly loved. The First Julia was the first woman to make me feel so tremendously inadequate, and that's how I thought knew I loved her. She was the first solid thing I learned to stand on. We decided to take the final road-trip to Cuyahoga in late July. I had the foresight to know that it would be our last adventure in the same way that owners know they'll put their dogs down when they put them in the car for the last time. The First Julia rested her hand patiently on my knee for all 336 miles of the trip. These days, if I can hit the speed just right, I can still hear her laughing.

I always knew she was a little crazy. I always knew that our relationship was mostly a bad idea. From the way she'd scream at me in debate meetings to the way she'd slap me around when we disagreed on something politically, I knew something wasn't quite right. Opposites attract, our friends would always say. Magnets repel, I would think to myself.

The Iroquois named the Cuyahoga River after its directional path, the way it snakes and careens around the state. "The crooked river" runs through Northeast Ohio and eventually feeds into Lake Erie. Its biggest claim to fame is becoming known as "the river that caught fire." Due to rampant dumping and pollution, the once-pristine waters turned crimson and lapped like desperate flames at the deteriorating banks.

The uncharacteristically wet Washington summer followed us west across the expanses of Maryland and Pennsylvania. As we drove north through Ohio, super-cell thunderstorms thwarted our progress. I remember that summer in accidental dive diners and cups of burnt coffee. Bypassing the miniscule map grid that represents the tail end of the Appalachian Mountains, we settled for flatter conquests. We were certain to make this last leg of our journey together replete with plateaus.

We camped near the mouth of the river. Pinioned between mounds of clay and salt-stained earth, the rust-colored, murmuring river shuddered at the sound of through-trains. The landscape surrounding the Cuyahoga is flecked with the faces of smokestacks, fuming like rival brothers at family dinner. We hiked down to the crooked river. The hot spit of a passing rail car utilized as a projectile at just the right angle, or the narrow lick of molten steel could have ignited it in an instant. Inhale: old flesh and ore. Exhale: wood swells and exasperated sighs.

I was never afraid of thunderstorms as a child. They were hallmark sideshows to the summers of my youth, and frequently lulled me into a deep and peaceful sleep. Thunderstorms on the road were an entirely different story. Between the gale force winds and the golf ball hail, I was terrified. And terrified was an understatement. Shocked awake in the middle of the night by the sound of lightning splitting century-old wood, I began to fear more than just the demise of my relationship that summer.

Just count the seconds between the thunderclaps. Every time you do it gets further away, the old adage goes. It is a simple fact. I spent most of that summer one-Mississippi, two-Mississippi-ing my way to peace and quiet. As we shared that six-person tent, just the two of us, it became more apparent to me how much space you can create in twenty by thirty feet. I felt her slipping through the cracks in my angsty high-school life like fine sand through clumsy fingers.

Five years later and the mountains still moan Cuyahoga.

Second Place — Fiction

Julia Timko

Unsteady

Climbing up my front steps I do my best to avoid the railings, which sway at the slightest touch. Like my grandmother when she encounters an open bar, it's always a dangerous endeavor. The stone is cracking and unstable in places so I always feel that I am fighting to get into what should be my safe space. The key is tiny, with sharp teeth and a peeling silver exterior. It always takes me two or three tries to get it into the lock.

Inside is dark and heavy, more like a cave than a house where four people live and breathe and laugh (on rare occasion). The ghost of my father is everywhere and I can feel him watching me as I go through the motions of taking off my shoes and sorting the mail. When he was alive I would often walk across the carpets he brought back from Kuwait in my mud-caked boots to spite him. Now it's an exercise in futility since he's not here to get angry.

My room is a mess and I can tell that my mother has been in there recently. Her perfume clings to the comforter and my collection of feather boas and there's a small clump of reddish fur where the cat must have sat next to her. I slam the door loudly to get her attention. That's about as confrontational as we get these days.

My cleaning strategy is simple, make piles and fill trash bags. I begin to throw everything that's on the floor into the hallway. I try to remember that I am graduating in a few days and I won't need my extensive notes on organic chemistry when I do, but the paper holds memories that I can't bear to part with. Like sitting at the dining room table while my father read Voltaire to me, heedless of the fact that I was trying to do homework that was supposed to be turned in three weeks ago.

My mother's feet brush softly over the kitchen floor and she pulls the cabinets open for a moment before closing them. They are cheaply made and lack handles, we are always pulling them from the bottom. She turns to look at me and we stare at each other across the space from my bedroom to the kitchen. The three-foot expanse morphs into an abandoned battlefield that conceals landmines for unsuspecting victims. When I blink, she's gone.

***

The smell of meat cooking greets me when I wake up. I don't remember falling asleep but the sun has gone down and my room is significantly colder. I get up and shuffle into the kitchen to see my sister standing there. She's heavily pregnant but doesn't look it with her slight figure.

"I don't remember asking you for help," she says as I edge my way into her space. I hand her the spice she's been trying to find for several minutes and take a step back.

"You didn't ask for it but man do you need it."

She stabs the ground beef with the spatula and jumps when a drop of oil spits out of the pan and onto her forearm. I shake my head and start to get out the dishes, one for me, one for her and one for her husband. The oil snaps again and she curses. This time I gently nudge her out of the way and let it cook while checking the forgotten rice.

The dining room table is in shambles and she groans, as if she hadn't noticed it before. Most of it is bills and junk news. We never know what our mother has or hasn't gone through so it all gets piled into the basket outside her door. I go back into the kitchen to finish slicing up vegetables and leave her to finish the job of making a place for us to eat.

The front door opens and heavy footfalls make the wood floors creak. She jumps up from where she had been sitting and hops into his arms. A shiver of annoyance and anger runs up my spine before they've even spoken a word. She's such a simpering idiot when he's around.

He steps into the kitchen, a smile on his face as fake as my own.

"Grab me a beer, Chrissy?"

I bite the inside of my cheek and turn away to hide the sour look.

"My name is Christina and no. Get the damn beer yourself."

He takes a beer from the fridge and laughs. That fucker knew exactly how it would make me feel and he did it anyway. I add it to the list of reasons she needs to leave him.

***

When dinner is over I retreat to my room and begin going through the package that arrived a few days ago, full of travel books from my grandmother.

The shelf hanging over my bed is heavy with the treasures she brought back from the jet-setting adventures she had after divorcing her husband. There's a fan from China, so stiff and fragile I have never taken it down or closed it. Next to it is a wooden comb, painted to resemble a tiny, demure Chinese woman with pink cheeks and an elaborate robe. A carved wooden elephant stands guard over the petrified wooden figurines from Argentina that are supposed to ward away evil spirits. The Spanish doll has tipped over and I straighten her, smoothing out her white lace dress and running my fingertips across the porcelain.

These treasures have sat above my headboard for as long as I can remember. Each time my grandmother came home she brought something new, with a story. The carved elephant came from Kenya, where she was almost eaten by a hippo. Thinking back on it, I am sure that the story was exaggerated. I can't remember which one of us grew the tale so tall. But I knew that I wanted nothing more with my life than to travel and make stories. This pile of travel books is the first step in the planning process that I should have started months ago.

Picking through the pile, I am reflecting. One by one, the friends who made plans with me dropped out of the picture. They have orientations to go to, and barbeques to attend with their functional family units. They have futures. And I have a dead father, a mother whose soul is still trying to catch his ashes in the wind, and a sister consumed with the joy of new life. An eternal optimist, I have decided to turn the negatives into a positive. No one is going to notice or care when I don't come home.

There are about fifteen books in total and most of them have green sticky notes poking out of them somewhere. My grandmother put them into the books that she has finished or used in some way and I picked up the habit at age seven. Sticking pink slips of paper into my Junie B. Jones books and the abridged classics with garish covers. Only two of these books are missing a note, Austria and Kosovo. The first bars of "Come On Eileen" start playing from my phone's speakers and I let it go for a while before checking it.

Our spot in 20. And for the love of God, bring pizza

***

I order the pizza from a tiny place on State Street, and drive west down to the park where we first met. Jane is lying on top of the great stone whale, chin tilted to the moon, soaking in the warmth from the smooth black concrete. The shouts and giggles of children have receded into the nearby homes and the faint wash of the ocean is the only noise. The Austria book falls out of my bag as we set everything down on the blanket I brought from home.

"You're actually going, aren't you?"

I'm blushing as she turns it over in her hands before giving it to me.

"I mean. That was the plan all along."

"Well yeah, but no one actually goes through with those plans. You don't see me getting ready to backpack through Scotland or joining the Peace Corps."

I ignore her as I open the pizza box and hand her a paper towel. She's wearing her Wesleyan t-shirt and the cut-off shorts we made together in 10th grade. The sharpie marks are faded now but the inside jokes have never gone away.

"I just want to do something crazy. Like my grandma. But I don't want to wait until I'm old and tired of having sex."

She rolls her eyes.

"Okay, number one, you hate your grandma. She's racist and tells you that you're fat. Number two, no one gets tired of having sex and number three, going to Austria doesn't count as doing something 'crazy.'"

I don't dignify her comments with a response After thirteen years of forced, begrudging, love/hate friendship, she already knows that what she's said has hit home. I start to make the fire with the driftwood. Though it's illegal, we've never been caught. When we first started coming here I convinced Jane that it was the magical powers of the emerald fire. In reality, the cliffs hide the light and the ocean masks any sounds we make.

I have more memories of this beach than any other. I know what parts get swallowed when the tide rises. I know which constellations hang above us, which oilrigs are still in use. Sometimes it feels like I have spent the better part of my life lying under the vast expanse of dead and dying stars that populate the nothingness. Jane takes my hand and we lay in silence until, "I miss your dad."

It's the first time we've talked about him in the months since he passed away. He liked Jane the best of all my friends, to the extent that he liked anyone.

"I miss him, too." My voice cracks and I have to take a deep breath.

"Sometimes I think about him." She waits, squeezing my hand and listening to me breathe. "I imagine him in this huge library. Full of sunshine. Waiting for you."

I laugh. Loudly. So loudly it bounces off the jagged dark and into the froth tickling our toes. Jane knows me more intimately than any girlfriend I've ever had. She knows my secrets and my joys. My shames. But she doesn't know my father.

"He isn't waiting for anyone. He never waited for anyone."

I pick up the Austria book again and start picking through it. Salzburg. That's a good place to start.

***

I wake up to my sister banging on my bedroom door. Pieces of paper with travel information, names of hostels and restaurants I *have* to try, surround me and I've fallen asleep with my glasses on. More banging on the door. I know it's my sister because she hits it with the palm of her hand instead of curling her fingers into a fist. The sound is distinctive. She bursts into the room after I ignore her.

"Aggression is bad for the baby," I tell her. She slaps several heavy pieces of mail on my comforter as a response. Official crests decorate the tops and my cheeks start to burn. "What the hell, Em?"

"When were you going to tell everyone that you got into Georgetown? Or Columbia? Or UCLA? Or Swarthmore? Or Pomona?"

She ticks them off by memory, eyes piercing through mine and into my headboard. I get up and put on the pajama pants I had tossed onto the floor before picking up the packets and throwing them into the back of my open closet.

"You know that opening someone else's mail is a felony, right?"

"I didn't have to open them to know what they meant. How could you not tell us?"

"It wasn't any of your business!" My voice rises to a scream and I try to get around her. She grabs my arm, tightly, the way she used to when we were kids. Now instead of anger, her eyes are filled with disappointment and frustration.

"Chrissy, I know it's been hard having Dad gone but you can't just—"

I rip my arm away from her and take a deep breath to bring my voice down. Every inch of my body is quivering with months of unrealized rage and I think of countless things that I could say to cut her down, but all I say is:

"Get out of my way, Emily."

***

I get out the door and down the porch before realizing that I've left the house with no keys, wearing only my pajamas and with no real plan. Before I can change my mind I march across the street to our neighbor's backyard. They're gone for the week and Emily and I have had a standing invitation to use their pool since our families became friends when I spilled grape juice all over their sofa when they were moving in.

Their backyard is closed in by a wooden fence and a luscious garden of rose bushes and orange trees. It didn't always look like this; they both got high blood pressure reports a few years ago and their doctor seemed to think that gardening was the answer to anything and everything. As angry as I am, the atmosphere is anything but soothing. I sit down in one of the poolside chairs and try to focus on the lack of noise, the sun on my freckles.

***

Emily waits for several hours before following me. She carries shame and an apology in the form of lunch, easing herself down into the chair next to mine. My clothes are drying from a dip in the pool and I am stiff from lying in the chair for so long. She allows the silence to go on past the point of comfort before speaking.

"I talked to mom."

That gets my attention.

"Yeah? What did she say? I bet she just wanted to tell you to be quiet." I try not to let on how curious I am. She hasn't left the house in over three months except to go to therapist appointments and she never speaks to us. I'm not even sure if she knows she's going to be a grandmother.

"That if you wanted to call the FBI to report her felony, she wouldn't fight it."

Laughter spills over my teeth before I can stop it. She made a joke.

"Mom was the one who opened the letters?"

Emily nods and takes a deep breath.

"She also said that she hopes you wanted to go to Pomona because that's where she sent the deposit."

I have read the word "speechless" countless times in my life and I can probably give you the word-for-word definition from the dictionary, but I have never experienced it myself. Until today. The air has been sucked out of my lungs by a cosmic vacuum and everything is spinning, just a little bit. My mother. My absent, frail, empty mother.

Emily hands me the travel book and gingerly heaves herself out of the chair with the grace of a beached whale.

"Orientation is in August. You'll be an aunt by then. But I guess if you want to go, then go." Her voice is soft but the blows land heavily. One anvil after another.

The section for Salzburg is bookmarked with a neon pink sticky note. I open it up, chlorine fingers sticking to the pages. The music festival, the birthplace of Mozart, the place where they filmed *The Sound of Music*.

I get up and find the spare key to the house, following the familiar contours to the library. There's a stack of books by the fattest armchair, topped with *1,000 Places to See Before You Die*. I set the book down, wiping off a bead of water that fell from my hair, and walk out.

Jen Jolles

Terminal: A Myth of Futility

I'm standing in the kitchen attempting to cook as I fight with her over text message about how much I hate chemotherapy. The return rate of messages is comparable to machinegun fire in hostile territory. I jab a knife into the cutting block with force and watch the handle sway like I do after an encounter with an open bar. I am certain that I've reached my wit's end—with her, with this disease, with myself. As I look out the window to see the city covered in a blanket of winter's dandruff, I exhale loudly—my breath freighted with exasperation. I fucking hate the winter.

When she shows up to my apartment the next morning for breakfast, she's still fuming. I am, too, but I am much more subtle in my practice of this art. The smoke rises slowly and snakes around my organs and alerts me to the fact that I should stoke it. She, on the other hand, is furious. Everything from the collarbone up shares the same crackling fireplace hue of her hair and she wastes no time getting right to her objective.

"Did it ever occur to you how selfish you're being?" She paces around my living room, shouting.

"Did it ever occur to you that I could ask you the same question?" I sit, white-knuckled, in my favorite easy chair, listening intently.

"You can't just fucking not do treatment, Jen. That's not just an option you have."

"Well. Actually, Kate, it is. An intensely enticing one at that."

I am tired. Over the last four years, I have only spent 691 days without cancer cells in my body. I am in pain. On the days I don't have class, I pop a Percocet and spend all day reading, hoping that the pain between my ribs will subside. I am depressed. It is intensely hard to have any long-term goals when you have spent the last four years of your life living it six months at a time. I have done countless rounds of radiation, dozens of doses of chemo, and even dabbled in a few experimental trials. I am certain that I want this to be it. Eventually, everyone else's desire to fight my disease outweighs mine, and I submit to a few more rounds of chemo.

"Yeah, no, stage four is about as bad as it gets. It is as bad as it gets Remission is kind of a far-off dream, but I can buy some time." I'm defeated as I realize how much time costs.

I know that being so nonchalant about my potential demise is going to hurt more than I intend it to. In my defense, Kate forfeited her right to be hurt months ago. Despite the fact that we are rigidly associated and loosely involved, our relationship is predicated on the fact that we owe each other nothing. Still, to know is to be responsible for knowing. So we continue to pretend that these things in our chests are only used for breathing.

"Are you familiar with the story of Theogenes?" I'm not confident about much, but I'm pretty sure that in this department I'm better read than she is.

"The Brazilian beer? It sounds like it? Thee-og-what?"

It's all Greek to Kate. I make a fresh pot of coffee and begin to give her a lesson in mythology.

A prominent boxer in Ancient Greece, Theogenes consistently found himself in the most antagonistic human condition. Strapped to a stone slab and tasked to fight to the death 1,425 times, Theogenes fought and emerged victorious 1,425 times. I would assume that consistently toeing the deceptively thin line between existence and expiry would exhaust a man. It seemed to have a minimal effect on Theogenes, however. Time after time he would stand nose-to-nose with his opponent and beat them to death. I think often about the pugilist. I think about what kind of gall or what kind of stupidity must be required of a man to spend his whole life sparring with a ceaseless opponent. And then I realize—is that not the work of life itself?

Coffee didn't taste great today. And thus I have come to accept today as the beginning of the end. You could argue that after fifteen rounds of chemotherapy in one year, nothing would taste very good. Or perhaps you could argue that the end is rising up to meet me. I'll be honest, most days life doesn't have a very appealing effect on the palate, and I haven't been as hungry lately.

I don't know that comparing my experience to that of Theogenes is a useful exercise. In fact, to compare Theogenes' career as a pugilist to my status as a cancer patient would be feckless. Like Theogenes, I, too, have been strapped to stone. Unlike Theogenes, however, the only opponent I have to face is myself. The person who sits with the cold, exhausted body on the shower floor, clothes it, and tucks it into bed and the person who is simultaneously killing it from the inside out are in fact one and the same. Two sides of the same coin—the only thing that determines which side is seen is the amount of force put into the spin.

Three months ago when I found out that I had lost the genetic lottery for the third time, I was beside myself. *You gotta play to win*, the Lotto slogan goes, and I don't remember ever picking any numbers. It's a unique experience— being told you have six to eighteen months to live when you're twenty years old. I'm sure there's a lot of significance that I don't understand embedded in those numbers, but I'm not a math major for a reason.

"So whatever happened to Theogenes?" Kate's cut-glass eyes stand in stark contrast to the terra-cotta mug from which she slurps her coffee.

I deliberate for a moment when I realize that I don't actually know the fate of Theogenes. I know only of his posthumous legacy. Charged with murder and then tossed into the sea, it seems as though the statue of Theogenes erected in his honor has a more colorful history than the pugilist himself. I assume that he just grew old, grew tired, grew weary, and then simply dissolved.

It's six in the morning and I'm sitting in the chemo chair with one arm raised above my head as the nurse primes my port with saline. The metallic taste floods my mouth as the syringe empties out, and blood runs back into my line. Roberta takes the end-cap of my port with the tubing of the methotrexate bag and links them together with a satisfying click. The sound snaps me into a memory of the Legos I played with in my youth.

Looking out the window, I scoff at the sleet coming down in thick sheets. Fucking winter. Roberta's salmon scrubs are obscured by a gown that makes her look like a midget Smurf. She signals me to lower my arm and I rest as comfortably as I can in the pleather recliner. I can't help but chuckle at the irony—the nurse wearing two pairs of gloves, a gown, and a mask while putting these chemicals into ME. I'm never offered the opportunity to protect myself.

"Why do you always come here alone?" she asks, while making intense eye contact with the sixteen inches of rubber tubing cascading out of the hole in my chest.

"Never alone," I say, waving the curled newspapers in my hand.

It's true. I've not had a physical companion to chemo since the summer, my choice. I carry the obituaries of several local news sources to every appointment. It's the cancer equivalent of reading *Lolita* on a crowded train full of families with children. At the very least, it keeps people from daring to sit next to me.

Tom, the resident dad of my early-morning chemo cohort, shakes his baseball-capped head and chuckles at my interaction with Roberta. The promise of slow-growing, stage one testicular cancer keeps him fresh. Once a week he comes in with his Land's End catalog woman of a wife, they sit in the corner, and they eat breakfast while Roberta hooks him up to his Taxotere drip. He already has kids, so he considers himself thankful. Usually by the time I'm leaving chemo to head to my first class of the day, Tom's knocked out cold from some combination of Benadryl and Zofran. Tom may be 35 years my senior, but in this department, I'm the veteran.

In Sisyphean replay, I strenuously roll myself to the top of a clean bill of health once a year only to clatter back down in relapse whence I begin the climb all over again. I've begun to wear a nice, Jen-sized indent into my beloved pleather chair five times a week now that I've been told my previous chemo regiment wasn't working. The scene is always the same. Roberta or some other poor nurse will come over, prime my port, hook me up, tell me to knock back some biochemistry and they'll come back in an hour. The chemo room is always a revolving door. Folks come in, speed date with Death, and they head out, back to their deceptively benign realities.

Sisyphus was condemned to an eternity of rolling a boulder up a hill only to watch it roll back down. It was Einstein who said that insanity was doing the same thing repeatedly and expecting different results. Like my good buddy Sisyphus, I suppose I've gone insane. I am certain that Sisyphus recognized the futility of his own efforts. Every day Sisyphus was rollin', and every day, Zeus was hatin'. Day in and day out, rolling that boulder to the top of the hill, only to realize that the motherfucker has slipped back down to the bottom. One will always find their burden, wherever it may roll.

These days, I spend equal amounts of time planning my funeral and doing my homework. I firmly believe that, if I graduate, I should be able to declare a double major—one in English, my field of study, and one in funeral planning. There are certain tasks that you never want to leave up to your mom. Least of these tasks would be the types of things you want at your funeral. In an unfortunate turn of events, however, if you remove the burden from your family, you implicitly place it upon your friends. After all, they're the ones who have volunteered to put up with your shit; your family just has that requirement.

I am having dinner with Drew and Taylor on a Tuesday when I drop the Nagasaki of all cancer-bombs.

"If it's all right with you guys, I want you both to be pallbearers."

Drew chokes on his beer and Taylor drops his burger. I know it's a pretty unfair request. Drew's forearms are the equivalent thickness of pencils and Taylor hasn't done a complete push-up since high school. I am sympathetic to their discomfort. How do you soften the thought of carrying a coffin? As one of their best friends, I am sitting across from them, instructing them on how I want things done at my funeral. In these moments I am so alive, only to have to subject them to seeing me wither and die.

"Would you just shut the fuck up? Just. Stop fucking talking." Taylor finishes his fries and polishes off his beer. "You're not going to fucking die. And if you are, I'm not going to carry your coffin, you selfish bitch, you can walk yourself into the underworld."

There is no denying that Sisyphus' existence is sad. Perhaps what is most unfortunate about his story is that he is already dead. In spite of this, he comprehends his fate. Life never awards you a token proportional to your effort. When I am running back down the hill I am so free. It is only during my ascent that I am forced to face the gravity of futility. When I am required to weigh all that I have against all that I have lost, I am forced to acknowledge that life has seized me.

In the end, there is a 100 percent chance that one of your own organs will kill you. So, when I walk to chemo in the pre-dawn darkness, I've stopped looking over my shoulder. I am flying down that hill, knowing full well that my boulder and I will always meet at the bottom.

Gaia Faigon

Lovely and Broken

It's hard to wake up in the morning for class. It's even harder when you wake up an extra half hour early and decide to go to breakfast with your friends. On Tuesdays and Thursdays, we all go to breakfast together because we all start class at 9:30. I jump down from my bed to the cold, hard, gray tile, which reminds me that my roommate and I still haven't found a rug even though we've wanted one for a few months. I gather my toiletries and walk down the hall to the bathroom where I look into the mirror and frown. The harsh lighting brings out all of my imperfections. The dark bags under my eyes. The pimples that dot my cheeks. I'd be lying if I said that none of it bothers me, but it never concerns me that much. What does bother me is my body.

My biggest fear going into college was the dreaded Freshman Fifteen. I'm not overweight, heavy, or even chubby in any way. I'm actually quite small—both in height and in width. One of the boys down the hall was able to pick me up with one arm. I know I'm little, but I don't feel that way. I feel like a hot-air balloon. It was the same yesterday. And the day before. I want to be healthy, but I had an eating disorder in high school and it is starting to make a reappearance.

I brush my teeth and wash my face in a blur. All I can think about is how tight my pants are going to be today. *Am I going to eat lunch? No*, I decide. *Just coffee.* The two things I never feel bad about consuming are water and coffee.

Getting dressed is one of the most stressful parts of my day. I turn off the lights before I take off my pajamas. I don't want to see the fat hanging off my body. My jeans are getting looser. Relief swells in my stomach and I can't help but think that I don't want my stomach to swell.

Out in the hall, I meet up with the others and we groggily walk to the dining center. The cold air of the gray morning bites at my exposed fingers and the wind pierces through my jacket, which is perfectly warm for November back home in California, but not here. My shivering is annoying, but it means I'm burning calories.

We open the door to a burst of humid air and shed our outer layers. I feel too ashamed of my nonexistent pudge, so I leave my jacket on. I walk over to the bagels and schmear on a thin layer of cream cheese. I also grab an apple that I plan on saving for dinner.

I look around for my friends. They're still in line for omelettes and banana pancakes. I wait and look around awkwardly, pretending that I'm lingering with a purpose. *They're taking a while. Should I go get breakfast pizza? No, that would be a bad idea.*

As we all sit down, they dig in to their meals. I grab a coffee at the sandwich station. The coffee here is terrible and almost makes me feel disgusting for drinking it. When I return, I pick up my bagel and wonder if I should eat it.

People think it's all about starving. You want to be skinny because you're so caught up in appearances. But they don't understand.

There's an inherent need to be fragile—to look emaciated, only skin and mostly bone. But it comes with a complex: you are strong for going without. You are strong because you're working tirelessly and unwaveringly for what you want—to better yourself. In this case, that means losing weight without eating.

Taking up less space, not necessarily losing weight, was almost always my main goal. You feel unworthy of the space in the world you have been allotted in this life. You want to apologize for everything you do—it all feels wrong. Everything you say, think. Every move, every choice is wrong—except that of starving. You know it's wrong, but you've also never been more right.

The first time around, I knew I was beautiful—at least in some shallow sense of the word—but not enough. Not conventionally. I think I fell into the trap of thinking brokenness is lovely—an idea that somehow the whole world understands.

I longed for countable ribs and the 90-degree corners of my hipbones. I wanted a collarbone so prominent that my necklaces would change their angles as they draped over it. I'd stepped so far deep into an ocean of skeletal inspiration that I didn't understand why others found it so abhorrent.

Someone once told me that I am little but tough and that the words in my head are worth more than my weight. It made me cry—not only because of how nice and loved it made me feel, but also because I didn't—and still don't—wholly believe it. If I am tough despite my petite frame, why shouldn't I be smaller? Do my made-up words and awkward sentences really mean much to anyone?

I know it's sad that I think and feel such terrible things, but then I wonder: would anyone notice if I suddenly lost my soft stomach and round thighs and exchanged them for bony shoulders and angular hips? Would they care or even try to bring me back into their world where boys say they like curves even though you can see them lusting after the skinny girl who walked past them on the sidewalk?

When I was recovered, I was pretty open about my experiences. I talked about it emotionlessly. It was all fact and there was no point in dwelling on dark times. Even now, when I think about what I'm doing to myself, I think about it plainly. I'm starving myself and most people would say that's bad, but I don't. I ate less than 1,000 calories today, so I'm staying true to my illness. I'm sick and I like it that way. I want to be strong, but also weak—to look like just one little push could shatter me. I want to be small on the outside and on the inside, so I'm not a bother to anyone. I want to be broken and I know that's weird, but it's beautiful to be broken and I've never wanted anything more.

I look at my bagel and decide it's not worth it. I put it down and join the conversation at my table. Eating isn't important. I'm better without it.

Elizabeth Pollack

Five AM

I picked up my iPhone. "Hello?"

"We have an emergency. A huge emergency," my dad said on the other line, before I even finished saying the word *hello*. I was at my mom's house, sitting on my bed. My dad's voice was frantic. "I need your help."

I inhaled. "*What.*"

"They're dropping off our new window shutters on Tuesday. Nobody will be home. I need you to wait at my house from nine in the morning until five in the afternoon for the delivery guy."

Silence.

"Oh, was that the emergency?"

"Yes."

I pressed the end button on my phone and threw it on the floor. I let Dad's next four consecutive calls to go to voicemail.

***

A few weeks prior to my father's home improvement emergency, he called me while I was in school to finalize my flight schedule for coming home between spring and summer term. "I miss you terribly, Iz. Your flight is at 6:45 in the morning on Friday. Get to the airport by 4:30."

"Are you *joking*?"

"Please don't complain about this again. This isn't a big deal. Think you can get a friend to drive you to the airport so I don't have to pay for a cab? Oh, hang on, my client's on the other line. I expect you to get an A on all your finals. If you get on the Dean's List I'll get that discount on my car insurance again. Bye-bye!"

After my 6:45 AM flight home, my dad picked me up from the airport and was driving me to my mom's house. "I'm really sorry, Izzy. But I have to go to San Francisco this week for work. I have to."

"Oh." I was kind of bummed Dad would be gone while I was home, but my stepmom is a huge pain in the ass so I knew at least I wouldn't have to see much of her, and I would just hang out at my mom's house.

"Okay. Well, I need you to take us to the airport at five in the morning on Sunday. Okay?"

"*Nope.*"

"Iz, please. I'm your father. I'd really appreciate it. We have an early flight to San Francisco. It's much, much cheaper to have you drive us than to park the car at the airport for five days. It's so expensive."

"Work should pay for it," I realized.

"They are, they're paying for the flight and hotel. It's an optional convention anyway."

"If it's optional, why are you going? I thought you were too sad to leave me while I'm home?"

"Well, Shirley and I want to make a vacation out of it."

Of course.

He reiterated how I can just go home and sleep after I drive them, and how much money I would be saving him. Finally I just said yes, since he financially supports me and I've never actually had to get a job because of him. I figured the early mornings were a kind of thank you for paying my tuition and credit card bills for 22 years.

***

At 4:30 Sunday morning, when my dad opened my bedroom door and screamed, "Iz! Iz, are you up? Iz! Iz! Izzz!! Elizabeth!" I realized I was already awake. I was too nervous to fall asleep because sleep is so comfy and Dad always cruelly yanks me out of it. When I was in high school he used to just come into my room, turn on the lights, and say, "Oh, Iz! Hi!" to wake me up.

"Do I need to turn on the light?" he asked. I groaned some sort of no. "Good girl, Iz. You're a great kid. I'm so proud of you. I love you. We're leaving at 5:03 AM sharp." My dad has OCD and it makes him hate doing things at normal times.

I fumbled around in the dark in search of my glasses because putting in contacts after an all-nighter feels like stabbing ice-cold needles into your eyeballs. I stumbled down the stairs of my dad's house, my eyes still kind of closed. My dad was extremely energetic and wearing a baseball cap and socks rolled up halfway to his knees with tennis shoes and cargo shorts.

"Good morning, Iz. Great. So glad you're up. So proud of you. We're leaving in a minute. I need your help. Take this out to the car." He stuffed a suitcase in my face.

"Oh my God, it's like Noah's Ark out there," I said when I opened the front door and was greeted by thunder and lightning.

My stepmother came moping out of the kitchen, barely looking at me, acting as if she was sitting shiva and not about to embark on a free vacation to California.

"Shit. This damn rain. I hate flying," she yelled.

Dad's good mood fluttered away. "What do you want, Shirley? Want to stay home?"

"Why'd you book our flight so damn early in the morning? I only got three hours of sleep last night and if I don't get at least eight, my immune system will weaken, I can feel it weakening. And now this rain, the mold levels are so high, it will go into my lungs, and—"

"Iz!" My dad turned to me. "Put the suitcase in the car! Please! We're running late to the airport."

"I didn't have my Fiber One cereal this morning. I'm already feeling constipated, and you know how lack of sleep makes it worse," Shirley continued.

I rolled the suitcase out in the rain, wondering how frizzy and puffy Shirley's hair would get in the humidity. I collapsed into the backseat in the jeep. The jeep is 14 years old and none of the seatbelts work. Through my sleepy haze, I surveyed the neighborhood and noticed all the houses had their lights off. I was jealous. At five in the morning on a rainy Sunday, everyone else was still asleep.

Actually, my dad and stepmom probably woke them. I heard their arguing from the front door, even while in the jeep with the doors closed.

"Shirley! Go outside! Go! I turned on the alarm, we have fifteen seconds to get out—do you want the alarm to be broken while we're gone?!"

"I don't want to go out in the rain!"

"GO!"

I couldn't wait to spend the week at my mom's.

As my dad locked up the house and wheeled two suitcases out to the car while also balancing Shirley's carry-on luggage and purse, Shirley carried nothing except her sweatshirt and ran to the car.

"It's locked!" she screamed, "Shit! I'm getting wet! Open the door! Now!"

Shirley was looking at me through the car window as if I was the reason she was constipated and getting rained on. I was tired, so my reflexes were slow. When I saw her angry eyes, I started snickering and couldn't stop.

"Get in the car, Shirley!" my dad screamed.

"I can't! The door is locked! Elizabeth! Open it!"

Shaking in an effort to try and stop laughing, I slowly reached from the backseat to the passenger seat door and opened it. Shirley was a little drizzled on and very pissed. She plowed into the car and slammed the door shut. We sat in a somewhat awkward, huffy silence as my dad carried the rest of the suitcases to the trunk.

"Get out of the car, Iz," he shouted from outside.

"Huh?" I was still half asleep.

"I need you to hold up the trunk."

I stopped smiling and got out of the car and back into the rain. The trunk door of the jeep is so old that it literally cannot defy gravity anymore. Someone has to hold the trunk up manually while the other person loads something in it, or the trunk comes crashing down on your head. The rain started pouring down harder and, actually, Shirley ended up being the driest of all of us as we got in the car.

"Thank you so much for driving us, Elizabeth," my dad said, as he sped down the empty highway.

"You're welcome," I mumbled, while reading some Jesus billboards. "Just give me the money it would have cost for you to park your car in the airport and we'll be good."

"It's thirty dollars."

My heart stopped beating. "You just asked me to wake up at four in the morning so you could save thirty dollars?!"

"Oh god, Iz, calm down. You're doing us a huge favor driving us."

Shirley sighed very loudly, and very obviously for attention. We ignored her. So she did it again.

"What, Shirley?"

"It's just these mold levels. They're so high, I don't feel well."

"Oh, come on," Dad said, merging into another lane.

"Don't you care?"

"No."

I always get scared riding in the jeep. My dad's brother bought it in 1999. He gave it to us a few years later when he realized what a crappy car it was and no longer wanted it. My Uncle Bill has two dogs—when one dies he replaces it with a new rescue immediately—and he always drove them to the lake and then piled them in this jeep afterward. Whenever it's hot outside, the car still smells of wet dog, even though it's been twelve years since one was last in it.

The air conditioner also doesn't work. In the summer, so as not to crash the car due to heat stroke, you have to drive with the windows all the way down. When driving on the highway, the car shakes from the pressure of the wind blowing through. As often as my dad tells me he loves me, I always note how many near-death experiences this jeep has subjected us to, and Dad's eagerness in allowing his three children to drive it. Once, I was driving with my brother, and the rearview mirror slid off the windshield and crashed into the cup holder.

"That's not a big deal," my dad told us when we called him from the side of the road.

"Are you saying I can drive without a rearview mirror?"

"Yeah, we can put tape on it."

This morning, my dad and stepmom started to feel bad for being assholes and forced me to join in their riveting conversations.

"Don't forget," Dad told me, "On Tuesday I need you to wait at my house for the delivery guy with the shutters. Be there at nine."

"Oh, God." I had forgotten about that.

"Oh, and Elizabeth?" Shirley started, "Please don't touch the produce in the bottom drawers. It's my organic peppers, they're very expensive, and I need them when I get back from California."

When we finally arrived at the airport and everyone piled out of the car, the rain had mostly stopped.

"I'm going to miss you so much," my stepmom said to me, staring at my face and looking into my eyes, pretending my absence was something that made a difference in her life. I looked past her cheek at the cars pulling out of the airport.

"Okay," I replied.

She grabbed me by my shoulders and into a hug. As her torso crushed mine, I realized I had forgotten to put on a bra that morning. The sun was rising and I didn't want my eyes to get used to the light because then I wouldn't be able to fall back asleep.

"Gah, enough." I tried to maneuver out of the hug.

My dad kissed my forehead and thanked me a hundred times.

"And don't forget," he said. "Be at my house on Tuesday at nine in the morning. Bring in the mail. When you leave, turn on the alarm, and run out in 15 seconds."

"Don't tell anyone our alarm password!" Shirley interjected.

I stared at her. "I'll put it on Facebook."

Dad continued. "Lock the door. Turn the AC way up. Don't waste money. And be back here on Thursday. Our flight gets in at 11 at night, and I need you to pick us up."

I blinked at him and grabbed the keys from his hand. The sweat on my back from the humid car was making me itch. My head started to hurt from sleepiness and my stepmom. I nodded that I understood my instructions.

"Thanks, Iz. Drive safely. I love you." He gave me a hug.

I waved and got back in the jeep to drive to my dad's house and feast on my stepmom's expensive, organic peppers.

Jason Ludwig

The Dawson Center

On October 16, 2002, Angela Dawson looked out of her window to see if anyone was outside of her house. Two weeks earlier, her home had been the target of an arson attempt. Since then, she and her family had locked themselves inside of their 1401 East Preston Street residence, located in the Baltimore neighborhood of Oliver. Angela had been a participant in the Baltimore City Believe campaign, an effort by then-Mayor Martin O'Malley to put a halt to the violence and rampant drug dealing in the city. The campaign encouraged Baltimore residents to alert authorities to any illegal activities in their neighborhoods. Angela had called the police numerous times about the drug deals and violence that occurred on a near-daily basis on her street. Despite the best efforts of Angela and the police, the corner of her block remained a popular drug-dealing location. For her efforts with the Believe Campaign, Angela and her family were targeted by the same drug dealers she had been trying to stop. Her home was vandalized on multiple occasions and the neighborhood punks threatened to kill her if she did not stop working with the authorities. The Baltimore Police Department lacked the resources to ensure the protection of witnesses who came forward during the Believe Campaign, so after the attempted arson of the Dawsons' home, they encouraged Angela and her family to move out of Oliver. Angela refused to be forced out of her neighborhood by a bunch of degenerates, so the Dawson family remained put.

At 2:18 on that October night, 21-year-old Darrell Brooks broke into the Dawson home. He poured gasoline around the staircase before setting it on fire, trapping the Dawson family in their bedrooms upstairs. The house was ablaze in a matter of minutes. Neighbors were awoken by the smell of smoke and the Dawson family's cries into the night sky. Angela died that night, along with her five children, eight-year-old twins Keith and Kevin; Carnell Jr. and Juan, both 10; and LaWanda, 14 years old. Her husband Carnell survived, but only for one more week, before succumbing to injuries sustained in the fire. In 2003, Darrell Brooks was charged with the murder of the Dawson Family and was sentenced to life in prison.

In 2007, the burnt-down remains of the house were transformed into the Dawson Safe Haven Community Center. The Dawson Center, literally raised from the ashes of what had once been the Dawson family's home, hosts an afterschool program for students from Kindergarten through 12th grade.

Pamela Carter, the program director, helps students with their studies and homework, as well as providing them with a hot meal which, for some of the 50 children she works with, is the only thing they will eat all day.

It is March 24, 2014, and a group of student volunteers from Drexel University is visiting the Dawson Center as part of an Alternative Spring Break program. I am a part of that volunteer group and this is one of our many stops during our weeklong community service project in Baltimore. The Dawson Center stands out from the other buildings in the neighborhood. While the houses on the block are composed of worn-out red bricks and cracking gray cinderblocks, the exterior of the Dawson Center incorporates vibrant blues and yellows. It has a bright outside staircase that would not look out of place in a jungle gym, which scales the height of the building. It adds a little life to a neighborhood that seems dead. Many of the other houses in Oliver are vacant, with boarded-up windows and doors. Bright orange signs warn would-be intruders not to enter these homes, which now house rodents, asbestos, and trash. Some streets in Oliver are completely vacant; the only signs that people ever lived there are the litter on the streets and the graffiti on the walls.

Before we begin our work, Pamela Carter invites us inside for coffee and to tell us about the history of the Dawson Center. Ms. Pam, as she prefers to be called, is a diminutive woman with an air of accomplishment. She stands no taller than 5'2, with a stern face and glasses. She has been involved in community work in Baltimore for years, devoting most of her life to trying to clean up the city. Before becoming the program director at the Dawson Center, she had been a member of the Baltimore City Council. She has been involved in numerous campaigns and organizations that aimed to improve the city, but she says that at the end of the day they have all failed.

"Everyone gets excited to start a project," she says. "But no one ever seems to care enough to finish it."

The Dawson Center is the perfect example of this. There was a great amount of excitement when the center first opened back in 2007. Residents of the neighborhood were glad to see that there was some effort to create something positive in the community. However, the program now struggles for funding, and Ms. Pam asks us all to say a little prayer for the Dawson Center, for it to remain open one more year.

After coffee, we get to work. Our task is to clean the Dawson Family Memorial Garden, which is located across the street. Ms. Pam tells us that when the Dawson Center was founded, the garden was built to be a beautiful reminder of the family that had lost their lives on this very block. The garden used to be filled with various trees and flowers of all different colors and in the very center were plaques to each of the deceased. However, no one ever bothered to tend the garden so the life inside began to wilt and die. Now, the plaques are nowhere to be seen, most likely buried underneath all the litter. It resembles a trash dump more than a garden and it is hard to imagine anything ever having grown in it. There is no shrubbery, but plenty of empty plastic bags and other discarded items that we are tasked with disposing of. I pick up an empty bag of chips, only to find a dead rat underneath it. Various empty bottles are scattered around the garden: Colt 45, Steel Reserve, and Hennessy, among others. There are syringes, used condoms and losing lottery tickets that need to be picked up. Ms. Pam tells us that she warns the younger children that ghosts live in the garden, so that they will stay out of it. I think about the ghosts when I pick up a photocopied black and white photo of a dreadlocked man with the letters "R.I.P." written across the bottom.

It starts to rain, so we decide to wrap up our work in the garden. It is not completely clean, but it certainly looks better than it did when we started. We even uncover the memorial plaques to the Dawson family that had been buried under years of trash. Ms. Pam gathers us around in front of the Dawson Center to thank us for our service. As she says bye, a hooded man walks by our group and eyes us suspiciously before standing on the corner that Angela Dawson had lost her life trying to keep safe and drug-free. Ms. Pam warns us that he is most likely dealing and that if we don't bother him, he won't bother us. So we don't. We silently walk back to our van and begin the drive back to the church that serves as our home during our week in Baltimore.

As we drive back, I pay special attention to every liquor store we pass, each one with a circle of people standing outside trying to hide from the rain underneath the cover of the store awnings. Most of them have a bottle in one hand and a cigarette in another. I notice each person standing on the corner: another hooded man standing on his own, then two men huddled together in conversation. I try not to make assumptions about these men, but having heard so much about the rampant crime in Oliver, my mind cannot help but infer what they are up to. Outside of Ms. Pam and the Dawson Center, these street corners and liquor stores are the only sign of life in Oliver. We pass by a colorful mural that reads "Root For Tomorrow." I don't imagine that Oliver's future will be much better than its present. It's been over a decade since the death of the Dawson family, and the neighborhood I look upon now is just as morbid and destitute as the neighborhood that Angela Dawson looked upon twelve years ago. Just as their plaques in the garden had been forgotten under all the garbage, so too has the martyrdom of the Dawson family become absent from the cognizance of the people of Oliver. Even the greatest memorial to the family, the Dawson Center, is on its last legs and seemingly destined to become nothing more than a memory. Lone crusaders such as Ms. Pam cannot save this stagnant community on their own. It seems as if the neighborhood has not received any type of assistance to help stimulate progress. I do not see a single library or even a grocery store during our drive. However, I do see innumerable amount of store signs advertising "Wine and Spirits," "Liquor and Packaged Goods," or "Beer and Liquor." Oliver's condition cannot be blamed on the people living in the neighborhood. This neighborhood, and the dozens of other neighborhoods in Baltimore just like it, was set up for failure. How much longer will it be before these neighborhoods are completely vacant and the people who once lived there are all forgotten?

When we get back to our church, I do something that I have not done since I was much younger. I pray. Just like Ms. Pam asked, I pray that the Dawson Safe Haven Community Center will remain open for another year. I pray that a Safe Haven will open on every block, to keep the children out of the streets and provide them with some hope for their future. I pray that the next generation won't have to drink or sell drugs to attempt to escape the bleak realities of their life. I don't know who or what I am praying to, but I hope that they can hear me.

Faculty
Writing

Introduction

Writers render their perceptions from far off places and times; rarely do they live close to us, and rarer still do we know them or have the opportunity to know them, if only because they have died. They're almost always strangers with disembodied voices to whom we have no easy access. This can be a source of frustration to anyone who has wanted to ask a writer to elaborate on a particular point or share his or her experiences with the nuts and bolts, from conception to execution, of a written subject.

In the following section, examples of the work by Drexel faculty have been included in *The 33rd* as representations of professional, creative, and scholarly writing. The authors are alive and kicking and on campus; some may be your teachers now or in the future. You can see from the pieces that the approaches range from original works of poetry and fiction to blog posts and scholarly articles. You can assume that each subject and genre presented particular challenges that the authors had to grapple with in the same way that all writers must, including, of course, those in a composition class.

Stacey Ake

Burning the Hydra

On July 16, at 5:30 AM, the sky lit up. At 5:32 AM came the sharp *craaack!* of the shock wave. "We are all sons of bitches now," said Kenneth Bainbridge. On August 6 and August 10, the bombs were dropped. The physicists started to wonder what they had done. But it was too late.[1]

The Manhattan Project, like another Herculean task—the destruction of the Hydra—ended in fire. The early-morning bomb exploded at the Trinity test site near Alamogordo, New Mexico, on July 16, 1945, was the product of the labor of over 600,000 people. Without the support of these thousands of employees from such companies as Du Pont, Eastman Kodak, General Electric, Westinghouse, and Chrysler Corporation, there would have been no Hiroshima, no Nagasaki. Without the theoretical groundwork of Einstein, Frisch, Bohr, Schroedinger, Born, and Heisenberg, Sadoka's thousand paper cranes would have no urgency, no meaning. Without the curiosity of Feynman, Oppenheimer, Alvarez, Fermi, and Peierls, there would have been no Japanese whose spontaneous combustion left a permanent shadow on the sidewalk.[2]

Without *Kristallnacht* and Hitler's genocidal persecution of Jews that resulted in a mass exodus of German intellectuals to the West, no human population would have been exposed to mass quantities of radiation. Without this exposure, Neel, Satoh, Goriki, Asakawa, Fujita, Takahashi, Kageoka, and Hazama would have been unable to calculate the mutation rate of genes in humans (specifically in hibakusha or "survivors of the bomb"). Without the post-atomic bomb disenchantment experienced in physics by Wilkins, Crick, Szilard, and Delbrück, the seeds for the present-day revolution in molecular biology and genetics would not have been planted. Without the work of Marie Curie on radium, which led to her death from radiation poisoning (cancer) in 1934, insights into curing the disease that killed her would be impossible. Without the deaths of Mme. Curie, thousands of Japanese, and millions of Jews, the very techniques I used to do my doctoral research would never have been developed. So, you see, it is true. We *are* all sons of bitches now.

The tentacles of the Hydra which is science are polymorphous and legion. They extend in a multidimensional matrix throughout time. Tentacles from boundless sources affect myriad outcomes. All scientists stand on an infinite number of nameless shoulders. Myself included.

---

[1] Schwartz, Joseph. *The Creative Moment: How Science Made Itself Alien to Modern Culture.* New York: HarperCollins Publishers, 1992. p. 117.

[2] Curiosity is rightly defined in German as *neugierig* or "greed for the new."

To criticize any particular aspect of science, such as technology or research or method or philosophy, as if it were the whole of science, is to attack only a single tentacle of the Hydra. To examine only one branch of science, whether it be biology, chemistry, or physics, is merely to assail a different tentacle. By what manner, then, can one examine the body scientific? Perhaps by learning from the story of Hercules and the Hydra that science, like the Hydra, is a living thing, and that to understand science within the confines of human understanding, one must control science as Hercules finally controlled the Hydra. He killed it. When science as we now know it is dead and gone, then those most-accurate-of-scientists *à la Heidegger*, the historians, will be able to tell us exactly what it meant. But not until it is dead.

Yet the death of science will only hail its end as a collective human endeavor. Expiring science might endure forever as an arcane curiosity, just as the occasional 20th-century scholar studies ancient Mayan stele or Akkadian cuneiform. However, these language forms—the stele, the cuneiform—although decipherable, are dead to this world, for there is no longer a community for whom their messages are existentially meaningful. Without a living community, a language is merely a code in search of a decoder, a subject of intellectual gamesmanship. But science is a living language expressing a living world understood by members of the scientific community. And science, like all other corporate human endeavors such as language, is a cultural phenomenon.

As a cultural phenomenon, science contains all of the attributes of human culture. There are local languages with slang and jargon; there are rivalries, gossip, and theft; there is camaraderie, wonder, and brilliance. There are cultural differences among people from different areas of science, just as there are cultural differences among people from different regions of a country.

Reminiscent of the way in which the word "Spain" evokes an idea-monolith represented by flamenco dancing and bullfighting for the unversed, the word "science" invariably spawns an idea-monolith represented by microscopes and equations to the scientifically uninitiated. But the idea of Spain being nothing more than flashy dancers and *picadores* is ludicrous to those familiar with its many facets such as the Catalán architecture unique to Barcelona, the Basque culture of the north, the risqué tourist beaches of the south. Furthermore, to those who live in Spain, the stereotyping proffered by the tourist and the critic is laughable, and the contemptuous comment of the outsider: "How can people live like that?" damns only the questioner. It merely reflects his ignorance.

Science, like any culture, is handed down from generation to succeeding generation. There are initiation rites, cliques, and excommunications. There are trends, oversights, and aversions. There are conmen, evangelists, and sticks-in-the-mud. There are ghettos and country clubs. Molecular evolutionary genetics is currently a Club Med. And I belong to it.

Science, like any other culture, is more than a way of talking about the world; it is a way of *seeing* the world. Moreover, it is a type of vision that has more in common with poetry, the fine arts, and philosophy than with technology, mechanics, or engineering. Science is not an activity for material production. It is, in fact, a leisure activity,[3] specifically a glass bead game played with ideas about the material world. The practical implementation of these ideas is found in technology and entrepreneurship, but not in science per se.[4]

The nature of science as leisure activity is best illustrated by comparing the intimate botanical knowledge of the rainforest held by the Yanomamö against the systematic botanical knowledge of the same biome held by a scientist. Detailed botanical knowledge is, for the average Yanomamö, a matter of life and death. For the scientist, it is a matter of curiosity and interest. Furthermore, while the Amerindian is more likely to find edibles and potables, the scientist is more likely to find a new antibiotic or an example of co-evolutionary species. The need for their questions is different, thus so is the nature of their answers.

This example of the scientist in the Amazon can be extended further. It can be used to demonstrate the difference between the scientist and the entrepreneur. A researcher's discovery of a new antibiotic may result from pure curiosity. Such was Sir Alexander Fleming's discovery of penicillin in 1927. Or it may result from the deliberate mining which is research *and development.* It is from this latter type of work that the other β-lactamase ring antibiotics (ampicillin, etc.) have been developed. For this reason, the search for pharmaceuticals in the rainforest is not primarily a scientific undertaking inasmuch as it is an economic one. It is an entrepreneurial use of technology as a means for obtaining a particular product. Thus, from a Kantian perspective, one might say that science differs from technology in that science is an end in-and-of-itself, if only because the questions that science answers begin with "Why...?" and not with "What for...?"

---

[3] By "leisure activity" I do not mean hobby or pastime. I mean any activity in which a member of a society can be engaged full-time because of the surplus productivity of the culture as a whole.

[4] The difference between science and technology can be compared analogically to the difference between philosophy and psychology. In the case of both psychology and technology, the goal is to get something done. Whereas, for science and philosophy, the goal (if there is one) is to find out what things are (or are like).

The pursuit of science or technology as a career is a question that every proto-scientist (and even established scientist) faces at some point, perhaps continually. Technology means patents. Technology means money. Technology means power. But it is not really science. Technology is research looking for its answers at the back of the textbook. The desired outcome is already known, and all surprises are errors. The questions of science are more like those of a child who, while capable of formulating a question within a particular range, may find the domain of the answer greater than his present understanding. Science, like the crew of the starship *Enterprise*, prefers to "go where no man has gone before." So do I.

The nature of science in its contemporary avatar, as I have outlined it, is one which is irreparably entangled with the fate of humanity—both its goodness and its evil. As such, science is a human, all too human, endeavor—the artifact of a living culture. It is also an art quantified, a fundamentally non-productive leisure activity, which can be distinguished from technology by its open-endedness. These elements of humanity—good, evil, art, leisure, and indeterminacy—combine to make good drama. The resolution to the question of whether Montagnier or Gallo first isolated the AIDS virus is the stuff of novels. The elucidation of the structure of DNA by Watson and Crick (who used cardboard cut-outs, paper clips, and other people's data) has the makings of slapstick. Richard Feynman's demonstration of how the O-rings on the space shuttle Challenger may have failed epitomizes the poignantly tragi-comic. But above all, these stories reflect the nature of science as one of narrative. Nonetheless, it is not the narrative itself, which is the aim of science. For science, the medium is *not* the message.

The message of science, like that of philosophy, is to represent what things are (or are like). However, the exigency of science demands a greater creativity than does philosophy on one point, and one point alone—the results of science must be *both* universally repeatable and universally communicable. For philosophy, the former is impossible, and the latter is optional. Because philosophy has no need to corroborate its claims with the material world, philosophy can rest in metaphor. Science, however, must be analogical. This analogical function of science has created a difference in temporality between philosophic and scientific narrative.

This distinction in temporality between the narratives of philosophy and science is that the claims of philosophy are static in time whereas scientific claims are not. In philosophy, all time periods are contemporaneously in parallel. Neo-Kantians can converse quite amicably with Kantians on all subjects (with a few exceptions), and they both can chat with Platonists. Scientific time is not only one of informed present, it is also a dynamic time in which the future may re-write the past at any moment. There are no Darwinians who converse with Neo-Darwinians, and there are absolutely no Galtonians or Lamarckians. In an almost Peircean way, the data lead the mind and not *vice versa.*

The authority of the data (the empirical) over the mind (the rational), and the constant return of the theoretical to the experimental, elevates scientific narrative above the level of mere heuristic device. Unlike philosophy, which, when bereft of rational discourse, is reduced to myth, science is simply reduced to plodding trial-and-error. Rational discourse is not the mainstay of science, but a stimulus for future trial-and-error. Scientific narrative is a means of communicating the culture, but it is not the culture itself. It is the doing of science, the actual corroborating of theory with data, that is science. All else is solely hints and guesses signifying nothing.

To me it seems highly unlikely that anyone would write a guidebook about Spain without having first visited that sunny, yet somber, country. Nonetheless, much is written about science by those who do not even darken the threshold of a lab with their shadows. To write about the phenomenon of science is not the same as writing phenomenologically about science. To deplore the results of the Little Man and Fat Boy bombs is not to critique atomic fission theory. To acknowledge intellectually that we are all sons of bitches now is not to understand experientially the reason *why* this is true. There are no armchair scientists. There are only game players. All others simply do not know what it is like...to be a tentacle. But I do.[5]

---

[5] This essay was written by the author just as she was making her transition from biology to philosophy as her primary area of interest.

Jan Armon

Toomey Gave Up Too Easily

To the Editor:

As a writer, I imagine conversations...

"Unless I take the lead on gun control, I cannot win re-election," whines Senator Pat Toomey. "Ninety percent of Pennsylvanians are ready to turn against me."

Senator Toomey's NRA handler listens quietly.

"Please, let me reach across the aisle, and sponsor a background check for purchases on the Internet and at gun shows."

Toomey's handler sits impassively. Toomey is pleading now.

"There's a risk it might pass, I know. But do you want me to lose my seat?"

Finally the handler speaks:

"Here's what. You approach a senator across the aisle. Eventually, there will be a vote on the floor. We'll make sure it gets defeated. You'll still look good. But you will tell the press that the matter is done."

Readers, the fact is that Senator Toomey gave up on background checks after a single vote by the Senate. That is not impressive.

Jan Armon
Rosemont

Paula Marantz Cohen

Glory at the Fountain of Coca Cola

This year, the 50th anniversary of the assassination of JFK, affords another opportunity to mourn the death of an optimistic, can-do America. America today is hobbled by schism and ineptitude. But then, as the many books about JFK released this year make clear, Camelot wasn't what it was cracked up to be either. That's part of the point. In a postmodern age, you can't look at the world without irony—even when looking back on it. Everything, even our history, seems soiled.

But visit The World of Coca Cola at Pemberton Place in Atlanta for a taste, figuratively and literally, of an un-ironic America. It's significant that you can't tell a Coke slogan from 1924 ("Refresh yourself") from one from 2010 ("Twist the Cap to Refreshment") and whenever politics gets hinted at it is mostly to underline how apolitical Coca Cola is. Consider: "The Great National Temperance Beverage" (1906) or "America's Real Choice" (1985). Coke promotes a chaste sort of pleasure, as in: "Enjoy life" (1923) and a modest patriotism as in: "Red, White, and You" (1985). Time and the tumult of history have no bearing on such inoffensive slogans as: "For People on the Go" (1954), "Always Coca Cola" (1992), "Make it Real" (2005), and "Life Tastes Good" (2001). This extends to that expression of global outreach, "I'd Like to Buy the World a Coke" amended into the musical number: "I'd Like to Teach the World to Sing (in Perfect Harmony)."

A song like that, emanating from a multinational corporation, might make you squirm (especially if you took a Postcolonial Studies course in college), but you'd have to be Scrooge to make a fuss at The World of Coca Cola. All those little children posing with the Coca Cola Polar Bear are cute; the old advertisements showing women in aprons and men in fedoras are nostalgia-inducing; and the chance to sample Coke-related drinks from around the world makes for comparative interest, not to mention a pleasant, sugar-induced buzz.

The drink itself has a tortuous history that The World of Coca Cola has edited into simple and heroic form. It had its beginnings in 1886 as the work of Colonel John Pemberton, a Georgia pharmacist. Not mentioned in the promotional literature is that Pemberton was on the Confederate side of the Civil War and, after being wounded in the Battle of Columbus, Georgia, the last battle of the war, became addicted to morphine. Hoping to alleviate his addiction, he developed Pemberton's French Wine Coca, which he marketed as a patent medicine and which gained particular traction among neurasthenic women. As temperance legislation began to be enacted in Georgia, however, Pemberton produced a non-alcoholic form of the drink, added carbonation, and had it sold at soda fountains. Unfortunately, he had failed to kick his morphine habit, and, short of money, sold all or part of the product to another druggist, Asa Griggs Chandler, who, with his son, went on to reap the serious profits.

Various versions of the drink as well as ownership disputes make it hard to fully trace the Coca Cola genealogy, although the World of Coke makes a point of making everyone involved an apostle. The linkage of Coke to cocaine is left unaddressed, even while the name of the drink rubs this in your face. We don't actually know how much of this substance was used in Pemberton's product—though presumably this was the real secret that gave Coke an edge over other beverages. It is interesting to note that cocaine was viewed at the time as a "cure" for morphine addiction. (Freud praised cocaine's curative properties in the 1880s, and became addicted to it in the process). But the company doesn't go into any of this, possibly for fear that younger visitors might want to purchase the stuff undiluted on the local street corner.

Part of what makes Coke's triumphal history go down so easily is that no one around today was alive before the beverage existed. Coke is "real," as the promotional slogans remind us, because, artificial sweeteners, colorings, and preservatives aside, it has endured in more or less the same form for as long as anyone can remember. It is moving to see those old, round-cornered Coca Cola machines and those small, green-tinted glass bottles. The red on white Coca Cola script is a kind of Madeleine experience for childhood. Even if you never experienced anything like the America of Norman Rockwell (who did many of the *Saturday Evening Post* advertisements for Coca Cola during the 1940s and '50s), there's something about that Coca Cola script that makes you think you did. I suspect individuals around the world feel this, even if they hate everything else that America stands for.

Coke, if I may extend my musings further, is the closest thing that exists to a religion of Americana. Not an American religion, but a religion devoted to the *idea* of America—which is to say, to those Norman Rockwell scenes of homecoming, fly fishing, and presents under the tree. Disney might be compared with Coke in having something of the same religious aspirations, but Disney has a more complicated apparatus—movies and theme parks (a visit to one of which is liable to bankrupt a family of four), not to mention the dubious figure of its founder, Walt Disney, a misanthropic anti-Semite (OK, Coke's Colonel Pemberton was a drug-addicted Confederate soldier, but never mind). To worship at the altar of Coke, you just have to like the drink and put out the paltry sum required to buy it—which, even if it may produce rotten teeth, diabetes, and obesity, isn't creating centuries of civil war and ethnic cleansing. It tastes good and it's refreshing, especially after you've spent the afternoon trying to assemble an IKEA cabinet or five hours in heavy traffic to eat overcooked turkey at your Aunt Leona's.

The World of Coca Cola is a temple to the religion of Coke and, as such, includes the requisite religious service. When you enter, you are herded into an auditorium to view a Coke cartoon. This stands for the liturgy. I am not partial to cartoons in general, but the Coke cartoon is the most awful cartoon I have ever seen. Just to give you an idea: It opens with an MC, a cartoon puppet version of a minstrel, who is wearing a waistcoat but no pants, and who is backed by a group of overweight chickens evocative of a Motown girl group. The MC has an apparently female sidekick, who resembles a cross between a firecracker with a face and Miss Piggy if she were run over by a steamroller. More than that, I can't tell you—the cartoon was utterly incoherent, if full of blaring music and frenetic movement. This supports Coke's religious status. Religions are supposed to have incoherent story lines. It's your job to impose meaning.

Our live host for The World of Coca Cola had the dark-rimmed glasses, high-belted pants and heavy-soled shoes of a Mormon missionary. He also had the gift of tongues—or at least for saying hello in a dozen or so languages. He announced that the cartoon we had just endured was about to be retired and replaced with a new one. He didn't say why. Religions don't explain themselves.

The museum itself contains the artifacts and rites associated with the cult. In this case, old advertisements, old bottles, and assorted other memorabilia. The crafting of a religion has as its basic premise the idea that nothing is too trivial to have significance—everything must be preserved and parsed. If you exhibit an item, say a bottle cap, with enough reverence and in a nice enough glass case, people will find it interesting and want to take a picture of it.

There must also be a mystery for Coca Cola to qualify as a religion. The formula for the drink serves this purpose—an idea that got a boost from a marketing calamity that occurred almost 30 years ago. In 1985, concerned that America's taste in soft drinks had moved to the sweeter side (where Pepsi resided), "New Coke" was introduced. New Coke had appealed to the company's focus groups but was vehemently rejected by the larger, consumer public. Protests were staged in which New Coke was poured down sewer drains, and much ink was spilt describing how upset the soft-drink version of Joe Sixpack was at having his beloved non-alcoholic beverage tampered with. If you excise all the Latin or the Hebrew from the religious service, you destroy the mystique; you make things too easy—in the case of Coke, too sweet. The outrage that resulted from the retirement of old Coke came as a surprise to company leaders, but it didn't take a marketing genius to realize that it could be capitalized upon. Coke Classic was revived 79 days after New Coke was introduced, and New Coke was quietly retired soon after that.

The Coke Museum spends a great deal of time talking about Coke's "secret formula," trying to whip this idea into something akin to the Trinity or at least the Virgin Birth. We learn, for example, that only a select number of people know the formula—or perhaps know only parts of it in the way revolutionary cells operate without full knowledge of the larger sacred mission. The museum features an iron vault where the secret formula is presumably held and in front of which you can have your picture taken.

The last stop in the World of Coca Cola is a large room with lots of soda dispensers, where you can sample Coke-related drinks from around the world. This portion of the visit is likely to disarm even the most cynical visitor. You'd have to be a complete killjoy like Cuba and North Korea (the only two countries in the world that presumably don't sell Coke) not to get excited sampling Coke products from Uganda, Chile, and the entire European Union. This is what Coke's high priests—i.e., its marketing experts—count on.

Ingrid G. Daemmrich

Humor as Celebrity-Maker: Recreating Lewis Carroll's *Alice in Wonderland* and *Through the Looking-Glass* in Multi-Media

Lewis Carroll composed his two children's tales, *Alice in Wonderland* (1865) and *Through the Looking-Glass* (1868) specifically to entertain two young girls, both named Alice. Why of all nineteenth-century children's books have these two narratives inspired so many immensely popular re-creations in multiple genres throughout the world? There are, I suggest, two interrelated answers. First, filmmakers' adaptation of Lewis's tales in a series of movies beginning with Cecile Hepworth and Percy Stow's silent film, *Alice in Wonderland* in 1903 and continuing until the present has given these narratives a celebrity that can compete with that of any living movie star or sports hero—except that unlike the latter, Carroll's characters never grow old. Second, the charm of Carroll's humor has inspired creators to invent their own versions of the tales to amuse their audiences.

Cultural critics and sociologists have identified four features that create celebrity: (1) an engrossing narrative, (2) an iconic image, (3) promotion by the media, and (4) the potential to be commodified and marketed, thereby turning a celebrity's immaterial value into material goods and the audience into eager consumers. (See Boorstin, Bowrey, Gorin and Dubied, and Kurzman et al., among many other scholars.) I would argue that another essential characteristic is the ability to amuse an audience ranging from young children to sophisticated adults and reaching around the globe. Today this extraordinary range requires adapting the celebrity's narrative and image to a wide variety of media extending from traditional literary genres to films, TV shows, animated cartoons, digital games, YouTube videos, and Twitter tweets. The latter three genres invite the audience to produce as well as consume the entertainment. Carroll's *Alice* narratives owe their celebrity specifically to four humor techniques: (1) comic naming, (2) word plays and riddles, (3) intriguing games with the interplay between fantasy and reality, and (4) the absurd, specifically the ability to meet the challenge of a puzzling, alien, threatening Wonderland with "corrective laughter" that views the territory as nonsensical, invented for our entertainment.

1. Comic Naming

One of the most consistent games played by adapters of the *Alice* narratives is linguistically superposing a new title on top of Carroll's. This technique makes fun of both Carroll's fantasy tales and an entirely different context. To name just a few of the hundreds of examples that carry on Carroll's predilection for phonetic play:

- Audrey Mayhew Allen's *Gladys in Grammarland* (c.1897), mocking a schoolgirl learning grammar;

- Two anonymous satires of the British Boer War: *Clara in Blunderland* and *Lost in Blunderland* (1902 and 1903). They were parodied by John Kendrick Bangs in his satire of American big business, *Alice in Blunderland* (1907)

- Robert Gilmore's *Alice in Quantumland* (1994), aligning Carroll's figures with quantum laws

- Tad Williams' science fiction series aptly named *Otherland* (1998)

- Brian Talbot's graphic novel *Alice in Sunderland* (2007)

- Johnny Tay's webcomic *Seven Years in Dog-Land* (2007). Featuring dogs as the protagonists, it combines horror with satire

- Douglas Cohen's steampunk novellette *Steaming into Wonderland* (2012)

- The appropriately named horror films *Alice in Murderland* (2010) and *Malice in Wonderland* (2008)

- Shin Megami Tensei's computer game *Alice in Horrorland* in which Alice controls the players (1992)

- Starting in the fall of 2013, ABC's series *Once Upon a Time in Wonderland*, a spin-off of both Carroll and the popular TV show, *Once Upon a Time*

By contrast, Carroll's comic names for his characters have mostly remained constant in the later adaptations, even while their appearance and character at times change radically. The eternally grinning Cheshire Cat embodies a common saying in Carroll's day, "grinning like a Cheshire cat," possibly, as Gardner speculates in *The Annotated Alice* (83), because Cheshire cheeses often bore the image of a grinning cat. The grin can be friendly as in Hepworth and Stowe's 1903 silent film or menacing as in Tim Burton's 2001 Gothic adaptation of Disney's 1951 animation. The Mad Hatter, originally capturing the fact that hat-makers became insane from working with the glue in the hat's inner binding, inspired both the cartoon "Mad as a Hatter" in the Batman series and Johnny Depp's clowning performance in Burton's film. Burton animates the Jabberwock, a name that Carroll invented for his nonsense rhyme in *The Looking-Glass*, as a monstrous villain, while in *Alice in Murderland*, the Jabberwock first befriends Alice, then murders her. Likewise, the Queen of Hearts, whose silly mantra, "Off with their heads!" ironically contrasts with her name, seems harmless in Carroll's narrative but actually chops off heads in Willing's 1999 *Alice in Wonderland* film. Variations of the brothers Tweedledee and Tweedledum have become a staple of political cartooning, starting with Thomas Nash's "Tweedledee and Sweedledum," published in *Harper's Weekly* the same year as *Through the Looking-Glass* and recurring as an effective visual lampoon for politicians without distinguishable platforms ever since.

2. Word Plays and Riddles

From Alice's first word puzzler as she falls through the rabbit hole, "Do cats eat bats? Do bats eat cats?" (28), to the White Queen's last command in *Through the Looking-Glass*, "Un-dish-cover the fish, or dishcover the riddle" (333), much of Carroll's humor resides in word play. It appeals to both children, who love playing with words, and adults, who enjoy solving word puzzles. Certainly the one that has attracted the most attention is the Mad Hatter's question to Alice during the "Mad Tea Party": "Why is a raven like a writing-desk?" (95). Conventionally, there is no answer. But Gardner reports that Carroll wrote in response to exasperated "parlor speculators": "Because it can produce notes" (95). Another answer: both have bills and legs. The "Mad Tea Party" chapter is famous for other word plays, such as "beating time" to learn music vs. beating Time as a person; "Twinkle, twinkle little bat" as a parody of the children's song, "Twinkle, twinkle, little star"; the play between "more" and "less" tea, when there isn't any; "in the well" and "well in" and Alice's oft-repeated response: "curioser and curioser." They all become amusing matter for successors, beginning with Disney's groundbreaking 1951 animation. It vividly brings to life the energy of the riddles and word play by adding the eye-catching exuberance of singing and dancing Technicolor cartoon figures. The audience, both young and old, is encouraged to sing and dance along.

By adding the novel concept of an "unbirthday" to the mad tea party, Disney initiated updated word plays for later adaptations. In one of "unclesporkums" "Funky Tales," for example, when Alice is puzzled by the conundrum of closed doors and a key that doesn't fit, she remarks, "This is worse than a game show" and "I'm the size of an ant and that key might as well be on the moon." In one of the The Muppets' *Alice* TV shows, Alice says to the Rabbit: "I'm looking for a hole." The Rabbit responds: "A hole? A whole what?" The darker adaptations meant for adults are perhaps the most inventive. The detective thriller *Murder in Wonderland* portrays the Queen of Hearts as a gay man and the tarts in the

Knave of Hearts' trial as loose women. The science fiction thriller *The Matrix* plays with the double meaning of "bug" for computer scientists by implanting a robot bug in the protagonist's chest, thereby "bugging" his trajectory into wonderland. Most recently, hashtag "WorldAliOfMyOwn" posts such word games as: "Cheshire Cats reign over copy-cats any day." Her followers are invited to respond with their own riddles.

3. The Interplay between Reality and Fantasy

Like other popular nineteenth-century fairytales, *Alice in Wonderland* begins with the reality of an ordinary white rabbit that without transition exhibits such fantastic actions as wearing a waistcoat, consulting a watch, speaking like a harried human before popping down a "rather large" rabbit hole. The hole becomes the conduit to a wonderland filled with unpredictable figures, objects, and settings. These present seemingly real objects that immediately become fantastic, such as the hallucinogenic mushroom crowned with the smoking caterpillar, the mysterious potion, or the pebbles that turn into cakes. Ingesting any of them results in Alice alternately growing to monstrous proportions or shrinking to minute size. In *Through the Looking-Glass*, the Red Queen begins as a chess figure that can randomly cross squares, a fearsome tyrant who challenges Alice as a pawn and in the conclusion, becomes her naughty black kitten. The fantastic penetrates the real and the real lurks in even the most outlandish fantastic.

Carroll's centering of his two narratives on card and chess games has inspired successors to play with endlessly amusing coincidences and clashes between fantasy and reality. Later versions capitalize on this interplay to create different games. Instead of characterizing the two soldiers who paint the white roses red in the Queen of Heart's garden as fearful and submissive, Hepworth and Stowe's early film shows them as children having fun at play. The 1951 Disney film entertains old and young audiences with a talking doorknob, dancing and singing teapots in "The Mad Tea Party," and a family of honking horns in the Tulgey Woods. In his musical video of the "Mad Tea Party," the Korean pop singer Seungri accompanies his song by throwing into the air first five, and then a whole bunch of credit cards. In Burton's film, the Mad Hatter plays an entertaining clown complete with top hat and makeup. The Japanese digital game *Alice in Horrorland* shows a dark Alice asking players: "Will you play with me?" Players click on "yes" to continue Dark Alice's chase; "no" to end it.

Perhaps the most intriguing games between reality and fantasy are played in the science fiction thriller *The Matrix*, because the boundaries between the two are totally confused. When Neo's mouth dissolves (much as the mirror does in *Through the Looking-Glass*) and the small bug-like robot is inserted into his belly button, is some unknown force playing with him? Trinity sucks out the robot with a tracking device, but also confides that from now on, he will be tracked. Reality or fantasy? Instead of answering, the film plays with viewers' minds, and viewers seem to love it.

4. The Absurd

The most daunting challenge faced by Carroll and his adapters involves the absurd. This is the humor that responds to an incomprehensible, alien, hostile world that undermines meaning and order. Can Alice persevere in her journey through Wonderland, when, for example, she loses her sense of self-identity? Repeatedly she asks herself, "Who am I?" The mismatch between her ever-changing anatomy, her goal to explore Wonderland, and its chaotic, incomprehensible environment gives rise to ludicrous scenes, such as attempting to fit her oversized body into the Rabbit's house or trying to comprehend how a tossed baby can turn into a pig or how the King of Hearts can convict the Knave of Hearts of stealing tarts when they are on the table. It all becomes part of an absurd card game. Particularly telling is the play with the concept of "nothing." Can one have more tea if one has had none? Does Alice exist if the Red King has stopped dreaming of her? Can Nobody be a person, as the White King proclaims in *Through the Looking-Glass*? The illogic of these snowballed "nothings, nobodies, and nohows" cause Alice to cry but also to recognize that all this illogic is in reality "nonsense."

Carroll's uncanny ability of superposing laughter on the distinctly non-humorous absurd has found many admirers among his adapters. The influential Disney animation of 1951 led the way by changing the knob of an impenetrable door into a harmless, helpful gnome and a flock of menacing vultures into umbrellas that take a bath in a waterfall. Even Alice's disappointment with her half cup of tea turns into the silly action of eating the saucer and cutting the teacup in half. Imitations in YouTube amateur musical videos such as "Derek W's" *Three 6 Mafia: Alice in Wonderland*, ratchet up Disney's superposition of humor on the absurd by combining dancing images that belonged to different scenes into one chaotic scene, disturbing and entertaining at the same time.

The opportunity to link horror with amusement has spawned many innovative approaches that take advantage of new media. Johnny Tay's webcomic *Seven Years in Dog-Land* portrays Alice in a cruel "wonderland" where dogs are the masters. Making blankets from the skins of "sapiens," for example, may make the cartooned Alice look sick, but the comic format diverts the painful allusion to the Holocaust to a casual diversion. Dark Alice in Shin Megami Tensei's videogame, *Alice in Horrorland* entices gamers into an alien, hostile world to play life-and-death games with her. Her magical tricks and repeated cliché "Could you please die for me?" trap the gamer into saying "yes," and thereby ending the game. An ongoing play on absurdity is offered by WorldAliOfMyOwn's tweets starting with the first on February 23, 2011: "A world in which everyone has a dozen blue birds is near .. thanks to Twitter." A year and many tweets later: "I dreamed an entire mad world in my head," followed by her last tweet, in German, "Wer ist normal hier und wer ist krank?" (Who is sick and who is normal?).

So, why have the *Alice* tales become celebrities? First, Carroll's imaginative narratives of Alice's encounter with a strange world that is both frightening and amusing have intrigued readers around the globe. Second, thanks to Disney and other animation illustrators, her image has become instantly recognizable to citizens worldwide, and third, as a result of the happy union between innovation and the Internet, the *Alice in Wonderland* "industry" has become self-perpetuating around the globe. A quick search of the Web will bring up hundreds of products with the Disney Wonderland image, ranging from ubiquitous mugs and t-shirts to flip-flops and iPhone covers. This celebrity, I would maintain, depends substantially on the humor techniques of comic naming of titles and characters, memorable word play and riddles (these are especially suitable to Twitter and other social media), intriguing games of fantasy and reality, and the "corrective laughter" that recognizes even the most puzzling and disturbing features of existence as nonsense invented for our amusement. Ultimately, these humor traits illuminate E.B. White's insight that "humor, like poetry, plays close to the big hot fire that is Truth, and sometimes the reader feels the heat" (174).

Works Cited

Allen, Audrey Mayhew. *Gladys in Grammarland*. Westminster: Roxburgh Press, 1897. Print.

Alice in Wonderland. Dir. Cecil Hepworth and Percy Stow. 1903. Silent film. Web. 30 June 2013. http://www.youtube.com/watch?v=zeIXfdogJbA

Alice in Murderland. Dir. Dennis Devine. 2010. Film.

Alice in Wonderland. Walt Disney Animation Studios. 1951. Film.

Alice in Wonderland. Dir. Nick Willing. 1999. TV movie.

Alice in Wonderland. Dir. Tim Burton. 2009. Disney studio. Animated Film.

Bangs, John Kendrick. *Alice in Blunderland*. New York: Kessinger Publishing, 2003. Print.

Big Bang. "SEUNGRI - V.V.I.P. M/V." YouTube, 20 Jan. 2011. Music video. Web. 30 June 2013. http://www.youtube.com/watch?v=ygkhxUItiUM.

Boorstin, Daniel. *The Image, or What Happened to the American Dream*. New York: Atheneum, 1962. Print.

Bowrey, Kathy. "The New Intellectual Property: Celebrity, Fans and the Properties of the Entertainment Franchise." *Griffith Law Review* 20. 1 (2011): 188-220. Print.

Cohen, Douglas. *Steaming into Wonderland*. YouTube. 2012. Web. 30 June 2013. www.youtube.com/watch?v=aqgtx7bXohk

Gardner, Martin. *The Annotated Alice*. New York: Bramhall House, 1950. Print.

Gilmore, Robert. *Alice in Quantumland*. New York: Copernicus, 1995. Print.

Gorin, Valerie and Annik Dubied. "Desirable People: Identifying Social Values through Celebrity News." *Media Culture Society* 33 (2011): 599-618. Print.

Kurzman, Charles, et al. "Celebrity Status." *Sociological Theory* 25. 4 (2007): 347-367. Print.

Lewis, Caroline. *Clara in Blunderland*. London: Heineman, 1902. Print.

Malice in Wonderland. Dir. Jayson Rothwell. 2008. Film.

The Matrix. Dir. Lana and Andrew Paul Wachowski. 1999. Film.

Scooterpiety. "The Muppet Show." YouTube. 3 November 2010. Web. 30 June 2013. http://www.youtube.com/watch?v=HFD3TkuPR8c

Shin Megami Tensei. *Alice in Horrorland*. Atlus: 30 October 1992. Videogame.

Tay, Johnny. *Seven Years in Dog-Land*. 2010. Web. 30 June 2013. http://www.webcomicsnation.com/john_avatar/dog-land/series.php.

Three 6 Mafia. "Alice in Wonderland." 2010. Music video. Web. 30 June 2013. http://www.youtube.com/watch?v=iOpkxbVl5Ik

"Tweedledee and Tweedledum Political Images." Google Images. Web. 30 June 2013. http://www.google.com/search?q=Tweedledee+and+Tweedledum+political+c artoons&tbm=isch&tbo=u&source=univ&sa=X&ei=H_LIUaSOAoW54APik4H4Cw &ved=0CDQQsAQ&biw=1600&bih=783

Unclesporkums. "Funky Fables: Alice in Wonderland." YouTube (21 Feb. 2011). Web 30 June 2013. http://www.youtube.com/watch?v=hbExb1yKe1E

White, E.B. *The Second Tree from the Corner*. New York: Harper and Row, 1954. Print.

Williams, Tad. *Otherland*. New York: DAW, 1998. Print.

WorldAliOfMyOwn. *Alice in Wonderland* tweets. 23 Feb. 2011-22 Feb. 2012. Web. 30. June 2013. https://twitter.com/WorldAliOfMyOwn

Blythe Davenport

The Lost Folk Tales of Laurel Hill

JOHN NOTMAN, the perfectly named planner of the city's prime necropolis,

where souls go to not-be, presents the folk stories that have been long buried

with their owners in his memory yard on the hill.

I. Caleb and The Fox

One night in winter CALEB COX watched a mysterious flame burning

on a hill far down the river valley. The next day he climbed

to a spot of earth scorched from the snow. The wily red Fox appeared.

"Devil Dog," said CALEB. The Fox replied, "You will be buried

in the dirt beneath my feet, your sons beside you." Then he was off,

a fire flashing against the snow, each step shrilling CALEB'S blood.

II. The King's Reward

When ALPHA WILLIAMSON rescued the king's lost

pearl from the sylvan giant with vast hands and miles for legs,

who made a night sky when he stood between you

and the sun, the king said, "You have my gratitude and your reward

will be my daughter's hand in marriage," but ALPHA

wanted nothing but the king's son and he said this,

and the king nodded and they lived happily ever after.

III. The Longest Night

Once upon a time, there was a god who made death into a long, dark oblivion. The dead molted their skin, the earth dug into their meat

until hollow skeletons populated the boneyards. Stone engravings

blurred, a tree swallowed the marble block of an infant's headstone.

One day a man decided to challenge the god's cruel dictate,

and dug down along the magic beanstalk's roots to his realm. The god ate him.

And anyone who might remember the dead—their laughter or their dullness—

and anyone who might remember anyone who might remember the dead—

their dances, the feel of their hands—indeed, anyone who might remember

anyone who might remember *these* people, they were dead too, and the wicked god

laughed to see the living make Death into an elegant thing, then gathered up his bony treasures.

Tim Fitts

Stripping Roses

The job paid five dollars an hour, but it paid cash, and Mrs. West promised future employment at West Farms Florist if things stayed busy after Valentine's Day. Mrs. West had a Southern bouffant that I didn't trust, but the next morning, I met her husband at their shop on Archer Road, and he drove me and a guy named Bankowski to the farm way out past I-75 into horse country. Mr. West picked us up at six-thirty, and the morning Florida fog seethed in and out of the Spanish moss and live oaks all the way down Archer Road to the farm. Mr. West took us to the shed where we met Harold, his cousin, who was going to be stripping roses with us. If the wind blew right, you could get a steady waft of horse manure. They kept the roses bundled up in boxes where they had been shipped from Peru. Mr. West told us they had to order extra roses, because they rammed steel blades into the sheaves at Customs to make sure they aren't loaded with cocaine. Predicting how many roses would be destroyed was impossible.

Mr. West told us to strip the five boxes here. When we were done with these boxes, separate them into long, medium and short stems. Take out the longest stems and put them in a stack. The long stems need the thorns intact. Once we had a stack, tie them into dozens. Then he pointed to the barn where the boxes had been stacked in three columns 10 boxes high. On average, he told us, stripping 20,000 roses required three 10-hour days, so it came out to 50 per day. If we finished early, it was 50. If we finished late, it was 50.

Mr. West handed us each a metal tool to strip the thorns. He demonstrated, fitting the mouth of the gadget around the stem, then pulled down in a swift tug, shooting thorns out the sides. Thorns nicked your hands no matter how you held it, so Mr. West told us that we had better use our gloves. I had forgotten to bring any gloves, and he told me that I should have brought them. I asked if they had some in the barn, but Mr. West told me that it would be better to use mine. I asked him if we could check, and he said that I should have brought my own gloves. Harold told me that if I rubbed my palms at the end of the day with garlic juice and Vitamin E they'd be good as new in the morning, which I tried when I got home that evening, but he failed to report that the sting of garlic shoots down where the nerves meet the joints and makes silver and purple lights light up behind your eyelids.

The three of us drank coffees and listened to the morning news, and broadcasters announced that the trade embargo against Iraq had caused perhaps more damage to archeological sites than the war itself. Harold said *boo-hoo*. Assholes like Saddam Hussein rape their own women, gas their own people, *spy* on their own people, and then people get bent out of shape because of archeological sites. Boo-*damn*-hoo. "Give me freedom, or give me archeology. I'll take freedom," he said.

We listened to music until lunch. Mrs. West fixed us tuna sandwiches that had a funny taste, but they worked. I took a stroll to work the stiffness out of my legs. I thought about bolting and even walked a half-mile towards Bronson to see if maybe they didn't have a bus, but decided against it. On the walk back, I counted over 250 tiny cuts on the palms of each hand. When I returned, somebody had put it back to the news channel.

"Hey there, latecomer," Harold said.

"How long have you two been back at work?" I said.

"Long enough," Bankowski said.

"Listen," Harold said, nodding at the radio.

I placed the gadget around a stem and jerked. The broadcaster repeated the announcement. The report was in from the Alachua County Police Department. They had made an arrest. Neighbors had called complaining of violence next door, and a young man had beaten up his grandmother. During the arrest, an altercation had ensued. The man was 22 years of age, and his face had been badly scarred, and witnesses claimed that he was wild-eyed. After some speculation, the police determined that the young man in question was the prime suspect for the killings. They had him. The fear that had gripped central Florida was over. "It is a good day for daughters. It is a good day for parents. It is good day for all of us," the radio said. The radio announced that the moratorium on walking alone was off, and young people could once again frequent Lake Allison after dark, but still, lock your doors and use your best judgment, but the relief, the broadcaster said, was palpable. The newscaster recounted the entire scene of the murders and repeated all the details of which we were all familiar. The radio man revisited the crow bar and gore, the couple locking themselves inside to wait for help that never came.

"Gas him," Harold said.

"Gas him nothing," Bankowski said. "He needs to feel more than gas."

Harold said it was times like this that they needed to suspend due process. Look at those girls he had cut up. Did we know what he had done to those girls? Harold said he had not seen the pictures, but he did not want to see the pictures, but what he had read was enough.

"Did you hear what he did with the scalps?" Bankowski said.

"Don't talk about it," Harold said.

"You don't want to know," Bankowski said.

"I think I can use my imagination," I said.

"I don't want to use my imagination for that shit," Harold said. "Unless you're some kind of sicko. Leave me out of it." Harold said that the killer had rearranged the girls after, and anybody who used their imagination for that was probably just as guilty. Harold said the monster they had picked up, had put them in positions, and *monster* wasn't really the word.

Harold dumped the empty cardboard and Bankowski fetched a couple more from the barn. We ripped open a new box of roses, and you couldn't help but do the math as you stripped and bundled. I didn't want to think about how much we were earning per rose, but after a time, you can't help but start calculating. Twenty thousand divided by 12. Five times 10 times three. Sixteen hundred divided by four-fifty. I kept getting my figures mixed up, but there was plenty of time to mix and match the numbers, and I didn't even want to think about it. They put the music station back on, then after a time it seemed like somebody was always ripping open another box and taking one down from the barn.

I liked bundling the long stems. I told Harold I wouldn't mind sticking around. I could do this kind of work all the time. I told him that Mrs. West had said something about taking me on permanently, but he didn't answer. I could see myself doing that kind of work. Snip the stems, keep the water fresh, wrap the bundles in Mylar, tell people they made a beautiful selection. How hard could it be? Harold seemed preoccupied, and I could tell he was thinking about the killer. I was right. He zipped a stem of thorns then said he wasn't sure what kind of asshole lawyer would go around defending somebody who either beats up his grandmother or cuts people up. "How do people stand in front of a judge and jury and look them in the eye and say that they should just walk free?" Harold said that due process was not established for people like that. Laws were made for normal people. They had him, they knew it was him, and they didn't need to waste any more of taxpayers' money on him. They had wasted enough. Take him out back, that's it.

"I don't know," I said. "I don't know about that guy."

"What don't you know?" Bankowski said.

"I don't think he did it."

"Oh, no?" Harold said. "This guy that beats up his own grandmother? He sounds like a real prince. I tell you what. My heart is not exactly bleeding for this creep."

"Just because he beat up his grandmother?" I said.

Harold gave me a look and asked what kind of asshole beats up his grandmother. Bankowski raised his eyes at me. "Did you listen to the radio?" Harold said.

"I know," I said. "I never said it was good to beat up your grandmother. By general rule, one should never 'beat up their grandmother.' However, my greater point is that nobody beats up their grandmother without provocation, unless the grandmother has touched some nerve."

"Christ," Harold said. "This guy."

We kept stripping roses and bundling, and after a while, Bankowski changed the radio to a Top Forty station. They played Richard Marx, the Bangles, Amy Grant, and then broke for a millennium of commercials. Then they returned from the break to play more Richard Marx. I tried to crawl into a deep space in my mind and pretend the music wasn't happening, but sometimes one is powerless. I told the two that if they played one more Richard Marx song the police were going to have to come and pick *me* up for questioning.

On Thursday, after three shifts from morning until mid-afternoon, Mr. West dropped me and Bankowski off at the shop on Archer. I counted the money on the bike ride home and was happy that they had not charged me for the sandwiches Mrs. West had made for us each day. I tucked 50 dollars away for the electricity and water, and when my roommate, Charles Russell, came home, we grocery shopped. I bought a 20-pound sack of potatoes, onions, two dozen eggs, a 10-pound bag of apples, two pounds of black beans, three pounds of pintos, a tub of fat from the butcher, a gallon of whole milk, a quart of buttermilk and a quart goat milk and some onions. That night we ordered two large pizzas and split a 12-pack.

Charles Russell sat on his barstool eating pizza from the countertop, and I sat on the beanbag in the middle of our empty living room, facing the sliding glass doors that looked out on the woods. I could see Charles Russell's reflection behind me. I could see him bobbing his head to the music, holding a slice with one hand and raising his other hand a foot from the wall, opening his palm and slamming it against the wall—punishments he doled out to our neighbor for constantly complaining about noise from our apartment.

Moments later, when the phone rang, I watched Charles Russell pick it up and talk to our neighbor. He said he had not heard anything at all. He talked further, and then brought the phone to me. I told Selene, our neighbor, that I had not heard thumps or any sounds, either, but I would be happy to be on the lookout. I agreed, I said, that it was strange.

I told Charles Russell that he had better stop doing stuff like that, or people would start calling the cops, and they would have a new murder suspect.

Charles Russell responded by giving the wall another thump. We waited, but Selene must have been too tired to call.

"I'll tell you what," I said. "If that was me out there. If I was the killer, I would take this opportunity to go south. Or north. Or any direction. I would walk right down to the bus station and buy a ticket for the Keys, or Miami, or Okeechobee or something like that. I would not stick around for a heartbeat."

"They got him, already," Charles Russell said.

"That's not him," I said. "They're just trying to cool off the hysteria. A killer does not beat up his grandmother. Killers get lazy, or wreckless, or careless, but they don't go around beating up grandmothers."

"We'll see," he said. "We shall see."

"If that was me. I would go anywhere but here. Nobody's looking for him, now. Nobody's thinking about anything. I would go anywhere else and let them think they had their man. By the time they realized their mistake, I'd be gone."

"Keep talking like that, people are going to think you're the killer. I'm serious," he said. "I'd keep my clam shut if I were you." Charles Russell took another bite of pizza, then said, "It probably is you. You take walks in the woods. You take odd jobs. You do shit like shuck roses. You're like a day laborer. You do drifter work."

We sat for a few more minutes, and then Charles Russell went upstairs for bong hits, and I stayed downstairs for a few more beers, and then I went in the kitchen and ground up a garlic clove and rubbed the juice into my palms. It was worse the first night when I wasn't expecting it. The juice touched the openings and turned into instant fire—white light, white heat, blue flash, then sustaining, then holding, then giving, finally cooling into red, the pain subsiding and coasting into pleasure. Sweet pleasure.

Valerie Fox

Two Important Questions on Ant Individuality

Ever since the Ant volunteered
for the sleep and efficiency experiment
he's been tired.

The lab coats defined ennui
for him. He'd like to forget that,
just can't let go.

He's a dullard, he feels.
In his animal trance
he is no scholar's finding,

no culmination of tidy field-notes.
At least he has no memory
of first love.
One ant asks the other:
Are you happy?
Why can't you sleep?

Valerie Fox

Two Important Questions Concerning Seahorses

If we were seahorses and the men were impregnated
what would you take advantage of first?

And what would you be afraid of?
?????

I would take the grand tour
and visit many large bodies of water

those I could reach in as many days,
and keep a diary.

I'd want to visit the Black Sea
and Lake Michigan, just to name a few.

I'd take advantage of all the latest
transportation thingies.

There must be some companies catering
to this kind of travel. I'd keep in touch

with Papa Seahorse, a good guy
I wouldn't have to worry about while on tour.

He would basically refrain from consuming
alcohol and freefall amusement park rides.

If I were a sea horse, I'd be really into motherhood,
what the hell, and meeting my own assorted needs

higher and lower, and sometimes the needs of others.
I might forget about my family

while in the Black Sea,
or somewhere like that.

That old fear of forgetfulness might linger
in my seahorse consciousness.

Henry Israeli

New Year in the Old Country

Have you ever seen a lion carrying
a baby in its mouth, the tender pink bed
of its tongue raised high to keep
the infant elevated above its curved incisors,
then laying it gently onto a pink toile blanket
next to a woman who sits half reclining
with one arm behind her, a book perched in her hand,

so engrossed she does not so much as look up
when the baby rolls over onto its back
and plugs its little lips with a glistening thumb?
Have you seen the lion walk away on padded paws
stepping up to a trot only when it becomes a silhouette
against the distant blue and pink backdrop
of a night unpinning its long black locks?

Have you seen the woman,
pushing her rectangular glasses up
the bridge of her nose and lifting her right hand
to the top of the book to turn the page?
When she tells the child,
not averting her gaze from her book,
that when she is done reading she will eat it,
are you shocked to tears or secretly delighted?

Do you mistakenly assume these questions
are theoretical, or are you too polite
to interrupt the writer's thoughts?

The lion stands up and sheds its skin,
a countess removing her cape
before stepping into a glittering hotel lobby,
and drops it to the ground, a puddle of fur,
a map of a continent on a distant planet
so familiar we call it our home.

Lynn Levin

Stay Lucky

One rainy evening in April as I headed through Philadelphia on the West Trenton local, a very large man bent over me and asked in a very small voice if he could sit next to me. "It's only three stops," he said.

I lifted my eyes to a meek and plaintive face. In his dingy gray and white sweats, the stranger called to mind a parade balloon of a downcast Mickey Mouse. He smelled like a Goodwill Store, basement-aged humanness on old clothes.

"Just as much your train as it is mine," I replied, wondering if other passengers farther up in the car had refused him.

"That's the way you see it, and that's the way I see it, but that's not the way everyone sees it," he said, settling in. Glancing at the school folder in my hands, he asked if I were a teacher.

I allowed that I was and began to feel relieved that we only had three stops together. It meant he'd be getting off at Elkins Park, way before me. His musty aroma made my nose twitch.

"I used to be a teacher, too," he said. "Middle school industrial arts. But then I won a million dollars in the New York State lottery and quit my job."

Startled, I turned to look at him more closely. He seemed to be in his upper forties. His shaggy, slightly curly, light-brown hair fringed the collar of his ragged sweatshirt, which was dappled by raindrops. His eyes were pigeon-feather gray, but focused. He needed a shave. His big meaty hands looked soft. Relating his good fortune, he sounded more regretful than boastful.

"You won a lottery. You're lucky!" I said, trying to sound bouncy and cheerful. "And if you don't have to work...." I let my voice trail off. With chatty strangers you should try to keep it light and positive. Well, with chatty strangers you should try not to chat. On the other hand, this man knew how to drop the breadcrumbs of small talk, and I pecked them up like an eager bird. But why the vow of poverty, the street-person look? Outside of the rummage smell of his clothes and lack of barbering, he appeared clean. He enunciated clearly. He speech was educated.

"They don't like me on this train," he groused. Then he told me that the day before he fell into an argument with a conductor for trying to buy a ticket with a $100 bill. The conductor wanted to throw him off the train. My companion didn't say how it ended. Probably not in his favor, but I rolled my eyes as if to say, *Yeah, people and their rules.* I guess he thought that, being rich, he could act like a jackass if he wanted to.

Still, he intrigued me. And only three stops.

"So after you quit work what did you do?"

"Not much. Watched a lot of TV. Did a little handyman work for neighbors."

I imagined that he was good at handyman work, being a shop teacher. But the idleness, the TV watching made me sad.

"Right around that time my wife divorced me, and I went to live with my mom."

I tilted my head in sympathy for the divorce and offered a hopeful nod for the mom move-in. The guy, I did not ask his name, had the air of being a very large son. I've read of the misfortunes of lucky people who won tens of millions, sometimes over one hundred million dollars, in lotteries. Most of them squandered it on cars, houses, boats, lavish gifts, bad investments, and went bankrupt in a matter of years. Some fell prey to con artists. Their spouses often left them. A few committed suicide, and some were even murdered. Others lapsed into alcoholism and drug use or gambled their winnings away, still addicted to chance.

"Then you won't believe what happened to me."

"What happened?"

"One day I was changing a tire for an old lady by the side of the road, and a car came and ran me over."

"Oh my God," I gasped.

"I spent three years in the hospital." At this point, the rain was sloshing down so hard that the train windows looked like the portholes of washing machines. Lightning illuminated the city, but in the torrent everything was out of focus.

"Three years!" What terrible luck, I thought. I didn't know how you spent three years in a hospital unless there were many complications, readmissions, months in a rehab hospital. Maybe he spent two-and-a-half years in the hospital and rounded it up. He didn't go into details. His story was as strange as truth, and so I believed him.

"Then, a few years after I got out of the hospital, I won an eight-million-dollar settlement."

My expression froze in surprise. The guy was rich again. His good luck had returned. A poster for a personal injury law firm hung at the front of the train. My eyes darted to it, then returned to my companion. His hospital and medical bills, no doubt, sailed off the charts. Then pain, suffering, loss of income. Not that he was employed at the time of the accident. More likely, the accident had left him unable to hold down a job. In any case, the man had a way of winning cash.

Or did he? At the time, I didn't stop to consider that he might have been luring me into conversation with made-up million-dollar stories and invented tales of disaster. He was one heck of a storyteller.

"Not long after I got the settlement," he continued, "I was in the kitchen eating pancakes with my mom, and the doctor called. The doc said to my mom, are you sitting down?" I leaned in to catch every word. He was a very soft-spoken man. "So she sits down, and the doctor tells her that I have a neuroblastoma." My companion shot me a very serious look. I didn't know what a neuroblastoma was, but it sounded grave. Later that night, I looked it up and learned that it is a kind of nerve tissue cancer. In children, where it is most common, it often goes into remission, but in adults it is rarer and the prognosis is bad. Sitting there on the train, I didn't need to know the natural history of the disease to understand that the pendulum of luck had once more swung against him. He spoke as a man not long for the world. "I don't know why things happen like they do, but they do," he said giving me a look like a sigh.

By this time, we had passed the second stop.

"So I guess you're wondering what I do," he said.

"I was wondering."

"Every day I go to an ATM and take out a lot of cash. Hundreds of dollars. Then I go to the ghettoes of North Philadelphia or West Philadelphia, the food deserts. You know how many supermarkets they have there? About three. They have the bodegas, but the bodegas rip people off with their potato chips and packaged cookies and high prices. No fresh fruits or vegetables." He was speaking from the ramparts now. The meekness and self-pity in his voice had fled; the pistons of righteousness powered his speech.

I hoped he'd have time to finish his story before his stop came up. The rain continued to sheet down, and I saw he had no umbrella.

"So every day I go to one of those supermarkets in the ghetto. I stand by the checkout, and I pay the tab for random shoppers." He took a breath and looked at me for acknowledgment, to make sure that I knew that he was doing his part for a better world.

"You are helping so many people," I said. I was in awe of this guerrilla philanthropist.

"You should see the looks on their faces. The smiles. The gratitude. Sometimes they come up and hug me." A glow spread over his face.

I imagined the scene at the checkout aisle: people pushing carts laden with boxes of breakfast cereal and frozen waffles, packages of ground beef, chicken, bread, oranges, broccoli, milk, diapers, laundry soap. I imagined the guy standing by the cashier like a tree green with dollars, reaching out to the shoppers like the hand of good fortune. The lucky people fluttering around his leafy sheltering arms, their hearts light as birds, thanking him, wishing him God's blessing, then flying off to their families to whom they would recount the story of the loony rich white man who bestowed upon them free food. I saw multitudes of instant friendships, bright and brief as struck matches.

Each dollar he gave was his lucky ticket, too. Each happy countenance lifted his soul with a fleeting bond of joy. Was I being too dour to compare the jolt he felt to the high a gambler feels before the die come to rest, to the lift the lottery player feels before the numbers are drawn? He was a dying man, and he was not buying cars or boats or taking around-the-world cruises or even purchasing decent clothing for himself. I wondered if he still had his mother, if he had anyone to shop for and cook for. His whole enterprise was noble, beautiful, and terribly sad.

Then his stop came up. I wished him well. He nodded slightly, then he shambled down the aisle, off the train, and into the stormy night.

I only saw him one more time, a week after our train ride. It was early in the evening as the West Trenton local pulled away from Temple University station. My companion, his charitable work, I supposed, done for the day, stood in the crowd, limping in the twilight, checking his old-fangled flip phone. I had the impression that he was trying to look busy, the way people do when they are self-conscious about having nowhere in particular to go, no one in particular to meet.

Weeks later, I began to suspect that the man suffered from some type of delusion or savior complex that involved charitable heroics. The episodes he recounted to me might have been stand-ins for other things. The lottery win and the big-money damages: were those really Social Security or SSI payments? The long post-accident hospitalization, perhaps a stay in a psychiatric hospital? The neuroblastoma, the diagnosis of a personality disorder?

What did seem real was his desire to help others. That is the part of his story I still believe. He may very well have visited the ATM for grocery-gifting cash. He might have doled out bits of his disability money to poor people and lived cheaply so that he would have enough to give away. If he saw himself as a savior, amen. It was not a bad thing. And his mission afforded him human contact, fleeting though it was.

The way the man's luck went, I guessed that some future disaster or windfall—real or imagined—would strike him and that he would stay lonely, supplied with funds, and mostly good. The way the man's soul went, I guessed that he would keep providing for needy strangers; he would keep lighting little flames of fellowship, which he would have to relight with new strangers again and again. Maybe he also hoped that someone would tell his tale. And that I have tried to do.

Donna McVey

Can Mass Shootings be Prevented?

I was deeply saddened but not entirely surprised by the shooting at Sandy Hook Elementary School in Newtown, Conn., Dec. 14, 2012. A few days after the shooting, I received an e-mail from a coworker asking me to sign a petition on gun control. The e-mail made me reflect on the shooting; I thought more deeply about what had caused the shooting and how tragedies like this can be prevented. Finally, I ended up signing the petition because I felt it was a step in the right direction. While I'm not opposed to people owning guns for hunting or other purposes, I see no need for people to collect guns or own assault weapons. Yet I don't believe that gun control alone can solve the problem of random mass shootings, which have been on the rise in the past decade in the U.S. I would like to propose a multipronged approach to this problem based on my experience of living in Europe. In addition to gun control, in my opinion, we need to address health care, higher education and individualism in order to reduce gun violence.

I believe that health care is a right, not a privilege. I've lived in Germany and Romania, where quality health care is not only accessible and affordable to everyone but practically free. For instance, while I was teaching at a Romanian university on a Fulbright fellowship, I injured my shoulder and was able to get free health care. Although I was uninsured and was a U.S. citizen, Romania, like most European countries, has national health care. My mother had a similar experience in Germany, where she was able to get free health care as a tourist. In contrast, I have a friend who has a son with bipolar disorder, who is a U.S. citizen but cannot afford to get treated in the United States because he doesn't have health insurance. And if someone who has a mental illness can't get treated, won't he pose a greater danger to himself or those around him? Fortunately, the Affordable Care Act is a step in the right direction. Let's hope that in the future, everyone living in the U.S. will be able to afford health care.

I also believe that higher education should be a right rather than a privilege for every qualified student. Both the individual and society as a whole would benefit because a well-educated person has better prospects of being gainfully employed and is less likely to commit a crime. I envy my relatives in France, Germany and Romania, who attended universities in those countries tuition-free and graduated debt-free. While I also got a great education at the University of Pennsylvania, I had to take out substantial student loans, which I have been paying back for many years. Why is it that a U.S. citizen can attend a university in Germany tuition-free but cannot do so in the United States? Several years ago, I had the opportunity to attend a German university for a year, where everyone, regardless of their citizenship, attends tuition-free, and that university was typical of German universities. Therefore, I applaud President Amy Gutmann for recently making my alma mater affordable to everyone by making up the difference between what students have to pay and what they can afford to pay in grants rather than loans so everyone can graduate debt-free. Let's hope that more universities follow her lead.

Last but not least, let's cultivate a sense of community rather than individualism in this country. People who grow up with a strong sense of community are more empathetic and altruistic and are more inclined to help rather than hurt others. As a child growing up in Bucharest, Romania, I lived in an environment where people cared for and looked out for each other. As a result, there was hardly any crime. Also, I remember feeling secure and relaxed knowing that I was surrounded by people who cared about me. In contrast, after we moved to New York when I was in my early teens, I felt vulnerable because I had to look out for myself.

While I don't believe that we can entirely eliminate tragic mass shootings in the U.S. like the one at Sandy Hook, I think that we can reduce their occurrence by controlling who has access to what type of guns, but more importantly by creating a society where people care about one another and where health care and higher education are a right rather than a privilege, as they are in most European countries.

Usha Menon

Hinduism, Happiness and Wellbeing: A Case Study of Adulthood in an Oriya Hindu Temple Town

For most Americans, the phrase "the pursuit of happiness" holds enormous evocative significance. In contrast, for many Oriya Hindus living halfway across the globe in the temple town of Bhubaneswar in the eastern Indian state of Orissa, these words carry little resonance. Instead of happiness, many of these Oriya Hindus value wellbeing, a sense of satisfaction with life, but even this, as they describe it, stops being a valid goal as one approaches the end of life.

In this essay, I focus on Oriya Hindu understandings of happiness and wellbeing from the perspective of the women who live in the temple town of Bhubaneswar—an urban settlement, dating back to at least the 11th century (see Panigrahi 1961). This settlement centers on a 10th-century temple dedicated to the Hindu god Siva represented here as Lingaraj, the Lord of the Phallus. The temple town is distinct and separate from the modern city of Bhubaneswar, the capital of the Indian state of Orissa, which was planned and built after 1948. It is a fairly important pilgrimage center, attracting substantial numbers of the devout from North India, Bengal and Assam.

The attitudes and actions of the women who live in this temple town provide the ethnographic foundations for this essay. The essay demonstrates that, for these women, happiness as an emotional experience does not possess the same salience and significance that it does in mainstream Anglo-American society because the meanings they attach to it are so radically different from its Anglo-American connotations. Instead of happiness, Oriya Hindu women work toward achieving wellbeing. Therefore, I present in this paper a cultural model of wellbeing developed through analyzing these women's conceptualizations of the life course, the family roles associated with particular life-phases and the levels of life satisfaction that they achieve during these various phases. According to this cultural model of wellbeing, many Oriya Hindu women enjoy the greatest wellbeing when they exercise power and dominance within their household, when they are central to its productive activities and when they feel morally and emotionally coherent. Thus, for Oriya Hindu women, dominance, centrality and coherence are the three key elements that constitute wellbeing. I also demonstrate that access to wellbeing shifts across the life course, being low for young adult women, peaking for mature adults and declining once again for old women.

Before moving on to discuss the significance of happiness in Orissa in greater detail, it is instructive to identify certain features of Hinduism and the influence they have on the meanings that many Hindus tend to attach to this emotion.

Hinduism and Happiness

Hinduism, an ancient tradition that goes back more than 4,000 years, encompasses great diversity in beliefs and practices. Considered by many scholars to be both a way of life and a highly organized social and religious system (Zaehner 1966; Flood 1996), it lacks a single historical founder and possesses no single unified set of beliefs, no centralized authority and no bureaucratic structures. Instead, what Hindus share is a worldview—a set of metaphysical and philosophical concepts orienting them to life and the world. Thus, many Hindus believe that *samsāra*, the never-ending cycle of rebirth and re-death, binds all living creatures; that maintaining *dharma*, in the sense of upholding order in this world, is a worthy human goal; that *karma*, an impersonal calculus of good and bad actions undertaken over past and present lives, decides one's present and future life circumstances; and that the ultimate goal of all humans should be to break out of *samsāra* and achieve *moksa* or final liberation.

While this goal of *moksa* remains distant for most Hindus, it is still thought possible to savor the transcendental bliss (*ānanda*) associated with it through cultivating the self in this world. And this is where the ancient Hindu theory of the emotions—the *rasa* (juice, flavor) theory—influences the emotional life of many modern Hindus. It does so in two ways: first, by suggesting that through cultivating an aesthetic sensibility one can savor the *rasas* of various emotions and, thereby, the divine bliss immanent in all humans, and second, by classifying the mundane experience of happiness as both subsidiary and transitory.

The *rasa* theory was given literary shape some time between 200 BC and 200 AD by the sage Bharata, in the *Nātyasāstra*, the Treatise on Dramaturgy (see de Bary 1958). It states that there are eight (or nine) basic, enduring emotions (*sthāyi bhāva*), and thirty-three transitory and subordinate emotions (vyābhicari bhāva) [*bhāva* meaning "emotion," "being," "existence"]. The eight basic emotions are sexual passion (*rati*), mirth or amusement (*hāsa*), sorrow (*soka*), anger (*krodha*), fear (*bhaya*), dynamic energy or perseverance (*utsāha*), disgust (*jugupsā*), and wonder or amazement (*vismaya*)—and a ninth (added some centuries later), serenity (*sama*). More importantly, each basic and enduring emotion is said to have its own flavor, its own *rasa*; thus, the basic emotion sexual passion has eroticism (*srngāra rasa*) as its *rasa*, while sorrow's *rasa* is compassion (*karuna*).

Bharata, and later commentators and interpreters of his text (see Datta 2006, and Sreekantaiya 2001, for more on these philosophers) sought to understand the relationship between the eight or nine basic and enduring emotions and their *rasas*. How was the flavor of sorrow, when witnessed as part of a dramatic performance, different from the direct experience of sorrow? And they concluded that the experience of *rasa* and the direct experience of the emotion are incommensurable. They maintained that the main purpose of dance, drama and poetry is to enable performers and spectators to cultivate an aesthetic sensibility in order to transcend the humdrum concerns of the workaday world and taste the flavor—the *rasa*—of the different basic emotions. Tasting the flavor of emotions in this way was, and still is, thought of as an opportunity to apprehend the essence of ultimate reality, to experience the divine bliss of final liberation. This, in a sense, is one interpretation of happiness among Hindus.

The other interpretation stems from the fact that the list of eight (or nine) basic and enduring emotions does not include happiness; it does, however, include mirth or amusement. But, as Bharata describes it, Hindu mirth does not approximate happiness in the way that Americans might interpret it: the former has elements of mocking laughter at the flaws and failings of others, while the latter, as we all know, connotes celebration and joyfulness. That is not to say that ancient Hindus ignored happiness or joy (*harsha*) as delight and celebration, the Anglo-American sense of this emotion-state: they just did not consider it to be a basic and enduring emotional experience. They placed it on the list of thirty-three ephemeral and secondary emotions, which are the affective changes that, together with the antecedent situation (*vibhava*) and the somatic changes (*anubhava*) coalesce to constitute the experience of a basic and enduring emotion (Gnoli 1956; Pandey 1935). Happiness, therefore, is a fleeting mental state that could be a component of a basic, enduring emotional experience, although it does not itself rise to that level in terms of stability or primacy.

Another reason for discounting happiness and preferring wellbeing can be found in the Oriya Hindu view of life and its meaning. A core element of this view, as mentioned above, is the belief that every rebirth is an opportunity for humans to work toward the ultimate goal of liberation, or *moksa*—to break free from *samsãra*, the never-ending cycle of rebirths and re-deaths. This belief assumes that the world around us, enchanting and seductive though it may appear, is ultimately illusory. It also assumes that worldly entanglements mire us, blinding us to the singular truth that the really real lies beyond this manifest world. Notwithstanding this belief, Oriya Hindus are urged to pursue this-worldly goals. Thus, they are encouraged to experience sensual pleasures (*kãma*), to pursue profit and material prosperity (*artha*), and to fulfill their religious and moral duties toward family and society (*dharma*). A well-lived life requires that one pursue and achieve all these goals, especially during the early phases of one's life when one marries and raises a family. The significance of *moksa* as an ultimate aim of life lies in its engendering a particular orientation to this world and its activities. So, while enjoying the pleasures that this world has to offer has its place and is important, many Oriya Hindus recognize that, in the end, such enjoyment is unlikely to be truly satisfying. As one grows older, it behooves one to begin paying attention to one's ultimate destiny, to what will happen to the imperishable divine essence (*atman*) that resides within all of us—will it be reborn or will it, finally, be able to break out of *samsãra*?

Indigenous wisdom has it that one can achieve *moksa* only through cultivating non-attachment to the affairs and relationships of this world. No god or goddess can guarantee such liberation—it is entirely the result of one's own individual efforts. And non-attachment is cultivated through the exercise of self-discipline, through working through the importunate cravings of one's nature to produce a refined human being—the most perfect of all cultural artifacts. It should not come as a surprise, therefore, that women tend not to value happiness as a desirable emotion. If there is a state of mind that is desired, it is wellbeing—but even wellbeing loses meaning as a woman approaches the end of life when she is supposed to focus on what lies beyond, not on the mundane trivialities of this world and its small satisfactions.

The Oriya Hindu Concept of Wellbeing

Wellbeing or *hito*, the Oriya word for it, and its contrary condition, *ahito*, are fairly common concepts in the temple town: they express satisfaction or dissatisfaction with the way life is moving. In traditional Hindu thought, wellbeing is a clear and precisely formulated category (Zimmermann pers. comm.). The Sanskrit term for wellbeing, *hita*, has many meanings, the more prominent being that which is "beneficial, advantageous, salutary, wholesome" (Monier-Williams 1899: 1298). More particularly, ancient Hindu texts claim that "appropriateness...produces wellbeing" (Zimmermann 1987: 23-25), appropriateness here implying a convergence of attitudes of mind and behavior with the demands and circumstances of one's life.

The Oriya language, with its roots in Sanskrit, has maintained this causal connection between appropriateness and wellbeing. Having, however, dropped the physical component of wellbeing—referred to in Oriya today as *svãsthya*—it defines *hito* as the kinds of emotions and mental orientations (*manobhãbo, manobrutti*) that result from fulfilling one's responsibilities (*dãitva*) according to one's station in life, from being involved in the exchanges and distributions appropriate to one's life circumstances. Such a transactional definition of wellbeing among Oriya Hindus is not surprising, given as Marriott has remarked, the "explicit, institutionalized concern for givings and receivings of many kinds in kinship, work and worship" (1976: 109) in Hindu culture. Thus, when a woman both controls and is intensely involved in social and familial exchanges and distributions, she enjoys substantial wellbeing; when she either does not control such distributive networks or is marginalized from participating in them, her sense of wellbeing declines. For many Oriya Hindu women, this period of intense involvement coincides with the middle years of their life; thus, young adult women look forward to being middle-aged and old women look back on middle age as the most satisfying phase of their lives.

The Setting

The temple town is the research site for the present study. Most families here, even today, continue to derive their power and prestige from their hereditary connections with the temple. Several scholars (Mahapatra 1981; Shweder 1991; Seymour 1976, 1980, 1999; Menon 2002, 2010, 2011) have described the Oriya Hindus who live here as fairly traditional in their beliefs and practices.

Thus, together with other traditionally minded Hindus, they tend to believe in the permeability of the human body. They conceive of bodies as relatively porous containers that are partially shared and/or exchanged with others through events like birth and marriage, and experiences like sharing food and living together (Daniel 1984; Lamb 1997, 2000; Mines 1993). Such events and experiences are thought to alter continually and reconstitute one's physical substance.

Corresponding to this understanding of the human body, Hindus conceive of the person as open and less bounded, constituted of heterogeneous "particulate" substances and therefore, "dividual and divisible" in nature (Marriott 1976: 111). This conception of the person is clearly distinct from dominant Western notions that think of the person as a bounded, self-contained individual (Geertz 1984). For Hindus, personhood fluctuates during the life course, waxing and waning depending on whether one initiates, controls or at least regulates the exchanges in which one participates thereby, controlling the transformations one experiences.

While nuclear living arrangements do occur in the temple town, extended households are regarded as the ideal; the tendency is to maintain or move towards such living arrangements rather than the reverse. In terms of social organization, these households are patrilineal and patrilocal: descent is traced through males and a newly married couple moves in with the groom's parents. They are, also, most commonly three-generational, numbering at least 10 to 15 people who share a single cooking hearth (Seymour 1999: 63-69). They tend to break up when either the oldest male or female member dies, and adult sons set up separate households; these, in turn, become extended when sons grow up, marry and have children.

Arranged marriages continue to be the norm. Marriage initiates young women into adulthood, the rituals of marriage constituting the single most important ritual of refinement that an Oriya Hindu woman experiences. These rituals designate her the life sustainer of the family (by cooking and feeding family members) and the life maintainer of the lineage (by giving birth to sons). Highlighting Hindu understandings of the human body as a relatively permeable container, they also serve to remake and transform her substance unambiguously into that of her husband's family (*kutumba*) and lineage (*kula*), beginning her process of assimilation into these groups. This physical transformation is symbolized for a Brahman bride by the new first name given her by her husband and his family.

Literate in the local language, Oriya, but often not formally schooled, the women who participated in this study spend their lives within the compounds of either their natal or their conjugal families. However, it would be a mistake to assume that this seclusion implies isolation because many women are avid watchers of television, familiar with programs like *I Love Lucy* and *Oprah*. By virtue of belonging to the more privileged castes, these women exemplify a primarily Brahmanical sensibility: concerns about purity, auspiciousness and self-refinement influence much of what they say and do.

Moreover, the *rasa* theory's classification of happiness as a subsidiary and transitory emotion shapes their own understanding and experience of this emotion. These women believe that the adult experience of happiness, which is glossed in Oriya as *sukha*, is short-lived, fleeting, ending in a mere matter of seconds (*khyaniko*), lost as soon as one recalls the burdens of this life. Happiness is thought of as an immature emotion because only children, still unaware of life's travails and tribulations, are able to experience it fully and unreservedly. Not surprisingly, then, many of these women rarely talk of wanting to be happy; instead, their this-worldly goal is a sense of wellbeing—a sense of satisfaction with life, but even this, as mentioned above, stops being a valid goal as they approach the end of life.

The Sample

Data for this chapter was gathered through observation and lengthy conversations during two periods of fieldwork—four months in 1991 and 10 months in 1992-'93. I should also add that, prior to doing fieldwork, I lived for more than a dozen years in various towns and cities in Orissa. Therefore, although not an Oriya myself, I am familiar with Oriya culture and fluent in the Oriya language.

During the first stretch of fieldwork in 1991, I interviewed 66 women, ranging in age from 19 through 78 years, about a variety of subjects, including their conceptualizations of the life course and their levels of life satisfaction with respect to the past, present and future. In rating their levels of life satisfaction, the women chose from a typical five-level Likert item with scores ranging from 1 through 5. The choices were: negative life experiences greatly predominated over positive ones (score of 1), negative life experiences predominated slightly (score of 2), negative and positive life experiences were roughly equal (score of 3), positive life experiences predominated slightly (score of 4) and positive life experiences predominated greatly (score of 5). This sample was largely upper-caste: 53 of these women were Brahman while 13 belonged to what is referred to locally as "clean castes"—groups from whom Brahmans, despite concerns about pollution, will accept water.

For the second study in 1992-'93, I conversed with 35 women belonging to 10 extended families. Again, these 10 households were primarily upper caste: seven were Brahman, and the remaining three were "clean castes." Twelve of these 35 women were part of both samples. Using open-ended, loosely structured interview schedules, I asked these 35 women to describe, in detail, their daily routines and the extent to which they felt they had achieved wellbeing. In order to measure their experience of wellbeing, I resorted to a mode of estimation commonplace in the temple town. Folk here often speak of "not having even one anna of control over life's events" or of having "fully 16 annas of happiness in childhood", even though these coins are no longer in circulation. In pre-independence India, 16 annas made one rupee; therefore, a claim of 16 annas of wellbeing implies total wellbeing. Consequently, my questions about wellbeing and the answers I received were framed in these everyday terms.

These 35 women occupy traditional family roles: daughter, junior wife, senior wife, married mother-in-law and widowed grandmother. Thus, there are two daughters, 15 junior wives, five senior wives, nine married mothers-in-law and four widowed grandmothers.

Oriya Hindu Conceptualizations of the Life Course and Levels of Life-Satisfaction

Many Oriya Hindu women tend to conceptualize the life course in terms of five phases: childhood (*balya avastha*), youth (*kishoro avastha*), young adulthood (*jouvana avastha*), mature adulthood (*prauda avastha*) and increased or old age (*briddha avastha*). In addition, they view marriage as the most significant, transformative event in a woman's life, separating the first two phases from the latter three.

When talking of shifts from one phase to another, Oriya women speak in terms of changes in duties and responsibilities. Because such changes often accompany transitions from one family role to another, family roles are a significant part of the idiom for discussing lifespan transitions. Furthermore, the scores they gave themselves for levels of life satisfaction reveal that these women consider mature adulthood to be the most satisfying phase of a woman's life. Young women look forward to the future when they will become mature adults, old women yearn for the past when they were mature adults and mature adult women are quite satisfied with their present life circumstances. So, what is it about this particular life-phase—mature adulthood—that it provides women with their most satisfying experiences?

Representations of Different Life-Phases

My second stint of fieldwork sought a more precise answer to this question. In lengthy conversations, women occupying different family roles describe in detail their daily routines, elaborating on the degree to which they have control over their own lives and the extent to which they feel connected to their families, their community and divinity.

Through analyzing these data it is possible to develop composite representations of the later four phases of a woman's life course: youth, young adulthood, mature adulthood and old age. No single woman described any of these phases in the detail presented here. Each is a consensus of what many said—the points they agreed upon, illuminated by details that some of the more thoughtful women articulated.

Youth

According to local definitions, an unmarried daughter of marriageable age, living in her father's home, falls into the category, youth. Such a girl enjoys a carefree and irresponsible life, far more carefree, in fact, than that of even her brothers, for whom, the pressure to obtain a means of livelihood makes the years of late youth and young adulthood very difficult and stressful. She is indulged, she has no prescribed duties, and whatever she does, she does voluntarily. The daily routines of the two daughters in the sample make this abundantly clear. As one of them says explicitly, daughters have no responsibility towards anyone in their fathers' households: "My responsibility? What responsibility? I have no responsibility. As a daughter in my father's home, I have no responsibility towards anyone."

At the same time, they are keenly aware of the transitory nature of life in their fathers' homes. In this patrilineal, patrilocal society, women, after marriage, move from their natal to their conjugal homes. Thus, these girls know that vis-à-vis their natal homes they are temporary residents whose permanent homes lie elsewhere.

When asked to rate their wellbeing, daughters, unlike other respondents, preferred to say that they were happy rather than well. Both also claimed to have complete happiness, one saying she had 16 annas and the other refusing to quantify her happiness, saying, "When I get what I want, I feel happy, I have complete happiness. If one's desires are fulfilled then one is happy, and in one's father's house, aren't one's desires always fulfilled?" Because only one of the two daughters quantified her level of happiness, there is no average happiness score calculated for them (see Table 1).

Happiness, then, characterizes life in one's father's home, a life of non-involvement in household activities and no responsibilities. But this happy life is also, by definition, short-lived because all girls expect to get married, Hindu parents being enjoined by tradition to find suitable husbands for their daughters.

Young Adulthood

When an Oriya Hindu woman experiences young adulthood, her role is that of junior wife (sãna jã). A junior wife's most important challenge is to assimilate into her conjugal family. Given Hindu understandings of the permeability of the human body, this is a process begun during the rituals of marriage but that only time and she, through deliberate action, can complete. This challenge is important because, as many women claim, rapid and successful assimilation guarantees wellbeing.

The consummation of marriage is the first and necessary pre-requisite to assimilation. Another integral element in this process, and one that a junior wife engages in actively is performing sevã (service) to members of her husband's family (Cohen 1998). In the Oriya Hindu context, such sevã involves doing all the cooking and some of the serving of the food, much of the cleaning and washing, as well as performing explicit rituals of deference to her parents-in-law, most particularly her mother-in-law. Taking orders from the older woman, eating her leftovers, massaging her feet, drinking the water used to wash the older woman's feet before eating—all are seen as proactive ways of ingesting the physical substances of powerful family members, and all are thought to help assimilation proceed apace. A 36-year-old senior wife spoke for many when she commented,

We all did that as junior wives. For the junior wife, the elders are her gods. Just like you drink water from the Ganges, just like you drink *Lingaraj's pãduã pãni* (water used to wash the deity's feet), so too you drink the water used to wash the feet of elders. As junior wives, we all hope to get something from doing this...we hope to get their qualities, their abilities, their good thoughts.

In regarding household elders as her gods, whom she must serve with devotion, a junior wife is conforming to widely shared Hindu meanings about the relationship between superiors and subordinates (Alter 1992; Copeman 2009).

Oriya women claim, almost unanimously, that the early years of marriage are hard: being married into a family of relative strangers, being at the bottom of the family hierarchy, doing the hard physical work of cooking and cleaning, performing rituals of deference toward critical elders—all make this phase of life difficult for most women. This is also a time when a woman's geographic mobility is curtailed. She cannot leave the premises, not even to visit her natal home, except with the express permission of her husband's parents. Even within the house, she cannot move freely because she has to observe strict rules of avoidance with respect to the senior males of the family. As one junior wife told me, "These are our days of hiding." Even with her husband, a junior wife has to behave with extreme circumspection—avoiding conversation, and even glances, when other family members are present (Mandelbaum 1970: 74-79; Seymour 1999: 64).

This account of young adulthood would be incomplete if I did not mention the conjugal family's attitude toward the junior wife. In common with other Hindus, Oriyas believe that the sexual urge is both powerful and irresistible. Therefore, the sexual power a newly married woman supposedly exercises over her husband can potentially disrupt even the strongest of filial bonds. Most members of the conjugal family initially view an in-marrying woman with deep suspicion, fearing that she will cause the family's break-up (Bennett 1983). They subject everything she does—her cooking, her demeanor, her performance of *sevã*—to critical scrutiny. Only slowly, with time, after she has given birth to children, entrenched herself within the family, do their suspicions dissipate.

In terms of wellbeing, junior wives provide a wide range of estimates—from none at all to 15 or 16 annas, the average being 7.6. Not surprisingly, women who claim to possess substantial wellbeing belong to small conjugal households, having only seven or eight members, and have non-interfering and undemanding mothers-in-law. A notable feature of young adulthood is fairly clear evidence that some junior wives somatize their emotional distress, low scores on wellbeing frequently being associated with complaints of night fevers, chest pains and swooning.

Table 1. Distribution of Women's Wellbeing, in terms of annas, and According to Family Roles

	Daughter	Son's Wife		Mother-in-law	
		Junior	Senior	Married	Widowed
Household					
1		6	8	12	
2	–	12, 10		8	0
3			16	13	
4	16	0			
5		2, 16	14.5	8	14
6		10	–		9
7		10	16	16	
8		8, 8		16	
9		8, 8		6, 16	
10		4, 6, 6			8
Avg. Score	No score calculated	7.6	13	12	7.75

Mature Adulthood
(1) The Senior Wife

An older woman, after the birth of children, and the entry of younger sons' wives, ascends within the family hierarchy, becoming an "old"/"completed" son's wife—*purna bou*. While maturing and seniority happen on their own, a woman actively completes herself by giving birth to children. Senior wives experience a gradual relaxation in some of the restrictions that constrain a junior wife. Thus, when I asked them to identify the moment of transition from junior to senior, many laughingly said, "When we can go to the front door and call out loudly to our children playing outside to come indoors, then we have become senior wives."

Although a senior wife is not yet the senior-most woman of the household, she is well on the way to it, and she has begun to take advantage of the privileges that this position brings—the privileges of dominance and centrality (Lamb 2000).

Generally speaking, a senior wife is no longer involved in the drudgery of household chores; instead, she directs junior members to do them. However, she maintains her ties to the kitchen as the primary server of food, a distributive responsibility, steeped in prestige, which emphasizes her centrality within the household. This partial movement out of the kitchen coincides with an increase in her interaction with the world outside.

The senior wife is the public face of the family: she entertains guests, she shops for the entire family, and she represents the family at neighborhood celebrations such as weddings and sacred thread ceremonies. She no longer performs rituals of deference toward her mother-in-law—or if she does, they are casual and irregular. Now, in lieu of worshiping her husband's parents as gods, she begins to represent the family in its relations with divinity— although there are physiological and cultural limitations to this involvement. A senior wife is still young enough to menstruate, to be sexually active and to be involved in the feeding and care of her children. This inability to maintain bodily purity (Reynolds 1980; Lamb 2000) restricts her access to divinity, but even the limited access she has is highly significant because it indexes her successful assimilation into her conjugal family.

A senior wife often explains her non-performance of rituals of deference, and her role as family representative, as simply the result of her having become familiar to the family—a known quantity. An alternate, and to my mind more plausible, explanation is that "old" or "completed" wives have accomplished their transformations into full members of their conjugal families. Such transformations imply that senior wives are now "matched" (Marriott 1976, 1990, 2003) with their husbands and their conjugal families in terms of physical substance. Such matching has psychological and moral overtones because a woman experiences it as increased coherence within herself, coherence, here, referring, very specifically, to a woman feeling no psychological dissonance. Such coherence also implies feeling good about herself, feeling virtuous. Her conjugal family is now her family: her own self-interest and that of the family's finally coincide. The family reciprocates this self-realization by acknowledging her as a full member, an acknowledgement signaled by the non-requirement to perform rituals of deference, and by her elevation as the family's representative within the community and, occasionally, with divinity.

A concomitant of increased dominance within the family, greater control over the productive and distributive activities of the household, and inner coherence is having substantial wellbeing: On the average, a senior wife states that she has 13 annas of wellbeing, although there are some who claim to have fully 16 annas.

Before concluding this section, I need to emphasize that not all women will necessarily experience all of the privileges associated with mature adulthood. Usually, in a family with many sons, only the wife of the eldest son will do so. As an eldest son's wife, she will savor fully the power, coherence and wellbeing that come with being the senior-most wife—the privileges of primogeniture. If, however, the eldest son's wife is too meek or too incompetent, she is more than likely to be supplanted by the enterprising wife of one of her husband's younger brothers.

(2) The Married Mother-in-law

Mature adulthood reaches its zenith when a woman welcomes into her household the wives of her adult sons. As a married mother-in-law, a *sãsu*, a woman's position within her household is unassailable. Building on the privileges she enjoyed as a senior wife, a married mother-in-law supervises her household's activities and expenses, making sure that everything runs smoothly and efficiently (Vatuk 1987). The younger women do all the household chores, while she spends much of her day looking out watching the world go by—a pastime that she relishes and that is forbidden even a senior wife. She has considerable spatial mobility. She goes alone for her daily bath to the temple pond; she worships everyday, sometimes multiple times in a single day, at the Lingaraj temple; she leaves the neighborhood to visit relatives, staying over a few nights, if she feels like it; and, she goes on pilgrimages, accompanied by her husband or other relatives, to distant places.

In terms of dominance and centrality, the two family roles of senior wife and married mother-in-law are almost equivalent. Both supervise and control the activities of others and both are critical to the proper care of children and the production and distribution of food within the family. However, in terms of coherence, a married mother-in-law experiences greater coherence because she is better able to maintain bodily purity. This ability is relatively recent and the direct result of two factors. First, when a son marries and brings his wife into the family, his parents usually cease being sexually active: the job of reproduction has been passed on to the next generation (Vatuk 1992; Lamb 2000). Second, a married mother-in-law is usually past menopause and there is no time of the month that she is polluted (*mãrã*). While bodily purity, in and of itself, contributes to greater coherence—it does more than that. Bodily purity and her continued involvement in the household's productive activities make a married mother-in-law the best intermediary between the household and divinity. Most women relish this position. They feel and others within the family acknowledge them to be essential to its material and spiritual welfare. Dominant within the family, central to its domestic activities and emotionally and morally coherent, married mothers-in-law enjoy considerable wellbeing.

Consequently, the average wellbeing score for these women is 12 annas, three of them even claiming fully 16 annas of wellbeing.

Inevitably, time leads to sharp reversals in a married mother-in-law's situation. When a senior wife's adult son marries, she becomes a married mother-in-law in her own right. While she has been content, till now, to wait in the wings, she is more than ready to claim her moment and take center stage. And that is precisely what happens. When a senior wife welcomes her son's wife into the household, she displaces her own mother-in-law. The grandmother with married grandsons has aged out of mature adulthood—she is now old.

Old Age

The most notable feature about old age among Oriya women is that no familial duties are associated with this life-phase. The kin term for an old woman—the grandmother of married grandsons—is *burhi mã* (old mother/woman), not *sãsu* (mother-in-law). *Burhi mã* is an interesting kin term because while *mã* does connote 'mother', in the temple town, it often just means 'woman'.

Partly because of physical weakness, partly because there are younger women ready and willing to take over the obligations she previously fulfilled, an old woman becomes marginalized from the business of everyday living. A few old women remove themselves from the center of household activities on their own, curtailing their interactions with others both inside and outside the family. But many do not cede control and power that easily (Cohen 1998).

Of the three measures—dominance, centrality and coherence—that give mature adulthood its particularity, the most critical one is centrality. It is from being the linchpin that holds the family's productive activities together that all the other advantages flow. Thus, seniority per se does not guarantee dominance. It ensures autonomy but an old woman only controls her own activities, no one else's. Only when a woman is involved with the productive activities of the household in a managerial capacity does seniority imply dominance. No longer subject to menstrual pollution, an old woman can quite properly maintain continual contact with the gods, but only on her account. As a 72-year-old widow says, "When you stop touching the cooking vessels, you surrender your right to intercede with divinity; you can no longer intercede to ensure the health and prosperity of family members." For the first time in an adult woman's life, marriage no longer retains its earlier potent auspiciousness—and again, it is because, as an old woman, she is no longer involved in household activities.

Widowhood exacerbates further the conditions of old age. Many old widows are relegated even more severely to the background than their married counterparts, expected to contribute nothing to the family. Thus, a 78-year-old widow has no compunction in complaining loudly about her sons and their wives and children, "No one needs me for anything; no one asks me for anything, no one does anything for me...No one." Her complaints are not unique: many other old widows in the temple town echo them. Not surprisingly, she claims to have zero wellbeing (see Table 1).

With centrality and dominance slipping away in old age, coherence too, is threatened, partly because old women no longer mediate between their families and divinity and partly because they understand and experience the physical and mental disintegration that accompanies aging as increased incoherence. This idea that increased incoherence characterizes aging is part of Ayurveda, the indigenous system of medicine. There are well-known cultural practices, focused on withdrawal and renunciation, that old women can adopt to counter such incoherence—fasting, meditation, yogic discipline, scriptural study, attending religious discourses, going on pilgrimages, to name but a few—but they are not easy to maintain. And when old women fail at these practices, others castigate them for displaying a "second childishness."

However, there are some old women in the temple town who do not complain and who seem to be more accepting of old age and its various disabilities. The 72-year-old widow, mentioned above, is an excellent example of such an old woman. The reasons for her adaptability to the changing realities of life are, I think, to be found in her successful internalization of cultural meanings that speak to appropriate behavior in old age, those that elaborate on withdrawal and renunciation. Given this successful internalization, it is not surprising that she claims to enjoy substantial wellbeing, fully 14 annas of it. On an average, old women have slightly less than 8 annas of wellbeing.

Dominance, Productivity, and Coherence: A Cultural Model of Wellbeing

Given the data presented above, it appears that many Oriya Hindu women conceive of wellbeing as shaped by three measures: having control over one's self and dominance over others; being centrally responsible for managing the household's productive activities and its distributive networks; and, achieving coherence. Attaining the first measure facilitates attaining the latter two, such that, as senior wives and married mothers-in-law, women achieve wellbeing most comprehensively.

Both senior wives and married mothers-in-law report similar levels of wellbeing (see Table 1). Despite this similarity, I would like to suggest that a senior wife's experience of wellbeing may be qualitatively different from that of a married mother-in-law's because the three measures contribute differentially. Senior wives derive their sense of wellbeing from being fully assimilated members of their conjugal family, from being dominant within these families and from being intermediaries between their households and the community. Married mothers-in-law, however, derive their wellbeing primarily from their role as the household's best intermediary with divinity.

In addition, senior wives and married mothers-in-law may not experience the third measure—coherence—in the same way. As I described above, the coherence that senior wives experience is psychological: it is a consistency of the mind. In contrast, the married mother-in-law's coherence would be better described as moral goodness, the result of her ability to have regular, unrestricted access to divinity.

Finally, I would like to address the notion that age relaxes the constraints that hedge women's lives. Brown and Kerns (1985), summarizing cross-cultural data, explicitly state that middle age brings several positive changes in the lives of women who live in non-Western, non-industrial societies—geographical mobility, the right to exert authority over junior kin, the right to make decisions within the family, the possibility of occupying special offices and enjoying recognition beyond the household (p. 3-6; see also Minturn 1993). In the temple town, such relaxations do characterize mature adulthood, but not all women are fortunate enough to be mature adults. Widowhood, rejection by the husband and/or the husband's family, or the ordinary misfortune of marrying a younger son rather than the eldest often prevent a woman from becoming the senior-most wife in a family or the senior-most married mother-in-law, and, therefore, interfere with her becoming a fully mature adult. The women who miss out on the privileges of mature adulthood can enjoy geographical mobility and do have personal autonomy but they cannot exercise substantial authority over others, they rarely represent the family in its interactions with the world outside, and they hardly ever intercede with divinity. Thus, in the temple town, being older does not necessarily lead to a more satisfying life: as they say in the temple town, to be a mature adult woman requires a touch of divine grace.

Again, a comparison of the wellbeing scores of unmarried daughters and junior wives underscores the point that the significant relationship is between family role and wellbeing rather than between age and wellbeing (see Table 1). In extended households, unmarried adult daughters and junior wives are often of approximately the same age and yet, their sense of wellbeing differs vastly: daughters are carefree and happy while junior wives, at the bottom of the family hierarchy, have few culturally defined resources with which to access wellbeing.

Conclusion

I have presented in this essay Oriya Hindu understandings of happiness and wellbeing from the perspective of the women of the temple town of Bhubaneswar. I have shown that these women believe that only children and unmarried girls, unthinking and irresponsible, can experience happiness. Married women, with the burdens of life sitting heavily on their shoulders, may experience happiness for a few fleeting seconds but that carefree emotion of youth and childhood is gone forever. Thus, the meanings that these women attach to happiness are those of transience, immaturity, irresponsibility; they do not regard happiness to be a basic or enduring emotional experience of adulthood. Not surprisingly, perhaps, their thinking reflects ideas that Bharata, the ancient Hindu philosopher of the emotions, articulated, when he classified happiness as a subordinate and transitory affective state, not a basic, enduring emotion.

Instead of happiness, the women of the temple town seek wellbeing. The family roles of mature adulthood—those of senior or senior-most wife and married mother-in-law—provide a woman with the best opportunities to experience wellbeing. In these roles, senior women manage the family's productive activities, ensuring its material prosperity; they represent the family within the community, maintaining its reputation; and, they represent the family in its communication with the household gods, safeguarding its spiritual health. Through intense involvement in these activities and substantial control over such involvement, women experience dominance, centrality and coherence—the three key elements that constitute wellbeing. But life is unpredictable and not all women ascend to being the senior-most wife or a married mother-in-law, which implies that not all women enjoy the privileges of mature adulthood. Oriya Hindu women, therefore, value mature adulthood, not only because it is the most satisfying phase of a woman's life but also because not every woman is so blessed as to traverse it.

References

Alter, J. (1992). *The Wrestler's Body Identity and Ideology in North India.* Berkeley: University of California Press.

Bennett, L. (1983). *Dangerous Wives and Sacred Sisters: Social and Symbolic Roles of High-Caste Women in Nepal.* New York: Columbia University Press.

Brown, J. & Kerns, V. (1985). *In Her Prime: A New View of Middle-aged Women.* South Hadley, Massachusetts: Bergin & Garvey Publishers.

Cohen, L. (1998). *No Aging in India, Alzheimer's, the Bad Family and Other Modern Things.* Berkeley: University of California Press.

Copeman, J. (2009). *Veins of Devotion: Blood Donation and Religious Experience in North India*. New Brunswick, New Jersey: Rutgers University Press.

de Bary, W.T. (1958). *Sources of Indian Tradition*. New York: Columbia University Press.

Daniel, E. V. (1984). *Fluid Signs: Being a Person the Tamil Way* Berkeley: University of California Press.

Datta, A. (2006) *The Encyclopedia of Indian Literature* (A to Devo). New Delhi: Sahitya Akademi.

Flood, G. (1996). *An Introduction to Hinduism*. Cambridge: Cambridge University Press.

Geertz, C. (1984). "From the Native's Point of View: On the Nature of Anthropological Understanding." In R. A. Shweder & R. A. LeVine (eds.) *Culture Theory* (pp. 123-136). Cambridge, Massachusetts: Cambridge University Press.

Gnoli, R. (1956). *The Aesthetic Experience According to Abhinavagupta*. Rome: Instituto Italiano per il Medio ed Estremo Oriente Serie orientale

Lamb, S. (2000). *White Saris and Sweet Mangoes*. Berkeley: University of California Press.

Mahapatra, M. (1981). *Traditional Structure and Change in an Orissan temple*. Calcutta: Punthi Pustak.

Mandelbaum, D. (1970). *Society in India: Continuity and Change*. Berkeley: University of California Press.

Marriott, M. (1976). "Hindu Transactions: Diversity without Dualism." In B. Kapferer (ed.) *Transaction and Meaning: Directions in the Anthropology of Exchange and Symbolic Behavior* (pp. 109-142). Philadelphia, Pennsylvania: Institute for the Study of Human Issues.

Marriott, M. (1990). "Constructing an Indian Ethnosociology." In M. Marriott (ed.) *India through Hindu Categories* (pp. 1-39). New Delhi: Sage Publications.

Marriott, M. (2003). "Varna and Jati." In Gene R. Thursby and Sushil Mittal (eds.) *The Hindu World*. Routledge: London.

Menon, U. (2002). "Making Sakti: Controlling (Natural) Impurity for Female (Cultural) Power." Ethos (30), pp. 154-174.

Menon, U. (2010). "Dharma and Re-envisioning the Hindu Moral Code." In G. Misra (ed.) *Psychology and Psychoanalysis* New Delhi: Centre for Study on Civilizations.

Menon, U. (2011) "The Three Selves of Adulthood." *Psychological Studies* 56 (1), pp. 23-35.

Menon, U. & Shweder, R. A. (1994). "Kali's Tongue: Cultural Psychology and the Power of 'Shame' in Orissa, India." In H. Markus & S. Kitayama (eds.) *Culture and the Emotions* (pp. 241-284). Washington, D.C.: American Psychological Association.

Minturn, L. (1993). *Sita's Daughters: Coming out of Purdah, the Women of Khalapur Revisited.* New York: Oxford University Press.

Mines, D. P. (1990). "Hindu Periods of Death 'Impurity.'" In M. Marriott (ed.) *India through Hindu Categories* (pp. 103-130). New Delhi: Sage Publications.

Monier-Williams, Monier, Sir (1851). *A Dictionary, English and Sanskrit.* London: W. H. Allen and Co.

Pandey, K. C. (1935) *Abhinavagupta; An Historical and Philosophical Study.* Varanasi, India: Chowkhamba Sanskrit Series Office.

Panigrahi, K. C. (1961). *Archeological Remains at Bhubaneswar.* Bombay: Orient Longmans.

Reynolds, H. (1980). "The Auspicious Married Woman." In S. S. Wadley (ed.) *The Powers of Tamil Women. South Asia series,* no. 6 Syracuse, NY: Syracuse University Press.

Seymour, S. (1976). "Caste/Class and Child-Rearing in a Changing Indian Town." *American Ethnologist* 3(4), pp. 783–796.

Seymour, S. (1980). "Some Conclusions: Sources of Change and Continuity." In S. Seymour (ed.) *The Transformation of a Sacred Town*: Bhubaneswar, India (pp. 257–273). Boulder, Colorado: Westview Press.

Seymour, S. (1999). *Women, Family, and Child Care in India.* Cambridge: Cambridge University Press.

Shweder, R. A. (1991). *Thinking Through Cultures.* Cambridge, Massachusetts: Harvard University Press.

Sreekantiah, T. N. (2001 [1953]) *Indian Poetics.* Trans. By N. Subrahmanya. New Delhi: Sahitya Akademi.

Vatuk, S. (1987). "Authority, Power and Autonomy in the Life Cycle of North Indian Women." In P. Hocking (ed.) *Dimensions of Social Life: Essays in Honor of David G. Mandelbaum* (pp. 23-44). Berlin: Mouton de Gruyter.

Vatuk, S. (1990). "'To be a Burden on Others': Dependency Anxiety among the Elderly in India." In O. Lynch (ed.) *Divine Passions: The Social Construction of Emotions in India* (pp. 64-88). Berkeley: University of California Press.

Vatuk, S. (1992). "Sexuality and the Middle-aged Woman in South Asia." In J. K. Brown and V. Kerns (eds.) *In Her Prime: New Views of Middle-aged Women* (pp. 155–172). Urbana and Chicago: University of Illinois Press.

Zaehner, R. C. (1966) Hinduism. Oxford: Oxford University Press.

Zimmermann, F. (1987). *The Jungle and the Aroma of Meats: An Ecological Theme in Hindu Medicine*. Berkeley: University of California Press.

Harriet Levin Millan

Yalla!
(a story based on conversations with "Lost Boy" of
Sudan Michael Majok Kuch)

Dry Season (October) 1988, Juet, Sudan

Loud booming wakes me. I open my eyes. The inside of the hut is pitch-black. If I need to pee, I'll have to crawl to the door on my knees. Another loud boom. Bursting light. Flames shoot up. The thatched roof is on fire. I'm five years old. My mother rushes toward me holding my baby brother in her arms, shouting, "Kare! Run!"

Outside fire covers the sky. More huts are burning and people are screaming. I start to run then stop. Jeeps are lined up with men in robes leaning out of them holding rifles clutched to their chests. I'm not wearing any clothes, and I'm barefoot. The ground isn't wet, it isn't raining, but trails of lightning-like flashes leave people moaning on the ground. There're so many bodies, I can't tell who they are, my tall broad father, his face scarred in the Dinka ceremonial pattern, or my mother, her tongue fluttering against her teeth.

I'm crouched with my back against a tree crying for her.

"Over here," calls a villager named Manyuon—a man my father's age—running toward the swamp. To follow him means to not stay and search for my parents among the people on the ground.

What happens next, I would take back if I could.

A hot gust rises. It brushes my arms and chest. The huts to one side explode into flames. I spring out, running after him in one long jump after another.

Kicked up soil sprays my legs. Roots puncture the soles of my feet. Smoke sears my eyes. I follow Manyoun's shadow past smoldering huts as a sour odor—burning flesh—spreads across the field.

I splash down into water low and muddy reaching above my ankles, then deep and clear, almost over my head, every muscle in my body straining to reach the opposite bank. Crocodiles live in these shallows.

"How fast can you run?" my mother had asked, stroking my head and kissing me. She told me that I must run very fast but she didn't tell me that

Arab Jallaba armed with AK-47s and RPGs would attack our village in the middle of the night. They were cattle herders, and I was small enough to slip past them.

It happened on the evening of our harvest festival. Our relatives had traveled to Juet for the celebration. They came by foot. There are several small villages in Jonglei Province, most of them Dinka. They are a half-day's walk from one another. Our village is surrounded by Nile swampland. It takes maybe two hours to paddle a dugout canoe loaded with pumpkin, sorghum and maize through sinewy swamp to the town of Bor to trade.

Our relatives came from the outlying villages, women balancing baskets filled with yams on their heads and holding several chickens upside down in each hand. Some of them came with their cows, lifting gourds of water to their mouths to ease them on. Through the bush between villages, they encountered people fleeing who told them with quivering lips that the government in Khartoum was bombing Dinka, searching for the leader of the rebel army, John Garang, whom Khartoum believed was hiding among us. That night I watched their chests heave as they consoled one another and debated whether an attack was imminent.

Coarse sand slides under my feet. My hands become machetes tearing through leaves. I twist through mangroves so snaky, I think they're moving. I'm terrified that a python will grab my foot, the black night alive with cries and howls.

Hours pass this way. Shivering and sweating, I stop to rest. I hear a rustling and think it's Manyuon.

"Manyuon," I call out. No one answers.

My breath stops. I don't move. I don't know what to do. I stand there for a long time unwilling to acknowledge that the shadow I'd been following has been my own. I've never been alone in the bush at night. I cower as I imagine the sharp teeth of an evil spirit, a Nyanjuwan, cutting out one of my eyeballs.

"Majok, Majok," the spirit will call.

I grope for a tree, low enough to climb yet covered over with leafy vines to hide me. I scramble upward not even testing my weight as I lift onto the next branch. Perched at the top, I see images of our fields in Juet filled with bodies grow more vivid, as I hear noises born by wind—wails, moans, gunshots. No matter what shape Nyanjuwan assumes—a Jallaba or my mother—no one can reach me.

***

Morning. Evening. Morning. A voice through the leaves, crackling in the air, boomeranging between the branches.

"You, you, up there." It's a boy more than twice my age—at least thirteen years old, tall and lean in the way of our Dinka tribe dressed in khaki pants and a black T-shirt, with a Kalashnikov slung around his shoulders. He's a soldier, not a member of the army in Khartoum, but one of our Dinka rebels. He stands on tiptoe and stretches his neck up through the vines and waves for me to come down. I don't move. He shows me something in his hand—a strip of dry meat, and he tells me his name—Akol—and passes the meat up between the leaves.

It is veined and gristly, too dried out to chew. I roll it around in my mouth. Squeezing the rifle between his knees, he turns around so that I can climb onto him.

I swing off a branch and wrap my legs around his neck. He rides me on his shoulders. I slide off onto a log. I try to stand. He looks me over. Pain shoots through my foot. He watches me, then looks away.

A sound in the grass. I follow his face.

He laughs. "Heh heh heh, Nyanjuwan's coming to get you." He tilts his head, presses his rifle to his shoulder and aims. "She thinks she's so smart. I can't shoot her anyway. She's coming for you, but it's not worth the noise. Maybe next time, okay?"

I start to cry.

He drops back and turns around. "I'm joking," he laughs, lowering the rifle. "It's a squirrel."

Two days ago, I was preparing for a hunting trip with my uncle. He had given me some arrows to sharpen and I was sitting on a stool under the trees outside our tukul waiting for my cup of porridge as my mother poured it between two cups to cool it down for me.

I stare at Akol.

Akol stares back. "We can't stay here forever, you know."

I show him my foot. It's inflamed. I tell him that I stepped on a thorn the morning of the attack. It had taken my Uncle Matiop, a wrestler, to pull it out. Matiop had planted his spear in the ground, taken my foot in his hand and said, "I hope that is a thorn and not a curse." I watched Matiop strip some twigs off a branch and make twine. Binding the twine to a leaf, he tied it around my foot. He attached it in such a way that he left a space between the part of my foot where the thorn was lodged and the leaf. The idea was that as I walked the leaf would push down on the skin around the thorn and dislodge it. Sure enough, it popped out dripping blood.

I ask Akol if he thinks it is a curse.

"Don't you know?" he says. He pokes through the stalks until he rips one and breaks it in half. He squeezes out the sap and rubs it on the wound. It bubbles up as if to take away the pain. "See, you're getting better. Let's go," he says in Dinka, then firmly in Arabic, "Yalla."

I spit out the meat. Tears fly down my face, fast and hard. I point behind us. "Where are we going? The village is that way."

Out across the swamp, the village is thick with smoke. The gunshots that echoed through the night have left an eerie quiet. "We're going to Ethiopia."

"Ethiopia?"

"Yes, the country next to ours."

The way he says it, Ethiopia doesn't sound so far away, right next door, close enough to walk. I close my eyes and cover my ears with my hands. I refuse to budge. Exhausted and heartsick, I sink down, burying myself in the tall grass.

"Right this moment a big lorry is driving your family across the desert. If you want to catch up with them, you need to keep walking." As Akol speaks, he juggles his rifle from hand to hand.

My tears flow and his voice grows tense. He nods in the direction of an umbrella tree with leaves sheathing it on every side. "Just to that tree. Walk to that tree. With every one of your footsteps, you come closer to your mother."

With every little step, pain shoots up my leg and across my spine. Limping round about through the wattle, I trail after Akol and struggle to keep up with him, side by side, until he tugs me by the arm and positions me in front of him.

We arrive at the tree. I huddle in to hide myself in the thicket of vines.

Akol paces and sighs. He reaches in to shake me by the shoulders then digs his hands under my armpits, his rifle striking my legs. He doesn't apologize. If he feels sorry for me, he doesn't show it. He laughs, "Turn around. Look over there."

A foot is poking out of the thicket on the other side of the tree.

Akol grabs it. It belongs to a boy. Akol laughs. "Hahahaha! Why do you cry? Don't cry."

The boy is broader than I am and taller. He is not as small as I am. He keeps looking at me as if he's trying to figure out something. He sobs and stares. A muffled "I know you" comes out of him.

"You know who I am?"

He walks forward, pointing to the V-shaped scar on my forehead. The wound isn't fresh anymore, but its memory is painful and I don't tell him that up until the attack, I could think of no greater injustice than the time I had an infection in my eye and Matiop held me down while my grandmother, a healer, slit my flesh with a razor blade, thinking she could cure me.

"I saw you at the festival. I wanted to play with you, but my father made me wait and eat with him," he says.

The evening of the attack, the dancers wore brown and white skins, their faces painted to look like leopards. A pack of us boys ran from hut to hut, snuck off with pieces of cow liver from our mothers' tukuls and roasted them over a fire. "You're from Juet?" I ask.

"No, I'm from Alian."

"My mother's family is from Alian. What are you called?"

"Madut. Madut Bol Ayuen."

"You must be cousins," Akol says.

Madut's hair is close-cropped like mine, but he has the round face and broad bones of my father's family, not my mother's. I have been told that I take after my mother's side. If we are cousins, we don't resemble one another. We stare at one another then shake hands and embrace.

Akol turns the back pocket of his shorts inside out and another small strip of meat tumbles down. "Ahh! Here cuz, here's some deep love for you."

Madut reaches for the meat. His fingers brush the tip of Akol's rifle.

Akol stiffens. He rears his head, "Hey, watch where you put your fingers."

"Sorry."

Akol grips the trigger, "Duk yot e rian e ang'auich. Don't jump on a tiger's raft."

"Come on, show me how to shoot."

"Watch it. Did you hear me? Do you want to get your head shot?"

Madut steps back. "Okay, okay."

"Jelku. Let's get going."

"What do you mean? Where?" Madut asks.

"Tueng. Forward. You want to learn to shoot? Once we get to Ethiopia, you can train to be a soldier."

"I don't want to be a soldier. I want to go back to Juet."

"You can't go back there, everyone is dead."

Madut's face lights up in horror. "But my father is there. My cousins. I need to be with them."

"No one's back there. Only Jallaba."

My voice stops in my throat but Madut's comes on with persistence. He takes hold of Akol's arm and pulls on it. "No, no, they're looking for me. Please..."

"You trying to take my arm off or something?"

"I need to go back. Please."

Akol holds the rifle across his body. "And what'll you give me, a donkey's salary?" He looks Madut in the eye, "Trust me, whoever is alive has gone to

Ethiopia. If your family is alive, you'll find them in Ethiopia. Once we get to Ethiopia, you will see them."

***

We start out and keep on. The lion grass gives us cover. It is yellow and brown and spreads in every direction above our heads. There are many ways to go, none of them marked. The way is brittle with reeds. The way is prickly. It is sharp with thorns. It is inhabited with cries and wails. It is twisted with wattle. The wattle is thin but tall, and it is thick but low. More scant if we walk uphill. But the way cannot be back.

I'm not the only one slowing us down. Madut keeps looking for other people who have escaped the attack. He stops walking and stands at the bottom of a tree, pushing through the vines that cover it to look for his cousins from Juet. He's convinced they must be hiding. I'm also convinced that there are other people hiding, maybe my parents, but I'm too afraid that Akol will get angry and shoot us if we stop and look.

"Shhhhh! Jallaba will hear you," Akol says. He quickly turns his head to either side, his rifle cocked, listens and watches. He yanks Madut forward by the elbow. "Come on."

I walk, mostly limp, afraid that we're being followed. Occasionally we hear shots ring out. And there are other dangers. Akol marks off a few paces, sniffs the air, then walks back to where grass has been trampled down. He stops and bends down and buries his nose in a clump of grass to detect whether an animal, most likely a lion, is near. No one says a word as he inhales the scent.

Madut reaches for my arm.

I'm in a panic. There's nowhere to hide, nowhere to consider hiding.

A sound comes from far away, then quickly comes closer. It's not an animal sound. We duck down in the grass. Madut digs his fingers into my arm afraid that Jallaba Murahaleen are approaching.

Something green flashes—khaki uniforms of at least twenty soldiers marching toward the village. Madut's tense body relaxes and he rises and points excitedly. "Come on, let's follow them. They're going into Juet!"

Akol shakes his head and waves his hands, signaling for Madut and me to stay down.

Madut hisses back at him and Akol rushes over and knocks us into the grass. He covers our mouths with his hands.

The soldiers appear, their eyes hidden behind dark pairs of glasses. They run past, but there are others who walk more slowly, lagging behind. One of them takes out a smelly tobacco cigar from a pack and licks the ends with his tongue. He lights it, takes an extra long puff and passes it around. They send it back and forth, flicking ashes in the grass. The grass is so dry that if a stalk catches ablaze, it will spread.

The last of the men pass and Akol removes his hands from our mouths and pushes up to follow the soldiers with his eyes. A branch snaps. Our eyes roam level with the grass. We dive down again, bowing our heads and hiding our faces, our stomachs flat against the earth.

Another snapping sound.

A long moment passes before two birds with tufted heads and speckled black feathers scamper out. They're guinea fowls. I laugh and begin to rise.

"Stay where you are," Akol whispers.

"They're birds."

"Get down."

Madut screws up his face.

Akol balls his hand into a fist, "I told you no one's back there."

"You have a rifle," Madut says.

"Yes, and if they saw it they'd take it from me."

"Why?"

"Don't question me. Even if you think you know something, you don't. You don't know anything."

We walk again, this time not in the lion grass at the edge of the bush but deeper in. The sun bakes, bringing on smoldering pains of hunger. We need to find a tree with fruit on it. Jackelberry or thoc. Sunlight flickers on patchy earth stricken with drought.

"I'm starving!" Madut wails. He squats to hack at a vine with his fingers, picking off pieces and sucking on them, expecting something edible. Toward nightfall we pile up leaves to make beds. I'm exhausted. My feet bleed and blister and the wound from the thorn is still sore. Akol hands each of us a chewing brush. Madut hisses at him, "If you think we're so hungry that we have to chew on something, why don't we go catch a fish?"

"Boy, you don't know what you're talking about. The river's way over there on the other side of the swamp."

"No, I can see it."

"Your eyes are playing tricks on you."

"No, there's fish out there. All we have to do is scoop them up in our arms."

He's thinking of the rainy season when the Nile floods and we can wade right in.

Akol toys with his rifle. "Fish? I'm holding out for meat. Wait until we get to the Sahara Ajaageen. It's a wilderness. You ever taste dikdik?"

"No."

Akol waves the rifle in the air and raises the barrel to his cheek "Well, you're missing something."

"How come I've never tasted it?"

"Where we are going is the land of dikdik."

"So?"

"Tomorrow, if you stop acting like a baby, I'll teach you to shoot."

Madut smiles, which he hasn't done since the attack on Juet.

***

Hunger is a searing pain. It drives in its spike and rips through your gut at full force. I've been asleep only a short time. I wake to Akol who stands over me, slides a finger across my face and presses down on my lips, "Shhhhh!" he whispers.

There are footsteps, the rustle of weeds and the crunch of twigs. The footsteps come closer.

"Run," Akol whispers. There isn't time.

In a flash, something reels toward me. Rough hands squeeze my chin and pin back my arms. Bare feet press mine and pin me to the spot—a man's. Suddenly, the man pulls back and releases me.

Akol's rifle is pressed right up against the man's neck.

"Don't shoot, don't shoot!" the man pleads in Dinka. He speaks in the accent of the Bahr al Ghazal Dinka, who live far away from here.

Akol lowers the gun.

Tears run down my face. My arms hurt from where the man's pinned them back.

In a trembling voice, he says, "My son..." and in his funny accent, I'm not sure what he means until he finishes the sentence, "...got lost in the attack."

I lean against him and hold fast to his hips to feel the warmth of his skin. A few moments earlier, Akol might have shot him. The man hoists me up, and I put my arms around his neck, and we hug and hug and cry.

The man's first name is Panchol. He's been walking for two months. We've been walking two days. I worry that Akol is wrong, that our parents aren't on their way to Ethiopia. The man says that his wife and daughter are waiting for him in the grass while he goes into the bush for food. "Why endanger them all?"

"Have you been through Alian?" Madut says.

Panchol goes quiet. "I'm sorry, everyone who is still there will not survive. The Jallaba won't spare a single village. All the villages between Bar El-Ghazal and Manyideng will be destroyed. The government will take control of them."

Madut sobs.

Matiop had taken me to see the birds of Alian. He knew how to make his voice trill as birds with crested tufts and bright red beaks suddenly appeared.

"I'm sorry, listen, you can come with me. I don't want to leave you like this."

"You don't need to," Akol says.

"I can't leave you here."

"We're not staying."

"So where are you going?"

"We're going to Ethiopia."

"Ethiopia? Ethiopia's a long way off."

Akol passes his rifle between his hands, "I know that."

Each time he lets the rifle drop, the metal thuds against the heel of his palm. The sound is threatening and I'm wondering if Akol will change his mind and suddenly shoot him.

I put my hand in Panchol's and squeeze, hoping he will stop taunting Akol, but he continues. "Do you think Ethiopia is around the bend? Besides, it's a training camp for rebels. This is nonsense. You're children, not soldiers. Ethiopia is too far. It's through the wilderness. You'll never make it. Now listen, follow me and my family to Uganda. We're headed straight for the border. If one of your fathers found my son, I wouldn't expect him to leave him here."

Madut paces. His sobs fill the darkness.

"That's enough now. Stop your crying," Panchol says.

"Leave me alone!" Madut shouts.

"Don't disrespect me, child. If this were daylight I'd whip you with a branch. Now come with me. I will become your father."

There's a flurry of movement. "Stop it!"Akol shouts. He makes a grab for Madut who I think is trying to escape.

I feel betrayed. Madut is trying to get back to Juet without me. I can't see where they are, but I can hear their heavy breathing.

"Stop it, get off!" Akol sounds furious. His voice is cold and metallic and the sound of it makes me shiver.

Everything goes silent as pressure from a gunshot fills the air.

I fall back and Panchol covers my body, his body so light I can feel his bones, lighter than I expect for a grown man, much lighter than my father's.

The first sound I hear is Madut crying again.

Akol, still furious, yells, "You crazy fuck!"

"I'm ashamed," Panchol says. "I'm ashamed for our tribe. I will remind myself that you are just boys."

If Madut had fired the gun, it happened while Akol still held it. Akol's holding it now, thrusting it into the small of Panchol's back.

"Leave us," Akol says.

I feel a hand on the back of my neck. It's Panchol's. He's giving me some sort of signal. He's trying to get me to leave with him. I turn around to his shadow as it dissolves into darkness. I stand between Akol and Madut, afraid to leap forward and run away with Panchol. Before they can stop me, I've broken away, slinking forward where they can't see.

I've become invisible and none of them know where I am, even I don't know where I belong, yet I must make a choice, and I have always thought of survival like this, a choice in the pitch blackness. It's so dark, I walk by feeling the turns in the path. I hold my breath and let go, sliding downward, almost like swimming in a current, keeping myself upright until Panchol who's been waiting, calls out, "Shhh! Here, I'm over here."

I take his hand and think of my father whose authority is so firm, the whole time Madut and Akol were fighting over the rifle he'd have kept his arms folded over his chest.

Panchol steadies me and we walk until we reach the grass clearing, part of it flattened, almost flat enough for the lorry Akol promised. But instead of a lorry, there are dark clusters of slowly moving people, hundreds of them, retreating to the border under the cover of night, a caravan of men, women and children, mostly naked, their few possessions bundled in goatskins, and boys like myself, boys coming out of hiding.

It is a moonless night, a strong wind is howling. I stand next to Panchol with my head rigid and back arched, my ears sharpened to the sound of the howling wind. A chill pricks the back of my head, spreads up and down my spine, covers my arms with goose bumps. I stop walking and listen. Slowly, I realize it isn't wind that's howling. It's voices floating through the air, calling and calling, growing louder and more alive.

They are voices that I have heard in song over fast drumbeats. People danced, jumped in the air, jammed in between one another. Our cows joined in when there was a wedding. People brought their pride bulls and cows wearing special bells around their necks.

My mother and grandmother taught me the names of our ancestors, back ten generations. Dinka boys play a game to see who's smart enough to memorize all their ancestors.

My grandmother took my hand. "Come, Matiop is inside. He will teach you a song. You will learn it now for your initiation. This way you will not embarrass yourself by crying when your father picks up his spear."

There isn't any light surrounding the mass of people, not even moonlight, but their murmurs charge the dark sky and their outlines soften. I stare out, imagining my mother among them, the sound of her wooden bracelets clanking softly.

I'm about to run forward at full speed. Panchol scoops me up in his arms. His fingers, thin-boned and light, clamp my wrists. The feel of them is painful and disappointing. "Tomorrow my wife will lead you to your mother."

"But do you know who she is?"

"Any of these women can be your mother."

Kathleen Volk Miller

Choosing Childfree

I need to weigh in on the pseudo news of the moment: *Time* magazine's reportage on a 2010 study that showed "childlessness has risen across all racial and ethnic groups, adding up to about 1 in 5 American women who end their childbearing years maternity-free, compared with 1 in 10 in the 1970s."

I am not following why so much of the response to this pseudo news has been focused on childfree childbearing years as a woman's right, or discussing this issue from a feminist angle. Don't we all know a man who broke up with a woman because she wanted kids in the future or because she did not? Or someone who married a man with the hopes that he would change his mind—whatever that mind might be—on the "kid issue" or vice versa, and even—MY GOD—could it be possible?—a man and woman who jointly agreed to not procreate?

The silliest argument I saw was on CNN, by a 27-year old who decided to "come out" about her decision. She says this, about her mother's response: "She didn't understand right away. Later, she accepted it and now supports my stand for equality." I'm not clear on how her decision to not have kids helps me or even my daughters. Men are parents too. When did they pop out of her equation?

The idea that remaining childfree makes one selfish, or the perception that it does, is illogical to me. A strong argument can be made that *having* kids is selfish. Some people have kids to support their own egos, in the hopes of unconditional love, as a self-reflective mirror, or literally to have someone take care of them as they grow old. I'll get this bold: People who have children they cannot afford, or do not have time for, are far more selfish than those who choose not to have kids at all.

My many childfree friends, both male and female, are some of the smartest, generous, feminist-thinking people I know.

When I gave birth to my first child in my later twenties a friend just a few years younger said something like, "I don't want to offend you, but the reasons to *not* have kids are so real and concrete, and the reasons to...I can't see them."

Funny thing is, neither can I.

It's much easier to list the reasons not to have children. There is just so much "they" don't tell you. But I will:

1. There are prodigious amounts of poop involved, and not just diaper poop. Women, you are likely to poop on the table during delivery. Men, you are likely to see it. Sure, you know you will be changing a lot of diapers, but you simply cannot fathom the volume of actual shit you will deal with, of all colors, consistencies, and textures. You will dream of crap. You are likely to have shit under your nails for about six years, depending upon your child's intelligence and your own energy levels.

2. There were years of my life where I would look at the grocery check-out and think, "Where am I in all this?" Apple juice and graham crackers and goldfish and diapers and elbow macaroni and string cheese. I'd spend $120 on beige foods and have nothing I wanted to eat.

3. Even the most demanding partner is not as difficult to deal with as a two-year old. Your partner might insist on purchasing a wicker teapot as a souvenir from your trip to Maine, or watching *Restaurant Impossible* On Demand (On Demand!), but he would never go rigid in Wegman's, screaming for a Kit Kat bar while his head spins 360 degrees, not even on his worst day.

4. Your joy may be multiplied, but so is your pain, and it's worse than you can imagine. Take every bit of middle-school angst and multiply it by a bazillion. That's how you will feel when someone slights your kid, or your kid even thinks someone has. Imagine pain from loss, and how it made your heart itself hurt. Now imagine the surrounding veins and arteries being braided. Now, tie them in a Windsor knot. You're close.

5. Unless you own a farm or your own business, kids are not really helpful for very long. If you add up the few years they can mow the lawn or sponge mop the floor, thereby saving you a bit of time or money, they haven't even made a dent in their diaper costs (see above). Factor their allowance(s) in, and you're back in the red.

6. You give up your freedom in ways you cannot fathom. You are no longer free to walk out the door; to not worry about everything all the time; to take a shower or a shit when you need to (see, there's poop issues on both sides); free to not schedule work meetings around sing-alongs at the grade school where your second grader will stand on her tip toes every time she has to hit a high note.

Kids *are* good for excuses, though, that part's true. You can get out of demonstration parties by saying Emily has a fever. You can blow off other people's birthday parties by claiming you have to drive Johnny to a different one. You can even leave work early if little Henry has to see the school nurse.

Kids are a terrific excuse for not having met your original career aspirations, even if that's only true in your own mind.

I love my kids. I've told them that I believe raising children should not be an obligation or assumption and that there are plenty of good, solid reasons not to procreate. They know this does not mean I love them any less.

Anne-Marie Obajtek-Kirkwood

Banks and *Capital*: A New World Order

Money inspires filmmakers. Americans have given us, among others, *Wall Street, Wall Street 2, Cosmopolis, Arbitrage, Margin Call, Rogue Trader, The Wolf of Wall Street*; the French, *L'Argent*[1] (Marcel Lherbier 1928), *Le Sucre*[2] (Jacques Rouffio 1978), and more recently in 2011, a very good year: *Krach* (Fabrice Genestral), *Ma part du gâteau*[3] (Cédric Klapisch), *De bon matin*[4] (Jean-Marc Moutout), *Capital* (Costa-Gavras), and last year, *Le Grand retournement*[5] (Gérard Mordillat), to mention just a few. Costa-Gavras enjoys controversial topics, well illustrated by *Z, State of Siege, Missing, Music Box* and *Amen.* In *Le Couperet*,[6] he had already attacked shareholders for "downsizing" leading to the dismissal of personnel, including the executive, the protagonist of the film. This time with *Capital*, he was inspired by Stéphane Osmont's novel and *Capitalisme total*[7] by Jean Peyrelevade, former head of the Crédit Lyonnais,[8] without forgetting reality. He wrote the screenplay with Jean-Claude Grumberg and Karim Boukercha.

Capital traces "the resistible rise of a bank-valet in the fierce world of Capital." Marc Tourneuil, interim president of Phoenix Bank, foils plots and machinations from his French and American colleagues to win against and oust his opponents. This upward mobility is accompanied by moral impoverishment proportional to his business success. Costa-Gavras does not here depict small traditional banks, but those of globalized finance. According to the filmmaker, "fictional characters hold our truths." This study will therefore endeavor to analyze the diverse voices in the film and what they reveal of the financial world and human nature.

It all starts with an unfortunate golf swing that reveals the cancer of Marmande, president of Phoenix Bank, and catapults in his place Marc

---

[1] *Money.*

[2] *Sugar.*

[3] *My Piece of Pie.*

[4] *Early Morning.*

[5] *The Big Reversal.*

[6] *The Chopper.*

[7] *Total Capitalism.*

[8] A historic French bank: "In the early 1990s it was the largest French bank, majority state-owned at that point. Crédit Lyonnais was the subject of poor management during that period, which almost led to its bankruptcy in 1993. It was acquired by former rival Crédit Agricole in 2003." http://en.wikipedia.org/wiki/Crédit_Lyonnais

Tournier, a former graduate of Polytechnique[9] with five years at Goldman Sachs, New York, five years at Phoenix, Paris, who won the confidence of the president after writing a book for him ending with this sentence: "Money is a dog that does not require any caress. It just wants to be thrown the ball farther and farther to be able to return indefinitely," a conclusion which speaks volumes about his banking philosophy.

Marmande defines the role of a president: "A president signs checks, sacks and eats." Marc Tournier, whom his rivals at Phoenix wished to see as a straw man, quickly shows himself tougher than expected, taking his role really seriously and not as temporary, "a temporary stand-in," "a discount president," which infuriates his colleagues, especially when he claims Marmande's office, his personal plane and the same salary. While Marmande's salary was 2,400,000 euros,[10] his will not exceed 1,800,000. This substantial amount however will be increased by many bonuses, and stock options, throughout his various operations and transactions. Super-salaries are thus established, which have nothing to do with merit and emphasize the "violence of the rich"[11] described by Michel Pinçon and Monique Pinçon-Charlot,[12] a violence "which means poverty for some and wealth for others, which allows for the distribution of dividends at the same time as the dismissal of those who produced them, which allows Pharaonic compensations in millions of euros and increases of the minimum wage that number in cents" (9). This same violence impresses because it proceeds "in camouflage, in suit and tie, and good manners on the front stage, but shameless exploitation of the most modest as a golden rule behind the scenes" (9). This violence also permeates the minds, "makes the most humble respectful of power, knowledge, the elegance of culture, relationships between 'beautiful' and 'great' people" (9). This is well illustrated in the movie scene of the family meal where everyone is very respectful of Marc except for the former trade unionist uncle whom the diners would like to silence. These huge salaries have various explanations among which the consideration enjoyed by the "makers," as our sociologists underline it: "By building their image as leaders of men, whose authority is based on exceptional skills, that education in prestigious schools certifies, leaders of industrial and financial groups arise as supermen able to demand exorbitant pays compared to what the French earn. These rich have seceded: they stand outside of the common lot" (141-142).

---

[9] A prestigious engineering school.

[10] A euro is roughly $1.37.

[11] Such is the title of their book in French that came out in Fall 2013. Translation of parts of their text is mine, as is the translation of other books or analysts' quotations.

[12] Further references to these two sociologists will just be given as Pinçon-Charlot.

Philippe Steiner concurs, denouncing the consequences of this situation on the rest of the population and the perverse reasoning which sets in: "The fiction that allows leaders to put an 'I' instead of dozens of thousands of employees, their work, their activity and their innovations without which the company is nothing, is now at the heart of the appropriation of profits as obscene remuneration in industry as well as in finance" (Pinçon-Charlot 144). Employees become too expensive, their payroll, their social benefits being too high, and Dittmar threatens Phoenix bank with relocation, as Americans who have interests in Phoenix, "like Paris but not France. Too much social legislation."

In his new role as manager of Phoenix Bank, Marc must navigate between two sets of opponents: on the one hand his French colleagues, including de Suze, hoping to "bury the dog with his master" and whose mansion is nicknamed "the mansion of knife-planters in the backs," and on the other hand, U.S. partners, including Dittmar Rigule, who appears as a friend to Marc against his French colleagues and wants to "buy" him with bonuses, a fact Marc is well aware of: "The Americans want me to lay off, the French that I take the fall, my coworkers are all saboteurs."

Upon taking office, Marc considers measures to clean up the bank, including gathering and placing on the market all toxic products, hybrid securities, which he calls "the legacy of the past." He thus wishes to adopt "a more ethical approach." He is nevertheless stopped short in his projects by the holders of a U.S. pension fund who represent a blocking minority in Phoenix and dictate their laws since nothing can be done without their consent. Their frequent spokesman, Dittmar, wants to see Phoenix evolve the American way, with only one diktat, that of numbers, profitability, under the pretext of having acquired debts because of Phoenix. He wishes for a quick return of funds, and thus satisfaction from the shareholders. This "cowboy capitalism" irritates his French colleagues who do not ignore that "this gang of villains [...] bought a quarter of Phoenix with a loan that Phoenix must pay back." Marc is thus trapped: he must lay off under the fierce shareholder pressure, or lose his job. Ironically, it is Diane, his wife, who will suggest how to proceed as she reads a book on Mao Zedong, the Chinese leader having used the rank and file to keep away the executives that annoyed him. Marc is convinced that he must lay off "without seeming to sack people" and that unlike Mao, he must also "streamline the rank and file." Diane comes to the rescue: "Hey, it's easy. Have you not learned that at Polytechnique? It's called a social plan."[13] This term of

---

[13] "Social plan," "un plan social" in French, is used as a term meaning "lay off."

"social plan" has Viviane Forrester react. She underlines all the fallacy of this expression in *La Promesse du pire*[14]:

How not to jump up every time—every time I jump up—when hearing the term "social plan" substituted to "dismissal"? The word "social," then as such a slap, supposed to define the project and the act of expelling, banishing, ejecting a human being from his social position, depriving a person from his means of living, presents each excluded being as the lucky recipient of altruistic projects developed by the most attentive of negotiators (37).

This linguistic deception is also commented on by Pinçon-Charlot: "Politicians of the liberal right or left hijack the meaning of words, invert moral values, having understood what power owes to the degradation of language and paralysis of thought. Political correctness is always linguistically incorrect" (154), the purpose of this Newspeak ultimately being the destruction of concepts (154).

And thus a social plan is put in place at Phoenix, accompanied by a very sly questionnaire (as in Laurent Cantet's *Human Resources* or *Brassed off* by Mark Herman[15]) inviting employees of any status to say "what prevents them from thriving in [their] work, whether material or in [their] relationships with [their] heads, [their] colleagues or [their] subordinates." And Marc, in this worldwide dialogue with his employees thanks to a giant connected screen, presents his initiative in glorious and friendly terms: "This is a family discussion to boost energies. We must break clans, so that Phoenix Bank be reborn from its internal contradictions, and put an end to unworthy leaders, despotism, moral and sexual harassment, the degradation of the individual, arbitrary promotions, insecurity of employment, suicides. My friends, it is time to open our hearts and minds, thank you." Bursts of applause in the room and on screen that would actually be deserved, if only this approach was sincerely desired and implemented...but it only serves to raise shares traded, from 10 to 12 % for 7,000 redundancies in the world, 22 to 26% for 10,000, and the reward of a 13th month-pay for Marc and a 30-million euros bonus for the layoffs (3,000 euros per laid-off employee). De Suze protests, attempting to reduce the number of layoffs to 7,000; Dittmar imposes the 10,000. Later, confronted with the remarks of "bleeding" and "social carnage" from his colleagues at Phoenix, Marc will remain firm on the figure of 10,000 layoffs, and the New York Stock Exchange will close with a 19% increase.

---

[14] *Promise of the Worst.*

[15] A French and an English movie, respectively.

Banks, like Phoenix, are part of globalized finance. Profit being their main goal, they are disconnected from reality and have little regard for human life; exchanges are no longer based on the circulation of goods, but on money itself. "Commodity itself has changed status, writes Forrester. It is no longer the object, the subject of trade: the exchange itself has become the commodity. The exchange, not its object but its own hallucinatory, evanescent fluctuations, its illusory material will be bartered, become standard" (33). The plan hatched by the U.S. pension fund that pushes Phoenix to buy the eroded assets of the Japanese bank Mitzuko to ruin Phoenix and then buy it out is another illustration, "speculation bets foremost on speculation, only aims for it, and is its only outcome" (Forrester 20), on behalf of "profitability, the true governing agent of reality" (Le Gall 130). To reach this end even more efficiently, the financial system has developed robots, high-performance software, faster working than the human mind, day and night, and not likely to go on strike. During his trip to London, Marc is very interested in the acquisition of new robot traders "that accomplish up to 40% of transactions without human intervention and outside of any regulation, allowing no control of financial flows." We are witnessing a civilization of the omniscient screen, whether it be for human exchanges—often in Capital Marc thus converses with various partners via the computer screen—or for stock trading, which prompts Forrester to utter this sarcastic comment: "A civilization of the screen? These windows mask substance and behind them a History unfurls based on figures without further reference to anything but themselves and their masturbations" (35).

Phoenix seems to only depend on the U.S. pension fund that has four key positions on its board of directors and blocking rights. Otherwise the bank pays little attention to rating agencies, though Sieg, a colleague of Marc's, thinks they should be taken into account, to which Marc replies lucidly: "Fuck this mafia." And he is pretty right as these agencies, Fitch, Moody's, Standard & Poor have no political office, their members vote anonymously (Forrester 22-24), are remunerated by the governments, companies, banks, hedge funds they rate, rather arbitrarily depending on the country (Paul Krugman). They are granted an omniscience that they have not evidenced during the crisis of 2007/2008, that they did not see coming or have hushed. They plunge so many countries into distress, forcing states to budget cuts and to giving up their social policy. Having pushed away the pressure of rating agencies, Marc is certainly not afraid of the government, given the cavalier way he talks to its members. To a colleague who reminds him that "the government requires that credit be opened," Marc replies: "Do you work for the government now?", taking no account of governmental requests. He also remains very elusive when a member of the Elysée[16] asks him about his future layoff plans, and fends off any potential criticism. The State representative submits to this dialogue of the deaf and somehow enters the game since he thus concludes: "Given the economic situation, good news, even false, would be welcome." The government does not react either to the announcement of the massive layoffs.

The press is no better treated either. Returning from his first trip to the United States, Marc does not even deign to talk to journalists but delegates Marmande's daughter with a "give them food for thought." During the evening at the Louvre, he feeds nonsense to a journalist about the "democratization of luxury" and tells us aside: "I did not know then one can have a ball bullshitting on TV. I will have to get used to it. Henceforth I will now accept all interviews." In these interactions, the press does absolutely not take a critical stance, but is rather too respectful, even servile, often relaying the "new economic vulgate" (Pinçon-Charlot 135).

Given the limited opening of Phoenix to the government and the press, and the little control these exercise over it, the bank really escapes any control, especially as far as taxes are concerned. It possesses four accounts in the Bahamas, one with 30 million euros belonging to President Marmande. At his death, the only employee who, with Marc Tourneuil, knew the codes, has disappeared and the account with him, emptied or debited of 13,500,000 euros. Marc does try to learn more about this, but in vain. So Phoenix, like many banks and businesses around the world, invests money in tax havens and hidden transactions. These tax havens, by keeping funds away from national taxes, considerably deplete States' incomes, as Pinçon-Charlot has it: "The rich not only want to get rid of their taxes, but [...] they now refuse the constraints of national identity that has become an impediment to the global identity of deregulated financial capitalism" (46-47). Banks rise above national constraints.

Phoenix and the American pension fund operate according to their own laws, in total opacity for the common man. To thwart the purchase of the failing Mitzuko bank, Marc causes insider trading to the benefit of French and to the detriment of the U.S. pension fund, much to the chagrin of Dittmar who wants to sue him, but Dittmar is caught in his own snare since he originally committed this offense, Marc having evidence in the form of records and documents. The general public will know nothing because the banking family does not prosecute its own members; this is just not done and would prevent advancing careers. Marc returns to the head of Phoenix, having triumphed over all his opponents on both sides of the Atlantic.

---

[16] Presidential palace.

In *Capital*, we are witnessing the triumph of money, and its power without any scruple, without any morality. According to Marc, only money gives respect; besides it nothing else exists. For Dittmar, money is the only master, and bankers, following the famous phrase of Lloyd Blankfein, chairman of Goldman Sachs, namely quoted in *Capital*, "do the work of God." It is "the great international financial takeover of humanity" (Vasseur 18), the triumph of "supermen" who rule the planet, of an elite "that does not touch ground any longer" (Vasseur 19). How long will this last? "Until all hell breaks loose," is Marc's lucid answer.

Works Cited

Forrester, Viviane. *La Promesse du pire*. Paris: Seuil, 2013.

Hayes, Christopher. *Twilight of The Elites. America After Meritocracy*. New York: Broadway Paperbacks, 2012.

Le Gall, Jean. *New York sous l'occupation*. Edtions Daphnis et Chloé, 2013.

Costa-Gavras. *Le Capital*. Dossier de presse.

Krugman, Paul. "The Plot Against France." *New York Times*, 11 November 2013. A25.

Michel Pinçon et Monique Pinçon-Charlot. *La Violence des riches. Chronique d'une immense casse sociale*. Paris: La Découverte, Coll. Zones, 2013.

Tisseron, Serge. *Le Capital. Cerveau & Psycho*—no. 55 janvier-février 2013. 14-19.

Vasseur, Flore. *En bande organisée*. Paris: Editions des Equateurs, Littérature, 2013.

M.G. Piety

On Death and Dying

One of the most frightening things, I think, about dying is that we do it alone. Of all the natural evils for which one would like to blame the creator, this seems one of the worst. It would have been so much better, wouldn't it, if we left this life in groups, left perhaps with the people we came in with, with the children we remember from our earliest days in school, and perhaps also with the people we have come to love, if they are suitably close to us in age. If we could go in groups, as if on a field trip, it would be easier.

But we go alone, even those unfortunates who die in accidents that take many lives die effectively alone because they don't have time, really to appreciate their fates as shared. They say the people who remained on the Titanic sang as the ship went down. That's what I'm talking about. It would be so much better, so much easier to bear if we were assigned a time along with many others. We could begin to gather a little before that time, all of us who were assigned to leave together, we could begin to gather and prepare ourselves and share with one another the joys and sorrows of our lives. If we did that, I think we would realize that our lives had really all been variations on the same theme, that we were not so different from one another as we had thought.

I'm not certain if I believe in life after death, even though I am very religious. I'm not certain what it would be for. I doubt I will be ready to leave this life when my time comes. I think I'd like to live much longer than I know I will, say three or four hundred years. I think I'd eventually get tired of living though, so the prospect of living forever is not all that appealing.

It seems to me, however, that if there is life after death, that that place where we will all go (and I believe we will all go to the same place because I am a universalist), wherever it is, that we will all actually arrive there together. Even though each of us will die individually, alone, if we go anywhere, it is to eternity and since there is no temporal change in eternity, there cannot be any arriving earlier or later. Where we will go will be where everyone will go at the same time, or where everyone, in a sense, already is. There will be no waiting for the loved ones who die after us. They will be there waiting for us, so to speak, when we arrive, even if they are in the bloom of youth when we leave.

When I think about death, which I do more and more as I get older, I wonder if perhaps part of the point of it, of the horrible specter of that trip one must take alone, is precisely to make us understand that we never really are alone. And by that I don't mean simply that God is always with us, although I do mean that also. I mean that we are all part of the whole of humanity, that we are connected to everyone and, indeed, to every living thing.

There is a poem I love by Molly Holden that conveys this sense of connectedness very well. It's called "Photograph of Haymaker, 1890." It goes like this:

> It is not so much the image of the man
> that's moving—he pausing from his work
> to whet his scythe, trousers tied
> below the knee, white shirt lit by
> another summer's sun, another century's—
> as the sight of the grasses beyond
> his last laid swathe, so living yet
> upon the moment previous to death;
> for as the man stooping straightened up
> and bent again they died before his blade.
> Sweet hay and gone some seventy years ago
> and yet they stand before me in the sun,

That's not the whole of the poem. I left out the last couple of lines for fear of violating copyright. You can read the whole of it though if you go to *Poetry* magazine. Of course the poem *is* about the haymaker in that it's about mortality, which is inseparable, I think, from temporality. Time passes, people pass, as they say. The haymaker will pass, just as the grasses he's cutting down in the vigor of his manhood. And he is gone now of course that man who was young and vigorous in that photo taken so long ago.

I love to read philosophy and learn that others who lived and died long before me had precisely the same thoughts that I have had. I feel suddenly linked to those people in a mystical way. I feel as if they are with me in a strange sense, that we are together on this journey we call life, even though they completed it long ago.

Kierkegaard speaks often about the idea of death and how one must keep it ever present in his thoughts. I did not understand this when I first read it, but I believe I do now. To think about death, really to think about it, to think it through, will bring you right back around again to life and what a miracle it is, and by that I don't mean your own small individual life, but all of it, life as a whole, and you will be filled with reverence for it. You will be kinder to every creature.

And you will feel less alone.

Sheila Sandapen

Rhetoric, Plato, the Fourth Doctor Who and How to Tell a Cracking Good Story

Author's note: The character The Doctor mentioned in this piece is the Fourth Doctor as portrayed by Tom Baker 1974-1981.

Conversation at its best is a true exchange of ideas and ergo understanding between two entities; it isn't always easy to achieve even when both parties are speaking in the same language; it may be challenging, as illustrated in this exchange in Lewis Carroll's novel *Alice's Adventures in Wonderland*:

> "Then you should say what you mean," the March Hare went on.
> "I do," Alice hastily replied; "at least—at least I mean what I say—that's the same thing, you know."
> "Not the same thing a bit!" said the Hatter. "You might just as well say that 'I see what I eat is the same thing as 'I eat what I see!'"[1]

This bit of absurdity from *Alice's Adventures in Wonderland* gets to the heart of Plato's criticism that the poet is "[t]he imitator or maker of the image [who] knows nothing of true existence; he knows appearances only."[2] We as authors—whether experienced or student authors—must move beyond the idea of mimicking and try and create work that, if not entirely original, serves a purpose of questioning and telling a story. One example of rhetoric at work can be found in the pop culture phenomenon show Doctor Who (which has been on the air for 50 years). The character the Doctor has an ability to travel in space and time and often finds himself in situations where he must uncover the true story. His inquiring mind, facility with language and the TARDIS universal translator gives him an advantage in understanding the local language, but he must acclimate quite quickly to the attitudes and undercurrents of a situation in order to gain a greater understanding. While the universal translator is a trope in science fiction, the Doctor doesn't always need it. For example, in season 14 serial "The Talons of Weng Chiang," the Doctor as played by the actor Tom Baker interrogates a man from China while his companion and another bystander clearly can't follow. (And this is where the author must step in—he or she must make the story comprehensible to the intended audience.)

In our modern-day sensibility we tend to think of poets as creative, freethinking types who create original poetry. For Plato, poets were professional orators and their job was to recite lengthy mnemonic state-sanctioned verses (epics) to the audience.[3] These epics had to be formulaic so they could be learned and repeated without variation. These "poets" were not authors of the poems; they were merely parroting the memorized verses. It is this repetition without knowledge that Plato—and the Doctor—rails against. The Doctor's disdain for repetition of words without reflection is clearly highlighted in the season 14 serial "The Face of Evil," in which two races, the Sevateem and the Tesh, live in hatred of each other and blind obedience to their god Xoanon.

Words of Discovery and Recovery

In episode two of the season 14 serial "The Face of Evil," the Sevateem call the Tesh their enemy. The reasoning is based on the fact that it has always been so. The creed the Sevateem repeat is nothing but a mantra they repeat to comfort themselves and justify the status quo between the two tribes:

Neeva: Our fathers of the tribe of the Seventeem were sent forth by God to seek Paradise.

All: And still we Seek.

Neeva: They searched and found it not. While they searched the tribe of Tesh...

All: Curse be the cowards of Tesh.

Neeva: ...remained at the place of land, betrayed our fathers.

All: Death to the betrayers of Tesh.[4]

This repetition without understanding sets up two races to constantly distrust and wage war, and is a practice that the Doctor questions. On first encountering the Sevateem, the Doctor is also intrigued by a hand gesture they use to ward off evil. He notices they move their right hand from the ear to the shoulder and chest. In episode one of the same serial, the Doctor notes the gesture is the sequence of how to check the seals on a Starfall Seven spacesuit and he muses, "What makes that particularly interesting is that you don't know what a Starfall Seven spacesuit is, do you?" He has noted the anachronism and now must answer the question what does it mean?

Anytime a writer or orator starts off by saying, "I have heard" or repeats a myth (as Plato himself does with the myth of Theuth[5]) or writes about something he has no experience of, what will follow is not truth, only a semblance of it. As Walter Ong wrote, the "Extratextual content is missing not only for readers but also for the writer."[6] What this means is if the reader is unclear about a passage, she cannot ask the author what he meant. The writer, critiques Plato, is also similarly constrained. The writer does not have a live audience, the "...writer's audience is always a fiction."[7] In turn, the reader must fictionalize the writer and assign feelings and intentions to the writer that may have been true at the time of the writing but may no longer be accurate and the author cannot defend him/herself.[8] The reader can only read and reread the same fixed words hoping to get at meaning, which is what the Sevateem and Tesh find themselves constrained into doing. The puzzle of a people who repeat by rote and without understanding catches the Doctor's attention and he of course becomes determined to solve the problem. In this he finds a kindred spirit in the character Leela who is introduced in the story and shows a distinct lack of willingness to fictionalize a "meaning" to justify a pointless and potentially deadly war.

The four-part episode season 14 serial "The Face of Evil" marks a high point in the Fourth Doctor's world of dialectic inquiry. We first see Leela, a member of the Sevateem tribe, in episode one saying, "Do not beg Tomas. What I said is the truth." Leela, who is a primitive stereotypically dressed in skins and quick with a knife and deadly darts, serves as a stark contrast to the Doctor. Primitives are cunning and instinctual but not rational, or so it is commonly assumed. Leela, however, is possessed of a fierce intelligence. She resents Neeva, "the Speaker of Law," and favors her own thinking over tradition. Her truth is her disbelief in the Xoanon god and she is unafraid to speak it even though it means certain banishment and death from her tribe. Right from the start Leela (as portrayed by Louise Jameson) is a companion with a sharp mind and no preconceptions. She may not have the trappings of a civilized culture or book learning, but she relies on her instincts and pure logic, which makes her a suitable companion for the Doctor. Although a "savage," Leela responds to the Doctor's ideas and finds a place of acceptance in his company.

Later in the same serial episode two, the following exchanges occurs:

Leela: I don't know what to believe anymore.

Doctor: Never be certain of anything. It's a sign of weakness."

And again:

Leela: Do you know the answer to everything?

Doctor: Yes. Well no. Answers are easy. It's asking the right questions that is hard.

Asking the right questions. The Doctor is full of them and ponders the questions until he comes up with the right ones. As the plot lines of "The Face of Evil" unravel we find out that the Sevateem is really a "survey team" and Tesh is short for Technicians. The Doctor reveals that originally the two races were human explorers who landed on the planet. The Technicians remained behind on the ship and the survey team ventured out never to return. Through the years memory had faded and the two resulting tribes lived in distrust and fear of each other. Plato's concerns of the written word and fallibility of memory could become a nightmarish reality if we don't practice good authorship and storytelling. After all, we must always be guided by the who, what, when, why and how of creating a good story and never stop asking questions.

Endnotes

[1] Lewis Carroll, *Alice's Adventures in Wonderland* (Boston: Branden Books, 1941), 82.

[2] Plato, *The Republic and Other Works*. Trans. by B. Jowett. (New York: First Anchor Books/Doubleday, 1973), 205.

[3] Eric Havelock and Walter Ong have further contextualized Plato's comment and read Plato's comments not as being a condemnation of poets in general but a condemnation of the limitations of an oral culture and a push toward a literate society.

[4] Episode 1, Doctor Who, "The Face of Evil," season 14.

[5] Theuth is an Egyptian god of the underworld who Socrates depicts in the *Phaedrus* as advocating mankind take up writing in order to preserve his memories. Plato attempts to illustrate his feelings on written discourse in *Phaedrus* by introducing the myth of Theuth, the god of, among other things, writing. Theuth comes to the Egyptian king and tells him about writing, saying, "This discipline, my King, will make the Egyptians wiser and will improve their memories: my invention is a recipe for both memory and wisdom." But the king demurs and says "...since you are the father of written letters, your paternal goodwill has led you to pronounce the very opposite of what is their real power. The fact is that this invention will produce forgetfulness in the souls of those who have learned it...so it is not a recipe for memory..." Plato. *Phaedrus* trans. by W.C. Helmbold and W.G. Rabinowitz. (New York: Macmillan/Library of Liberal Arts, 1956), 68.

[6] Walter J. Ong, *Interfaces of the Word* (Ithaca and London: Cornell University Press, 1977), 100.

[7] Walter J. Ong, *Interfaces of the Word* (Ithaca and London: Cornell University Press, 1977), 53-81.

[8] Walter J. Ong, *Interfaces of the Word* (Ithaca and London: Cornell University Press, 1977), 101.

Marshall Warfield

Motel Swimming Pool, Late Afternoon

As
we
enter,
the first waves
ripple out to strike
the walls with tiny claps. Then stars
explode on the surface around us. We inhabit
this universe as enormous drifting astronauts—so huge, God finally sees us.

Scott Warnock

Where do you keep your hoes?: Standardized tests are destroying education

So where do you keep your hoes, if you are lucky enough to have any in the first place or you have a living environment that requires (or at least facilitates the use of) them?

My friend teaches elementary school in a low-income, urban public school with a large Spanish-speaking population. "Low-income" doesn't really cover it: She works in one of the poorest, most dangerous cities in the United States. Of course, despite those characteristics, children still live there.

So, she soldiers on. Well, "soldier" doesn't really cover it: She loves her job.

But it is challenging. Recently, her fourth-grade students were faced with a multiple-choice question on a standardized language arts test that went something like this:

Identify the underlined word:
The farmer placed the <u>hoe</u> in the shed.
A) Garden tool
B) Calf
C) Bag of seeds
D) None of the above

Every child in her class chose "None of the above."

During lunch, she said, the kids were all talking about this particular question. So after lunch the fourth-grade teachers had a conversation with the students about, well "hoes." The kids were shocked to discover that the hoe wasn't the farmer's woman, but a garden tool.

One kid then raised his hand and said, "What's a shed?"

Let's boil this down to the micro level. Every child in the class got this question wrong. Thus, the state or whatever overseeing, administrative, non-educational body will thus record a 0% success rate for the class on this language arts test question (keep in mind, this was not a test of their understanding of the main ideas of the course "Garden Implements 101").

But their error isn't about language or understanding linguistic or grammatical concepts. It's not about reading comprehension. Conceptually, these kids were wondering what on earth a shed is and why a farmer (obviously a man to them, by the way) would put his "hoe," his *woman*, in it? Had the "hoe" been bad? Was a "shed" a place of punishment for naughty "hoes"?

Who knows what you think of this story. Maybe you think it's funny. Maybe you think it's sad. Maybe you're angry and you think anyone in America, right after knowing the words to the Pledge of Allegiance, should know what the hell a "hoe" is. Maybe you think everyone should be like you, even if they grow up with Spanish-speaking parents in one of the poorest, most dangerous cities in America. Maybe you don't care.

You may have any of those feelings, but you can't think they did poorly on the test because they don't understand nouns, verbs, or language arts concepts. These children, nine and ten years old, did poorly because of their particular cultural reality in America in 2013.

My friend wrote to me, "I guess it is difficult to understand the true meaning of 'hoe' and 'shed' if you live in an apartment in the city and you have never gone anywhere beyond the limits of the city."

So for that question, they got a zero. Aggregate a bunch of standardized test questions like that, and the kids bomb it, look bad, and the school is in trouble.

Remember, people who will never go near your school and never talk to its staff care a lot about test results, of which this hoe question is just an example. Money is doled out. Teachers and administrators get fired. Districts get redefined. This all happens regardless of whether the test measures anything other than the fact that a child never got a chance to see a farm, or maybe even a garden, firsthand, and maybe never even had a book about farms, or a book about anything, in their homes.

My friend added that her school overall is supposed to show yearly progress based on the test scores. The school's effectiveness is measured in that way. Yet, she said, the kids who succeed on tests like this—hoe questions aside, I suppose, since they all failed that one—normally transfer to a charter school the next year. So the top-scoring testers leave, yet each year the school is supposed to improve its passing percentage.

Warrior that she is, my friend still loves her job—because she loves her colleagues and those kids, kids who are consistently held crookedly next to a standardized testing yardstick.

What are we measuring? We can do better than tests that are more measures of the places and ways in which kids are raised than the potential in their little brains—or the efforts of the diehard teachers who work with them every day.

Next time, maybe she'll just bring a hoe into school. You and I both know that's a perfectly ethical way to help kids learn.

Contributors

Sarah Adigba is a chemical engineering major with eyes ready to see the world. She documents her findings in short stories not so anonymously at her blog femmeneu.tumblr.com. She is from Lagos, Nigeria with hopes of being a writer along with being an accomplished chemical engineer.

Stacey E. Ake is an associate teaching professor of philosophy in Drexel's Department of English and Philosophy. She holds two PhDs. One is in biology, with a specialization in populations genetics, and the other is in philosophy, with a specialization in the work of the Danish existentialist Søren Kierkegaard. She is able to combine these two areas of interest by means of her work in semiotics and biosemiotics.

Jan Armon received his bachelor's degree in English from the University of Pennsylvania, followed by a law degree from Boston College. One evening, seven years into practicing law, Jan received a phone call from another attorney asking if he would take over her commitment to speak to a political science seminar about a topic in constitutional law. He prepared and, arriving at the seminar, asked everyone to sit with him in a circle. A lively discussion ensued, at the end of which he knew he had to change professions. As he had long wondered how he might teach things he'd figured out about writing, he enrolled in a PhD program in English at the University of Michigan, writing his dissertation on the academic value of personal writing. All this notwithstanding, he is most proud of having raised a couple of kids.

Avital Breverman is an electrical engineering major from East Brunswick, New Jersey. She is looking forward to a career in industry. Avital enjoys running, exploring Philadelphia, and visiting National Parks.

Taylor Bush is a creative writing major hailing from Pottstown, PA. Upon graduating, he plans to write a lot and embark on lots of adventures.

Paula Marantz Cohen is Distinguished Professor of English and Dean of the Pennoni Honors College. She is the author of ten books, including the award-winning *Silent Film and the Triumph of the American Myth*, and the bestselling novel *Jane Austen in Boca* and Mystery Guild selection literary thriller *What Alice Knew: A Most Curious Tale of Henry James and Jack the Ripper*. Her most recent novel is *Suzanne Davis Gets a Life*. She is a co-editor of *jml: Journal of Modern Literature* and the host of *The Drexel InterView*.

Ingrid Daemmrich has taught humorous literature and writing for many years. As an active member of the International Society for Humor Studies, she has delivered a number of papers at annual meetings and published three essays in its peer-reviewed journal, *HUMOR*. "Humor as Celebrity-Maker: Recreating Lewis Carroll's *Alice in Wonderland* and *Through the Looking-Glass* in Multi-

Media," a revised version of last year's talk, owes much to students in her 2013 English 103 course. Many thanks for all the valuable contributions!

Blythe Davenport's writing can be found in *Chronogram Magazine*, the *Painted Bride Quarterly*, *Mad Poets Review*, and the PS Books anthology, *Forgotten Philadelphia: Art and Writing Inspired by Philadelphia Heritage Sites.* Her first book, *Second Oldest: A Poetic History of Philadelphia,* was published in 2013. Blythe is an adjunct assistant professor in Drexel's First-Year Writing Program and lives in Philadelphia.

Joe Esposito is currently an entertainment and arts management major at Drexel University. His concentration in performing arts is one of many "paints in his palette," for he has current interests that fall in the visual arts and writing realms. "Beyond the Panes" portrays his childhood perspective on his mother's experience through marriage.

Gaia Faigon is an English major from Los Altos, California. Her hobbies include reading, dancing, and enjoying a cup of coffee with her friends.

Alissa Falcone is a senior English major from Medfield, MA. She will be working as a communications specialist in Drexel University's office of University Communications after graduation. In her free time, she likes to ponder the meaning of life.

Tim Fitts is an adjunct assistant professor in the Department of English and Philosophy. He also teaches first-year writing at the University of the Arts. He earned an MFA in creative writing from the University of Maryland and a BA in English from the University of South Florida. He is on the editorial staff of the *Painted Bride Quarterly,* and his stories have been published by *The Gettysburg Review, Granta,* and *Cutbank,* among others.

Valerie Fox's books include *The Rorschach Factory, The Glass Book,* and *Poems for the Writing: Prompts for Poets* (co-written with Lynn Levin). *Poems for the Writing* was a finalist for the Next Generation Indie Book Awards (education category). Much involved in collaboration, Fox has published many poems and stories co-written with Arlene Ang, and also published *Bundles of Letters Including A, V and Epsilon,* which is a compilation with Ang. She teaches writing at Drexel.

Nidhi George is a freshman political science major from Portland, Oregon. She hopes to one day attend law school and subsequently practice corporate law. Her goals also include traveling the world, serving others, and (with any luck) being a very happy person.

Steven Goff is a psychology major and Garnet Valley, Pennsylvania native who enjoys reading and writing poetry. In the future he hopes to pursue a doctorate in psychology while continuing to develop his skills as a writer.

Henry Israeli's poetry collections include *New Messiahs* (Four Way Books: 2002), *Praying to the Black Cat* (Del Sol: 2010), and *god's breath hovering across the waters*, forthcoming from Four Way Books in 2016. He is the translator of *Fresco: the Selected Poetry of Luljeta Lleshanaku* (New Directions: 2002), *Child of Nature* (New Directions: 2010), and *Haywire: New and Selected Poems* (Bloodaxe, 2011). He has been awarded fellowship grants from the National Endowment for the Arts, Canada Council on the Arts, and elsewhere. His poetry and translations have appeared in numerous journals including *American Poetry Review, Boston Review, Harvard Review, The Iowa Review, Smartish Pace, Grand Street, The Literary Review, Tin House, Fence*, and *Verse*, as well as several anthologies. Henry Israeli is also the founder and editor of Saturnalia Books (www.saturnaliabooks.com). He is an assistant teaching professor and Associate Director of the Certificate in Writing and Publishing at Drexel University.

Jen Jolles is a junior English major from Silver Spring, MD. She has lofty goals of getting her PhD and wearing a lot of tweed someday. In her free time, she enjoys running long distances and living with intention.

Hajer Karoui is a freshman mathematics major from Souse, Tunisia. She is a member of the Drexel Red Cross club, Drexel African Student Association, Track and Field, and many other clubs. She plans to minor or double major in computer science. Her hobbies include singing, playing the piano, writing, and running. Her favorite things to do are travelling and learning languages. She knows four languages and one of her goals in life is to master as many languages as possible.

Allison Law is a freshman education major with a concentration and minor in biology. She is from Roxbury, NJ, and hopes to teach high school biology in the future. Her hobbies include playing the piano and flute, and spending time with her friends, family, and puppy.

Lynn Levin, a poet, writer, and translator, is an adjunct associate professor of English at Drexel. Her most recent book is *Birds on the Kiswar Tree* (2Leaf Press, 2014), a translation from the Spanish of a collection of poems by the Peruvian Andean poet Odi Gonzales. Her poetry collection *Miss Plastique* (Ragged Sky Press) was named a finalist in poetry in the 2014 Next Generation Indie Book Awards, and *Poems for the Writing: Prompts for Poets*, co-authored with Valerie Fox (Texture Press), was a finalist in the education/academic category in the 2014 Next Generation Indie Book Awards.

Jason Ludwig is a sophomore history major from Brooklyn, NY. He plans to go into teaching after graduation. His hobbies include reading, writing, and playing soccer and basketball.

Brittany MacLean is an international area studies major with a literature, culture, and the arts concentration. She is pursuing minors in both Spanish and writing so that she can simultaneously indulge her love of travel, writing, and language. She believes that if you let the world change you, then you can change the world.

Donna McVey has an MS in education from the University of Pennsylvania. She has 25 years of teaching experience both in the U.S. and in Romania, where she was a Fulbright Lecturer. At Drexel's English Language Center, where she has been an ESL instructor for over 20 years, Donna coordinates student testing and placement in addition to teaching both written and oral skills to international students at all levels of English proficiency. Donna has numerous presentations and publications in her name. Her interests include writing, teaching writing, and mentoring.

Usha Menon is professor of anthropology at Drexel University. Her research examines various aspects of Hindu society and civilization, and she has written widely on goddess worship, gender relations, emotional functioning, Hindu-Muslim religious violence, Hindu morality and Hindu women and Western-style feminism. In particular, her work on Hindu women reflects a multicultural feminist perspective in that it seeks to study the ways in which these women either do, or do not, empower themselves within the concrete contexts of their lives instead of focusing on questions of individual liberty or gender equality. She is the author of *Women, Well-being and the Ethics of Domesticity in an Odia Hindu temple town* (2013) published by Springer (India).

Harriet Levin Millan is the author of two books of poetry, *The Christmas Show* (Beacon Press), which won the Barnard New Women Poets Prize and the Alice Fay di Castagnola Award from the Poetry Society of America, and *Girl in Cap and Gown* (Mammoth Books), a 2010 National Poetry Series finalist. Her poems and stories appear in *Iowa Review, Kenyon Review, Antioch Review, Smart Set, Ploughshares, Prairie Schooner*—where she is currently blogging on a Drexel University study trip to Haiti—and other journals. She traveled to Kenya and South Sudan on a Summer Literary Seminars and Drexel University International Travel Grant to research "Yalla!" She holds an MFA from the University of Iowa Writers Workshop and is director of the Certificate Program in Writing and Publishing and teaches first-year writing and creative writing in the Department of English and Philosophy.

Kathleen Volk Miller is co-editor of *Painted Bride Quarterly,* co-director of the Drexel Publishing Group, and a teaching professor at Drexel University. Kathleen writes essays and fiction, with work in publications such as Salon. com, *Opium,* thesmartset.org, the *New York Times, Philadelphia Magazine, Drunken Boat,* and other venues. She is currently working on *My Gratitude,* a collection of essays. She rarely blogs, but profundity can occasionally be found at kathleenvolkmiller.com

Anne-Marie Obajtek-Kirkwood is an associate professor of French and head of French studies at Drexel. She teaches French and francophone 20th and 21st century literature, culture and film, and women studies and international area studies with a focus on the Maghreb, Middle East, and Iran. Her research and publications include the above topics but also minorities in France, autobiography, and war (WWII, 9/11, the Iraq War). She has published *Signs of War: From Patriotism to Dissent* (Palgrave MacMillan, 2007), and on many contemporary French writers.

Cindy Phan is a communications major from Mechanicsburg, PA. After college she hopes to pursue a career in public relations and, in following her personal dream, one day become a published author of young adult fiction.

M.G. Piety is an associate professor of philosophy at Drexel University. She translated Kierkegaard's *Repetition and Philosophical Crumbs* for Oxford University Press (2009) and is the author of *Ways of Knowing: Kierkegaard's Pluralist Epistemology* (Baylor, 2010) and *Sequins and Scandals: Reflections on Figure Skating, Culture and the Philosophy of Sport* (Gegensatz, 2014). She is also the author of numerous articles and maintains two blogs, *Reading Notes* (mgpiety.org) and *Piety on Kierkegaard* (pietyonkierkegaard.com).

Elizabeth Pollack is a senior screenwriting and playwriting major from St. Louis, MO. She recently won a New Works Competition through New Cavern Productions and is currently writing a play for their winter season show.

Gregory Przybylski is a freshman biology major in the seven-year medical program affiliated with the Drexel College of Medicine. When not found studying, Greg might be writing for enjoyment, playing chess, or refreshing himself with a cup of tea. He is still writing love letters.

Maria Raggousis is an architectural engineering student from Bensalem, PA. She is passionate about music and the arts and hopes to continue her hobbies wherever her career takes her.

Tirthak Saha, a recent transfer from India, is a current electrical engineering major with a minor in engineering management at Drexel University. He has a passion for the arts and cites his father as the biggest influence in that regard. He fully anticipates being involved with writing, reading, and, hopefully, thinking all his life.

Sheila Sandapen, PhD, is an assistant teaching professor in the Department of English and Philosophy at Drexel University. She primarily teaches in the First-Year Writing Program.

Edward Seamans is a fifth-year senior majoring in software engineering. He enjoys traveling and playing guitar.

Bhavya Sharma is a freshman English major from India. She works for *The Triangle* and plans to continue a career in writing after college. Other than writing, her hobbies include painting, reading, and telling inappropriate jokes.

Julia Timko is an entertainment and arts management major from Silver Spring, MD. She likes reading and eating, and has no idea what she'll do after graduation.

Alina Toporas is an exchange student at Drexel University where she is majoring in political science. Born and raised in Romania, she began her undergraduate studies at the University of Sheffield in England, United Kingdom. There, she studied international relations and politics. Her goal is to one day work for a United Nations agency such as UNESCO or UNICEF. Her free time is mostly spent traveling, writing, and learning new languages.

Joe Wang is a junior accounting major who is a recent transfer student from the University of Chicago. He credits his love for writing to his rather sordid history in composing Harry Potter fanfiction back in middle school. Aside from that, he has an ardent passion for writing fiction and marathoning TV dramas late into the night.

Marshall Warfield writes poetry. His work has appeared in the anthology *Poems for the Writing: Prompts for Poets* and the journals *Press 1* and *Transient*. Warfield teaches writing at Drexel as assistant teaching professor in the Department of English and Philosophy. He also collaborates with artists in other mediums, and has most recently been working with filmmaker David Kessler on a project about the Pine Barrens.

Scott Warnock is an associate professor of English at Drexel and Director of the University Writing Program. He writes the bi-weekly blog/column "Virtual Children" for the website *When Falls the Coliseum.*

James Warren is a junior environmental science major. His hobbies include distance running and birding.